T0151892

danger — **truth** at work

OSHO

DVD: *Knowing the Truth is to Experience Existence As It Is*, Copyright © 2009, OSHO International Foundation,
Switzerland

This book is a transcript of a series of original talks by Osho given to a live audience.
The talks in this edition were previously published as *From Ignorance to Innocence* (Chapters 1–15).

All of Osho's talks have been published in full as books, and are also available as original audio and/or video
recordings.

Audio recordings and the complete text archive can be found via the online OSHO Library at www.osho.com
OSHO is a registered trademark of Osho International Foundation, www.osho.com/trademarks

ISBN (paperback)   978-0-9818341-7-7
ISBN (hardback)   978-0-9844444-1-0
Also available as an eBook: ISBN 978-0-88050-764-6

OSHO MEDIA INTERNATIONAL

New York • London • Mumbai
an imprint of
OSHO INTERNATIONAL
www.osho.com/oshointernational

Distributed by Publishers Group Worldwide
www.pgw.com

danger — **truth** at work

the courage to accept the unknowable

OSHO

I am not interested in creating beliefs in you, and I am not interested in giving you any kind of ideology. My whole effort here is — as it has always been, of all the buddhas since the beginnings of time — to provoke truth in you. I know it is already there. It just needs a synchronicity, it just needs something to trigger the process of recognition in you.

Contents

About the Authentic Living Series

The "Authentic Living Series" is a collection of books based on meditation events in which Osho responds to questions from his audience.

He has this to say about the process:

How do you ask a question that is really meaningful, not simply intellectually but existentially? Not just to add verbal knowledge, but to grow towards authentic living? There are a few things that have to be remembered:

Whatever you ask, never ask a ready-made question, never ask a stereotyped question. Ask something that is immediately concerned with you, something that is meaningful to you, that carries some transforming message for you. Ask that question upon which your life depends.

Don't ask bookish questions, don't ask borrowed questions. Ask something that you want to ask. When I say "you," I mean the you that you are this very moment, that is here and now, that is immediate. When you ask something that is immediate, that is here and now, it becomes existential; it is not concerned with memory but with your being.

Don't ask anything that once answered will not change you in any way. For example, someone can ask whether there is a God: "Does God exist?" Ask such a question only if the answer will change you, so that if there is a God then you will be one type of person and if there is no God you will be a different person. But if it will not cause any change in you to know whether God exists or is not, then the question is meaningless. It is just curiosity, not inquiry.

As I see it, whether God exists or not, people remain the same. They are interested only for the sake of peripheral knowledge. They are not really concerned; the question is not existential.

So remember, ask whatever you are really concerned about. Only then will the answer be meaningful for you, meaningful in the sense that you are going to be different with a different answer. Will you be a different type of being depending on the answer? Will your whole life begin to have such a different shape that you cannot be the same?

Introduction

The true religion will help you to find your truth. And remember, my truth can never be your truth because there is no way of transferring truth from one person to another. And even if a Gautam Buddha knows the truth, there is no way for you to know whether he knows it or not. Yes, you can recognize somebody who knows the truth, if you also know it. Then you will have the capacity to smell it. Otherwise you are simply believing in public opinion. — Osho

*D*anger: Truth at Work goes straight to the heart of our most fundamental human concerns. Why can't we just live happily and be content? It looks like humanity has all the knowledge needed to solve all its problems and yet — the truth is — the problems are never really solved, and often they only seem to get worse. What's the underlying reason for our failure? Is it something intrinsic to human nature, or ... ?

The truth that Osho exposes here about the roots of our problems is uncomfortable, because he puts our noses directly into what most of us don't want to see — our religious conditioning! "Me, and religiously conditioned? No way — I am free from all that." Or, "I'm spiritual but not religious," or "I'm an atheist, and I agree that religion is at the root of so many problems, but it's not at the root of my problems." Or, maybe you're among those who would say, "Are you kidding? If it weren't for the influence religion, we'd be in an even worse mess than we are!"

Now, if you can manage to put aside whichever of those protests first occurred to you — or maybe it's "all of the above" — you can enter the journey of this book with an open heart. Each chapter has the potential open your eyes to truths that go against everything you have been taught. If you think you've already dropped everything you've been taught, you will encounter passages that push the envelope beyond the comfort zone you now know as your "freedom from your conditioning." You will find yourself seeing things in an unaccustomed way, hearing the religious conditioning that underlies the words of everyone from television pundits to politicians to the latest new age soothsayer. "Turn the other cheek" and "Do unto others" will take on nuances you never even thought about before. And with a little luck, you'll begin to see how much of the way you look at the world is truly your own, and how much of it is mere mechanical repetition and parroting of "inherited wisdom."

This is not just a book to read, in other words, it is a living experience of deconditioning. Osho calls it a "dry-cleaning" of your mind. You might ask — why do I need to be de-conditioned? Because only after we have rid ourselves of ideas and beliefs that have been drilled into us by others — often with the best of intentions — are we able to truly enjoy life as it presents itself to us each moment, to respond to it in a way that is natural and true to ourselves. To be authentic, in other words, living by your own truth rather than settling for the second-hand lie of believing in truths handed down to you by others.

The enclosed DVD allows a first hand experience of this process — to take part in an experiment with a contemporary mystic at work.

Chapter 1
Pseudo-religion — the stick-on soul

? *Why is humanity today becoming more and more miserable?*

The cause is very simple, perhaps too simple. It is very close, very obvious, and this is the reason most people go on not seeing it. When something is very obvious you start taking it for granted. When something is too close to your eyes you cannot see it. For seeing, some distance is needed.

So the first thing I would like you to remember is that it is not only today that humanity is miserable. It has always been miserable. Misery has almost become our second nature. We have lived in it for thousands of years. That closeness does not allow us to see it; otherwise it is so obvious.

But to see the obvious you need a child's vision, and we are all carrying thousands of years in our eyes. Our eyes are old; they cannot see afresh. They have already accepted things, and forgotten that those things are the very cause of misery.

The religious prophets, the political leaders, the moral lawgivers — you have respected them, not even suspecting that they are the cause of your misery. How can you suspect them? Those people have served humanity, sacrificed themselves for humanity. You worship them; you cannot relate them to your misery.

The causes of misery are camouflaged behind beautiful words, holy scriptures, spiritual sermons.

It happened when I was a student, the first prime minister of India came to visit the city. In Jabalpur, all the dirt of the city flows just in the middle of the city. The city is very big — ten times bigger than Portland — and just in the middle of the city, all the dirt flows like a river. There is a bridge over it, and to pass that bridge is to know something about hell. I have never seen any place so stinking.

The day Jawaharlal Nehru, the prime minister, came to visit the city the bridge was one of the greatest problems. He had to cross it — that was the only way to get to the other part of the city. So they covered the bridge with mogra flowers. It was summertime, and the mogra is so fragrant a flower. The whole bridge on both sides had garlands of mogra hanging. You could pass across the bridge and you would not be at all aware that just behind those mogras, the wall of flowers, was the dirtiest place possible.

I was just going to the university. Seeing people decorating the Naudra Bridge — that was the name of the bridge; it was called Naudra because it had nine pillars, nine doors through which the dirt used to flow — seeing the people putting those flowers up, I stopped there. I started working with those people who were decorating, and nobody made any objection; they thought I must be part of the crew. Many people were working, and it had to be done quickly — soon Jawaharlal was going to pass. So it was easy for me to get mixed in with the workers, the volunteers.

When Jawaharlal's procession came and he was standing in an open jeep, I stood in front of the jeep and stopped it. It would not have been possible in any other place because everywhere there were military police, guards, security. On Naudra Bridge the volunteers were on both sides; there was no crowd from the city because nobody wanted to stand there. The crowd was not aware of what had happened, that these mogra flowers had completely covered the smell. The place smelled of paradise! The people were not aware of it because nobody else was near there.

I told Jawaharlal, "Please get down from the jeep. You have to look behind these flowers — that is the reality of this city. You are being fooled; these flowers are not decorations for your welcome, they are put here to deceive you."

He said, "What do you mean?"

I said, "Get down, and just come close to the flowers and look beyond them." He was a very sensitive and intelligent man. Others tried to prevent him, the local leaders.

I said, "Don't listen to these fools. They are the people who have arranged these flowers here. Have you seen in the city, anywhere else, thousands of flowers arranged for your welcome? And here you don't see any crowd. The arithmetic is simple. Just come down."

He got down and went with me to look beyond the flowers; he could not believe it. He told the people, the local leaders, the mayor, the members of the corporation and the president of the congress, "If this young man had not been so stubborn, I would have missed seeing the reality of your city. Is this what you have been doing here?"

He said to me, "If you come to New Delhi sometime, come and visit me."

I said, "Not sometime — I will come just to visit you. But you will have to tell the idiots surrounding you that I am allowed in."

He said to his secretary, "You have to take care that nobody prevents him." That's how his secretary became one of my disciples. And whenever I needed, he was immediately ready to arrange it; the doors of Jawaharlal's house were open to me.

I have remembered this incident because that's what has happened with the whole of humanity. You see the misery, but you don't see the cause. The cause is covered with flowers. You see the flowers, and because flowers cannot cause the misery you turn back.

The second thing to remember is that it is not only now that humanity is miserable; it has always been so.

Yes, one thing new has happened — it is a little difference, but a difference that really makes a difference — and that is, a certain percentage of humanity has now become more aware than it has ever been before.

Misery has always been there; but to be aware of the misery is a new factor. And that is the beginning of transformation. If you become aware of something, then there is a possibility that something can be done to change it.

People have lived in misery, accepting it as part of life, as their destiny. Nobody has questioned it. Nobody has asked why. And before anybody could ask why, the religious prophets, messiahs and priests were ready with the answer. Christianity is ready with the answer: "It is because Adam and Eve committed the original sin; hence you are suffering."

Now, can you see any connection?

According to Christianity the world was created 4004 years before Jesus' birth — which is not at all accurate, which is absolutely stupid. The world is millions of years old — and by "world" I mean only our world, this earth; I don't mean the sun, the solar system, because that is far more ancient. And I don't mean the world of the stars, because they are not as small as they look. They are bigger than your sun — they are all suns and they all have their own solar systems. They are far more ancient than our solar system.

In fact, when you come to calculate existence, years cannot be used as a measurement, they are too small. A million years does not mean anything; when you start thinking about how vast the solar system is, you have to use a new measurement that is not used ordinarily because we never come across such a big thing. And that new measurement was invented by physics: the light year.

You have to understand what a light year means, because our galaxy is millions of light years old. Light travels at a tremendous speed, the greatest speed there is. Anything traveling at that speed will turn into light. The heat of that speed is such that anything at that speed will become light, so there can be no speed greater than the speed of light. We cannot invent any rocket that moves faster than light, because then it will turn into light itself, as soon as it reaches the speed of light.

The speed of light is 186,000 miles per second — one hundred and eighty six thousand miles! In one minute, light travels sixty times farther; in one hour, again sixty times more; in one day, again twenty-four times more; in one month, again thirty times more; in one year, again twelve times more — that is the meaning of one light year.

Even if the Christians are right, Adam must still have committed the original sin at least five thousand years ago. Somebody committing a sin five thousand years ago — how many generations have passed since then? And you are still miserable because of his sin? That seems to be absolutely unjust. If he did commit the sin, God made him suffer. Why should you be suffering? You were never a part of it. If anybody has to suffer, it should be God himself, because in the first place what was the need of creating those two trees? If man was not allowed to eat from them, it was so simple: God should not have created those two trees. He was committing the original sin — if anybody was.

Then, even if he had created them, what was the need to tell Adam not to eat from those two trees? I don't think that Adam, on his own, even by now would have found those two trees. Among the millions of trees, it would have been just a coincidence if Adam had found them. But God showed him the trees, saying, "These are the two trees, and you are not to eat from them."

And this God is Jewish. Sigmund Freud understands it better — he is also Jewish, born out of the original sin — he understands far better than this Jewish God. To tell somebody not to do something is to provoke them, is to give them a challenge, is to make the person fascinated. It is not the snake who really persuades Adam and Eve. It is God's "don't" that hits hard, and they become curious as to why.

And the trees are not poisonous. One is the tree of wisdom. There seems to be no logic in why the tree of wisdom should be prohibited to man. And the other tree is of eternal life. Both trees are the best in the whole Garden of Eden! God should have told him, "Don't miss these two trees! Anything else you can miss, but these two trees you should not miss." On the contrary, he says to Adam and Eve, "Don't do this." That "don't" is the real cause of their disobeying; the serpent is just an excuse.

But even if they did commit the sin, whether through God or through the serpent, it is absolutely certain that you are not part of it — in no way. You were not there to support them. The Christians have been befooling the whole world, the Jews have been befooling the whole world, saying that it is because of the original sin that man is suffering, he is in misery. He has to turn back, he has to undo what Adam and Eve did. They disobeyed; you have to obey God. Just as they disobeyed and were thrown out of heaven, if you obey totally, without any doubt, without any questioning, you will be allowed back into the world of bliss, paradise.

Misery exists because of the original sin, according to the Judaic religions: Judaism, Christianity, Mohammedanism. These three religions have come from the same source; they all believe in the same original sin, and that we are suffering because we are the progeny of those people who committed it.

Even human justice cannot punish a criminal's son because he is a criminal's son. His father may have murdered somebody, a major crime, but then you cannot punish the son too. The son has nothing to do with it. And Adam and Eve did not commit any major crime — they just had a little curiosity. I think anybody who had any sense would have done the same. It was absolutely certain to happen, because there is a deep need in man to know. It is intrinsic, it is not sin. It is in the very nature of man to know, and God is prohibiting him. He is saying, "Remain ignorant."

There is, in the same way, an intrinsic, intense desire for eternal life. Nobody wants to die. Even the person who commits suicide is not against life. Perhaps he is hoping the next life will be better. He is so tired of all this suffering and anguish that he thinks, "In this life there is no chance, so why not take a chance? This life is not giving you anything and is not going to give you anything — take the chance. If you survive and enter into another life, perhaps ... " That perhaps, that lingering desire, is still in the man who is committing suicide. He may be committing suicide against something, but he is not committing suicide against life itself.

These two are the most basic and deep-rooted desires in man, and yet he is prohibited from fulfilling his own nature and his nature is condemned as criminal, as a nature which is rooted in sin. If he fulfills it he feels guilty; if he does not fulfill it he will remain miserable. These people have created the background of your misery.

Let me summarize it: If you are natural you will feel guilty. Then that will be your misery, your anxiety, your anguish: what punishment is going to be there for you? You are disobeying God, because all your scriptures and their commandments are against your nature. So if you fulfill your nature there is misery. If you don't fulfill your nature, there is also bound to be misery because then you will be empty, unfulfilled, discontented; you will feel futile, utterly meaningless.

So there are two types of miserable people in the world: one who follows the religious prophets and one who does not follow them. And it is very difficult to find a third category, a man like me, who does not care one bit! I neither follow them nor am I against them. I do not even hate them — there is no question of loving them. To me they are absolutely absurd and meaningless, irrelevant to our existence.

Take either side and you will be in trouble. Don't take sides, either for or against; just tell those guys, "Go to hell! And take all your scriptures with you." Only then can you be free of misery.

In the East they have a different explanation -- explanations can be different, but the purpose is the same. In the East, the three religions of Hinduism, Jainism and Buddhism, all teach that your misery is because of bad actions in past lives. And you have lived millions of past lives, in different shapes, different bodies, animals, birds. In that way Hindus have a vast perspective. Eight hundred and forty million species of life exist. At least their perspective is vast, not small like the Christian: only 6000 years.

Their perspective is certainly great: 840 million species, and you have passed through them all; then you have become man. In all those long years — you will have to use the term "light years" with Hindus and Jainas and Buddhists — you have committed so many things, good and bad, and everything is recorded about you. If you are suffering, that simply means your bad actions are heavy on you. You have to suffer, that is the only way to get rid of them. You have to pay for your actions. Who else is going to pay? You murdered somebody in your last life, now who is going to pay?

Their explanation seems more mathematical, more logical, than Adam committing sin and you suffering 6000 years later. So many generations have passed, and still the sin is fresh. So many generations have suffered and been punished for it, and you are still being punished for it. Can you punish so many people for one man's sin? And this is going to go on forever and forever.

At least the Eastern vision seems to be more logical: that in your past life you have committed some bad actions and of course you have to suffer for them. I say it looks more logical, but it is not existentially true.

What do I mean when I say it is not existentially true? I mean that whenever you act, the result of the act is intrinsic in the act itself, it does not wait for the next life. Why should it wait? If you drink poison now, will you die in the next life? I have been arguing with Hindu shankaracharyas, Jaina monks, Buddhist bhikkhus, saying: "Tell me, if somebody hits his hand with a hammer, will he suffer in the next life or here, right now?"

Action brings its reaction immediately. It does not wait. Why should it wait, and why particularly for the next life?

They have been befooling people, of course more logically than Christians and Jews and Mohammedans. Hence no sophisticated Hindu can be converted to Mohammedanism, Judaism or Christianity — impossible, because all your ideas look very childish. He has far more logical explanations. But those logical explanations are only significant on the surface; deep down there is nothing much in them.

I have argued with all these people. Not a single one has been able to answer my question. If you put your arm in the fire, will you be burned in the next life? The action is here; the reaction has to be here. They are joined together, they cannot be separated. The moment you love, you are happy. It is not that in this moment you love and you are in deep misery now, and in the next life whether there you love or not, suddenly one day you will feel happy — the good karma of your last life.

You are disconnecting things which are not, in the nature of things, in any way possible to disconnect. You hate somebody and in that very hatred you are burning in fire. You are angry and in that very anger, not out of it, you suffer. My approach is that each moment, whatsoever you are doing you are getting the immediate reaction.

These people are befooling you because they cannot say many things which go against the vested interest. They cannot say that you are poor because the rich are exploiting you — because they are hired by the rich people. Now, for example, a Jaina monk, Acharya Tulsi ... Jaina monks don't travel in the rainy season. And in India, it is not like in America; the seasons are well divided. The rainy season is four months, the summer season is four months, the winter is four months. Lately the seasons have been disturbed because of atomic experiments going on everywhere; otherwise, exactly on the expected date and day, the rains will begin, and exactly on the expected date and day the rains will stop.

The Jaina monk does not travel for the four months of the rainy season. He travels for eight months, and for four months he does not travel because the earth is wet, the grass has grown and many small insects, ants, are there in the grass. He cannot walk on the grass because the grass is alive. And he cannot walk on the wet ground because there may be some insects, which the wetness encourages. He has to walk only on dry ground where he is absolutely certain that no life can be killed by his walking. So the rainy season is out of the question. He cannot even carry an umbrella because that will be a possession. So in the rainy season it will be most difficult. He does not have more than three items of clothing — and all three items will become wet, so he will not even have clothes to change into.

This Jaina monk, Acharya Tulsi, stays in one place. He has a following of 700 monks, and for eight months those monks move around the country and for four months they come to live with the master in one place. But it is a very difficult problem: only very rich people can invite Acharya Tulsi to spend the rainy season in their city, because those seven hundred monks will also come. And that is nothing — when the 700 monks are there, and the head of the monks, Acharya Tulsi — who is like a pope in that sect — is there, then thousands of followers will come to listen. Because in the rainy season in India everything is closed, you cannot do anything. The shops are empty; people start playing cards and chess. All kinds of festivals happen in the rainy season because everybody is free. People visit their relatives, because there is nothing in their business that is at risk.

People visit their religious leaders. And it is a tradition that whosoever comes to see the head of a religious order is a guest of the city, just as the head is a guest of the city. So to invite Acharya Tulsi means spending millions of rupees, and only very rich people can afford it. If they can afford it, they must be businessmen. A businessman is never a loser. He is not a gambler. He counts everything, with interest. If he is going to invest — and that's the right word — millions of rupees in Acharya Tulsi, then he is going to take as much juice out of Acharya Tulsi as possible, with interest, and he will not leave without it. Both the parties understand it -- it is understood, not said. Acharya Tulsi has to protect the rich person because it is the rich person who protects Acharya Tulsi and his monks. It is a simple arrangement.

The same is true about other religions in India. It is a very costly phenomenon. For example, another Jaina sect whose monks live naked cannot stay in any household or family, because to be so close to a family may create attachment. Some trouble may arise, they may be distracted. They can only stay in a temple. And Jaina temples are the costliest and the best temples in India. It is now difficult to build that kind of temple. At Mount Abu — a few of you may have seen the Jaina temples, because I used to have my meditation camps there — they are such masterpieces of art. So much money has been poured into those temples; they are all marble and a single temple may take hundreds of years to build. The grandfather may start, and the third or fourth or fifth generation may inaugurate the temple when it is complete. Thousands of workers will be working on it, artists, craftsmen.

To invite a naked Jaina monk — because the naked Jaina monk is thought to be of the highest order of monks ... Acharya Tulsi is not a naked Jaina monk. He is thought to be of a lower degree. Yes, he is a Jaina, but if you ask the followers of the naked monks, they will say, "There is not much difference between us and Acharya Tulsi. Perhaps he keeps three items of clothing and we keep six: that is all the difference there is. The real difference is between our monks." And certainly the naked Jaina monk tortures himself more than any other in the whole world. Nobody can compete with him; he is the best masochist possible.

To invite a naked Jaina monk means you need a temple that can do justice to his prestige, otherwise you are insulting him. So every big town, big city, goes on wasting money in raising temples because the naked monk can stay only in a temple. Jainas are not many, but they have so many temples all over the country that you will be surprised. Even in places where not a single Jaina family lives you will find Jaina temples, because the Jaina monks pass by there and they need some place to stay.

You will be surprised — it looks very funny to see the whole thing — a Jaina monk is not supposed to beg from anybody other than a Jaina. Now, Jainas are very few, only three hundred thousand all over India — just like a teaspoon full of salt in the ocean. There are thousands of towns and villages where there is not a single Jaina. But the Jaina monk has to move for eight months continually; he has to pass through villages where no Jaina lives.

So what do Jainas do? A procession of twenty families — twenty buses, fifty buses — will follow the monk. But why fifty buses? Just one bus or one car would be enough, if just one Jaina family were needed. No, the Jaina monk has to go begging and he is not allowed to beg from just one family. That is against his scripture. And when the scripture was made, it was quite right because there were so many monks, they were becoming a burden on society. So if a monk comes to one family, finds good food and starts going there every day, he will become a torture to that family. And if other monks come to know about it, they will also start going to the same family.

So the rule was made that no monk begs from just one family — not even a single whole meal. Even for a single whole meal, he has to beg from different families: little pieces from here, little pieces from there. And he is not supposed to beg from the same people again tomorrow. No monk is supposed to beg from the same place where some other monk has already begged. Now this creates trouble; each monk has to beg from many families.

So fifty families, sixty families, follow these traveling monks with all kinds of food. And of course everything is also needed for themselves, they have to carry tents and everything. And there are only twenty-two naked Jaina monks left because the whole thing is so arduous that when one naked monk dies, he is not replaced. It is very difficult. So fifty, sixty buses, a whole procession. Then the tents, and a whole city will be put together in the night because in the morning the monk will come. And they have to make temples in places where they cannot even find a Jaina worshipper. They have to hire a brahmin to worship in the temple.

Now, brahmins and Jainas are enemies — Jainism is a revolt against Brahminism — but brahmins are the only people who know how to worship, so they will be paid to do it. They are not really worshipping; you can see, how can they worship the enemy? This man Mahavira, whose statue is there in the Jaina temple, has been continually criticizing brahmins. Now, the brahmin worships for a salary. Perhaps deep inside he is cursing, but on the surface he is praising and showering flowers and doing whatsoever Jainism prescribes for use in worship.

Then the whole city will be ready by the morning. The monk comes, and the monk knows about all these buses and that this whole city of tents has been raised in the night. When he came by the previous day there was not a single tent at all. And all these people he knows, because they have been following him for four months. Now, these people have to be rich to drop all their businesses, to take their whole family around. And the season is really difficult. In some places there are two hundred inches of rain, and in some places, perhaps the worst, five hundred inches of rain — and they have to follow the monk even to the mountains, because Jainas make their sacred places on the mountains.

Hindus make their sacred places by the side of rivers. Because Hindus had already monopolized the rivers, Jainas had to do something to defeat them — the same competitive mind is everywhere. So they thought that the best thing would be to choose the highest peaks of the mountains and show these fools that the rivers are dirty. People in India even throw dead bodies, half-burned bodies, dead animals into the rivers, and these are your sacred places? So the Jainas made their sacred places on high mountains.

Those buses follow them, and tent cities will arise on those mountains, just there in the night when the monk is sleeping, but not before his eyes. I have asked these naked monks, "Do you really not know that these people are following you — the same faces, the same tents, the same buses — for four months? They are befooling themselves, but whom are you befooling? And what is the purpose of all this circus?"

In private they would say to me, "You are right, but what can we say about it? You always hit wherever it hurts most. You have a knack," they would say to me, "of hitting people at their weakest point. Now this is clear, four months ... I know, but I cannot say it in public, because then how would I survive?" He depends on these people. These people are businessmen, they are investing money. They want him to say to the poor, "You are suffering from your past bad karmas, and these rich people are enjoying their good karmas from a past life. If you want to enjoy yourself then do good karmas, obey the scriptures, follow the principles handed down by the great masters, and in your next life you will be rich."

I was trying to explain why the priests have to bring in the next life: because about this life they cannot do anything. And about the next life, one thing is good: that nobody knows what will happen — whether anything will happen or not, whether anybody will survive or not. This strategy was invented so that the explanation would remain rational. Otherwise, there are people who are doing all that the scriptures say, and yet they are suffering, they are poor, they are sick. They ask, "We are doing everything that you say — then why are we suffering?" Leaving them aside, even these Jaina monks ... One dies with cancer, now what is he suffering for? In his whole life he never did a single thing that can be said to be wrong. You have to find the explanation somewhere in his past lives.

Man is in misery because religions have not helped him to destroy the causes of misery. On the contrary, they have consoled him so that he remains as he is.

Revolt, revolution, are of the same order as disobedience, disorder, creating chaos: you will suffer tremendously in the coming life. You are suffering now, and you are preparing the ground for more suffering. So they created this gap between this life and the coming life, the past life and this life. And it is a beautiful strategy, because neither have you any evidence of your past life — that you committed any bad actions or good actions — nor have you any way to know what is going to happen to you in the next life, the coming life.

They have given beautiful explanations and camouflaged the whole stinking reality behind beautiful flowers, so that you smell the flower and you forget the stinking river flowing just underneath as an undercurrent. Throw away these flowers and immediately you will be able to see why humanity is in so much suffering.

The new thing that has happened is, as I said before, that one percent of humanity has come to a point where it can become a little alert, awake. And that one percent of humanity, becoming aware of the misery, seeing the whole of humanity already in hell, is asking: "What hell are you talking about? There cannot be anything worse than what is happening on the earth." This one percent of humanity has created such questions. Those questions have also reached those people who are not so alert, but the questions have reached them anyway. They have also heard and started feeling some little stirring of consciousness: "Yes, there is misery, and immense misery."

Politicians have been deceiving you. They say, "If there is democracy, there will be no suffering. If there is independence, there will be no suffering. If there is socialism there will be no suffering. If there is communism suffering disappears." But there is democracy, and suffering goes on growing, accumulating. Countries are independent — not all countries are in slavery — but even in the countries that are independent, the misery is not less. Perhaps it is even more, because now they cannot dump their misery on anybody else — they are independent. A slave country at least has a consolation. That is my experience.

Before India became independent there was such a feeling all over India. My house was a place of conspiracy. My two uncles had been in jail many times, and every week they had to go to the police station to report that they were not doing anything against the government, and that they were still living in the same place. They were not allowed to move out of the town -- but people were coming to them, and they all had so much hope.

I was a small child but I always wondered, "These people are saying that just by becoming independent, all misery will disappear. How can that happen? I don't see any connection." But there was hope. There was the promised land very close by; just a little struggle and you would reach it. There was suffering but you were not responsible for it, the Britishers were responsible. It was a great consolation to dump everything on the Britishers.

In fact, I used to question these revolutionaries who would secretly visit my house, or sometimes stay in my house for months. One of them, a very famous revolutionary, Bhavani Prasad Tiwari, was the national leader of the socialist party. Whenever he had to go underground he used to come to my village and just live in my house, hidden. For the whole day he would not come out — and nobody knew him in the village anyway. But I was after him. He told me again and again, "You bring such inconvenient questions that sometimes I think it would be better to be in a British jail than in your house. At least there I would get first class treatment."

He was a famous leader, so he would have received first class treatment — political prisoners' special class — with all the facilities, good food, a good library. And at least he would have some freedom, because first class prisoners were not forced to do any labor. They would write their autobiographies and other books: all the books these great Indian leaders have written were written in jails. And they would go for walks. They were put in beautiful places that were not even jails, places that were created especially for them.

For example in Pune there was a palace just opposite our commune there, on the other side of the river: the Aga Khan palace. It was a palace. Gandhi was kept prisoner there, and his wife too. His wife died there, her grave is still there in the Aga Khan's palace. You might have seen it in Pune — when you pass the bridge, just on top of the hill above there is a beautiful house.

I had asked the owner, because the owner lived in Mumbai and used to come to me, "Whatsoever you want you can take, but give that house to me before I move to Pune. I want that house" — because in the whole of Pune, that was the highest point from where you could see the whole city, and it was really a beautiful palace.

He said, "It is difficult because it belongs to my mother. She is the owner of the house and she will not sell it because Gandhi was kept prisoner there, and she is a follower of Gandhi. She wants to make it a national museum in the memory of Gandhi. It is impossible to persuade her — and particularly for you! Even your name is unmentionable in my family. When I come here I have to say I am going somewhere else. Your name is unmentionable." Gandhians will not mention my name because I have been speaking against Gandhi continually.

So these special palaces were turned into prisons. They had acres of greenery, beautiful views. So Bhavani Prasad Tiwari used to say to me, "It would be better if I stop going underground, because you ask such inconvenient questions."

I said, "If you cannot answer them, what is going to happen to the country when the country becomes independent? They will be the questions which you will have to solve. You cannot even answer them verbally, and then you will actually have to solve them. I asked him, "Just by the Britishers leaving the country" — and there were not many Britishers — "how is poverty going to disappear? And do you want me to believe that before the Britishers came to India, India was not poor?"

It was as poor as it is now, perhaps even poorer, because the Britishers brought industry and technology that helped the country to become a little better. They brought education, schools, colleges, universities. Before that, there was no way to be educated: the only educated people were the brahmins, because the father would teach the son. They kept everybody else uneducated because that was the best way to keep them enslaved. Education can be dangerous.

"How are you going to destroy poverty? How are you going to destroy the hundreds of kinds of anxieties and miseries which have nothing to do with the British? Now, a husband is suffering because of his wife — how is it going to help? The Britishers have gone, okay; but the wife will still be there, the husband will still be there — how is it going to change anything?"

He said, "I know it is very difficult, but let us first get independence."

I said, "I know that after independence the problems will be the same, perhaps worse."

They are worse. In three hundred years not a single British governor general was assassinated. Now you can assassinate the prime minister. Your independence has given you great intelligence! In three hundred years the Punjabi Sikhs never said that they wanted a separate nation. Now they want a separate nation. This is what independence has given to people. But the real question is about the Hindu minority who live in the Punjab. They will all be killed. Either they will have to become Sikhs, or they will have to be slaughtered. So it is not only a question of giving independence to a particular state, the problem is of the Hindu minority. Where to take them? They will all be killed.

That's what happened in Pakistan. When Pakistan was created, all the Hindus who tried to remain in Pakistan were slaughtered. And Pakistan was not enriched by it. These are not the ways to become rich. Pakistan now is far poorer than India. The poverty has become greater because the population has grown. Now, the Britishers are not responsible for the growing population. You go on producing children.

Political leaders have kept humanity hoping — always somewhere far away, the great hope. For the classless society Russia suffered everything for more than sixty years: "The classless society is going to happen soon!" When will those days of waiting be finished? This is an old strategy. Jesus used to say to his followers, "Very soon you will be with me in the kingdom of God. Very soon you will see that those who follow me are saved, and those who don't follow me fall into eternal hell." It has not happened yet, and we don't even know whether Jesus is with God or not.

He even promised that he would be coming back. I think he must have lost courage — once crucified is enough! Now again he will be crucified, this time in the Vatican, because this time he will be coming as a Christian. And the pope will be the person who will decide: "This man has to be crucified — he is a pretender, an anti-Christ. He is not our lord, because when our lord comes he will come with glory, sitting on a cloud. That's how the lord has to come. And this man is born out of a woman, and not even out of a virgin." They are looking for the cloud the lord will be coming on, and the lord has escaped!

But the hope... Politicians go on giving hope and nothing materializes. One thing has to be understood clearly: no hope is going to help; no false explanation is going to help. You have to put aside all this crap and see into reality as it is. The reality is that this earth cannot tolerate so great a population; the population has to become almost half the size that it is now. But the way it is moving, it will be doubled instead. Misery will also be doubled.

I would like the population to be half of what it is — but for that you need intelligence, understanding. You have to understand that children are not sent by God. There is no God who is sending children.

In fact, a single man has enough seeds, in his forty or fifty years' lifetime, while he is capable of producing children, to produce the whole population of the earth — a single man! In each sexual orgasm, millions of potential human beings are lost. This is not something that God is doing, otherwise he is a very stupid God. What is the point of giving so many seeds to a man when the woman normally can only have one egg fertilized in a year? This is what created the trouble: man started having many wives. But a woman cannot start having many husbands — because a man can make many women pregnant, but if a woman has many husbands, what will they be doing? One woman, one man makes her pregnant, so the remaining ones go to the pub — where else?

This has nothing to do with God, this is simple biology. People have to be told to understand biology and to use all the methods which are available to reduce the population completely to half of what it is.

Stop bothering to go to the synagogue, to the temple, to the church, because they have befooled you enough. Stop asking these people — the rabbis, the monks, the priests — because all that they know they have been giving as consolation for thousands of years and all their consolations have proved impotent.

You have to turn from politicians, from religious people, to the scientist. The whole of humanity has to focus on science if it wants to get rid of misery.

And my religion I call the science of the inner soul. It is not religion; it is an exact science. Just as science functions in the objective world, this science functions in the subjective world.

Remember, the outer science can help immensely to reduce your suffering and misery by almost ninety percent. And once you remove ninety percent of your suffering and miseries, which are physical, biological — science can very easily remove them — then the remaining ten percent of misery will be for the first time clear to you. Right now it is lost in the mess of this ninety percent of misery.

Then you will be able to see that all that misery was nothing compared to this ten percent; this ten percent is the real anguish. And that can be transformed only through inward movement: call it meditation, awareness, watchfulness.

But that ten percent misery is of tremendous weight. The ninety percent is nothing, it is just hunger — you need food, you need shelter, you need employment, and all these things can be tackled by science.

Remove the priest completely. He has no function for the future. He has already done enough mischief. Focus on science, and then immediately you will see a new dimension arising in you, of which you were not aware.

It was there — but a hungry man, how can he think whether life has meaning or not? A hungry man cannot think whether the flower is beautiful or not; he is hungry. You cannot talk to him about music and poetry and painting. That will be humiliating him; it will just be an insult, an outright insult. But once these problems disappear then he will start, for the first time, to inquire about real existential questions which can be answered only by a subjective science.

So there is no future for religion. There is a future for an objective science to deal with objective matters, and a subjective science to deal with your inward matters. One will take care of your physiology, biology. The other will take care of your psychology and your ultimate center: the soul.

Chapter 2
I call it reverence for life

? *What do you think about the philosophy of nonviolence, and particularly about the Christian idea of turning the other cheek?*

I am not a philosopher. The philosopher thinks about things. It is a mind approach. My approach is a no-mind approach. It is just the very opposite of philosophizing. It is not thinking about things, ideas, but seeing with a clarity that comes when you put your mind aside, when you see through silence, not through logic. Seeing is not thinking.

The sun rises: if you think about it you miss it, because while you are thinking about it, you are going away from it. In thinking you can move miles away, and thoughts go faster than anything possible.

If you are seeing the sunrise then one thing has to be certain, that you are not thinking about it. Only then can you see it. Thinking becomes a veil on the eyes. It gives its own color, its own idea to the reality. It does not allow reality to reach you, it imposes itself upon reality; it is a deviation from reality.

Hence no philosopher has ever been able to know the truth. All the philosophers have been thinking about the truth. But thinking about the truth is an impossibility. Either you know it, or you don't. If you know it, there is no need to think about it. If you don't know it, how can you think about it? A philosopher thinking about truth is just like a blind man thinking about light. If you have eyes, you don't think about light, you see it.

Seeing is a totally different process; it is a byproduct of meditation.

Hence I would not like my way of life ever to be called a philosophy, because it has nothing to do with philosophy. You can call it philosia. The word philo means love; sophy means wisdom, knowledge — love for knowledge. In philosia, philo means the same love, and sia means seeing: love, not for knowledge but for being — not for wisdom, but for experiencing.

So that is the first thing to be remembered. Nonviolence is a philosophy to Mahatma Gandhi; it is not a philosophy to me, it is a philosia. That's where I have been constantly struggling with Gandhian philosophers, thinkers.

Gandhi wrote his autobiography entitled *Experiments with Truth*. Now that is utter absurdity; you cannot experiment with truth. When you are silent, truth is there in its fullness, in its absolute glory. And when you are not silent, truth is absent. When you are silent, truth does not appear like an object before you. When you are silent, suddenly you recognize you are the truth. There is nothing to see. The seer is the seen, the observer is the observed; that duality no longer exists. And there is no question of thinking. There is no doubt, there is no belief; there is no idea.

Gandhi was trying to experiment with truth. The simple implication is: you know what truth is; otherwise how are you going to experiment with it? And for a man who knows truth, what is the need to experiment? He lives it; for him there is no alternative. To Gandhi everything is philosophy; to me everything is philosia. Gandhi is a thinker, I am not a thinker. My approach is existential, not mental. Nonviolence -- the very word is not appealing to me, it is not my taste, because it is negative. Violence is positive; nonviolence is negative. Nobody has paid any attention to the simple fact that you are making violence positive, solid; and nonviolence is simply negating it.

I call it reverence for life; I don't use the word nonviolence. Reverence for life — it is positive; then nonviolence happens just of its own accord. If you feel reverence for life, how can you be violent? But it is possible you can be nonviolent and still you may not have any reverence for life.

I know these so-called nonviolent people. You will be amazed to know that in Kolkatta, Jains have a very important place. In all the big cities — Mumbai, Kolkatta — the Jains are the super-rich people. In Kolkatta I came to know of a strange phenomenon; when I saw it for the first time I could not believe my eyes. I used to stay in the house of a very unique man, Sohanlal Dugar. He was unique in many ways. I loved the man, he was very colorful. He was old — when he met me first, at that time he was seventy years old, but he lived to ninety.

He met me in Jaipur, that was his home town, and he invited me to Kolkatta because that was his business place. From there he controlled the whole silver market, not only of India but of the whole of Asia. He was called the Silver King. I had heard about him, but I had no idea who the person was. When he came to me for the first time in Jaipur, he touched my feet — an old man dressed in the Rajasthani way with a yellow turban, very ancient-looking in every way — and took out bundles of notes from the pockets of his coat and wanted to give them to me.

I said, "But right now I don't need them. You just give me your address; whenever I need I will inquire and if you are still in possession of wealth and in the mood to give, you can give. But right now I don't have any need, so why unnecessarily give me trouble? I am going now to travel for thirty-six hours, and I will have to take care of these notes. I will not even be able to sleep because anybody might take them. So please keep them." He just started crying, tears pouring from his eyes. I said, "But I have not said anything that would hurt you so much."

He said, "Nothing else hurts me more. I am a poor man because I have only money and nothing else. I want to do something for you — I feel so much for you — but I am a poor man: except money, I have nothing. And if you refuse my money, you refuse me, because I don't have anything else. So take this money. If you want to burn it, burn it here right now. If you want to throw it away, throw it away right now — that is your business. But remember, never again refuse money from me, because that means you are refusing me. I have nothing else to offer." His tears were so sincere and authentic, and what he said was so meaningful, that I said, "Okay. Give me this money, and take out the rest, too. You have more in your pockets."

He said, "That's right! That's the man I have been in search of," and he took all his money out. He showed me his pockets, inside out, and said, "Now, right now, I don't have anything else, but this is the man I have been in search of." And he invited me to Kolkatta.

Where he lived was a Jaina colony. Jainas tend to live together in one place because they don't want to associate with "lower human beings." They think they are the highest, the purest, the most religious. There, he told me, "I will show you something which will surprise you." He took me to one of his rooms, opened the window, and said, "Look outside."

Outside I saw … I could not figure out what it was. There were at least one hundred cots, without any mattresses on them, and one hundred people on those naked cots trying to sleep. I said, "But what is the matter? Why are the mattresses missing, and why don't they have any pillows? They are certainly in discomfort; you can see they are tossing and turning."

He said, "You don't know the reality of what you are seeing. There is something more to it; these people are hired by Jainas."

I said, "Hired? For what?"

He said, "To sleep on these cots."

I said, "But what is the purpose of it all?"

He explained it to me. In India, in hot countries, insects of all kinds grow very easily. A certain insect, a parasite — what you call in English a bedbug — makes its home in these cots.

Jainas cannot kill them because of their philosophy of nonviolence. They cannot kill them, and if nobody sleeps on those cots, the bedbugs will die — so they hire people. They will give you five rupees per night: you sleep in a cot full of bedbugs and they will suck your blood the whole night.

Nonviolent people are not necessarily life-reverent. Now what kind of business is going on? They are saving the bedbugs — but what about these poor men? The Jainas don't think about that. They are paying them so there is no problem with it. The people have agreed to sleep on the cots, and they are paying them.

But just to think of the idea, that you will put a man in such a situation! And the man must be in trouble because why should he be ready, for five rupees, to destroy his whole life? Maybe his mother is dying, maybe his wife is in hospital, maybe his father had an accident and those five rupees are essential for medicine, for food, for something. And every day there is a line: not all the people get in. There are only a hundred cots; those who get in are fortunate. And these people who are paying them are earning virtue. Their bank balance in the other world is growing — they have saved so many bedbugs from dying. A strange love affair with bedbugs! And they don't think about this man, the whole night being tortured. No, they have paid him, so there is no guilt about that.

I want you to remember: a man believing in nonviolence need not be necessarily life-reverent. But one who reveres life is bound to be nonviolent — that is its necessary corollary. But his nonviolence will have a totally different flavor. It will not be Mahatma Gandhi's nonviolence.

For example: Gandhi is continually trying to teach nonviolence to his disciples, and following it himself. He is not a fraud; whatsoever he believes may be wrong, but he does it with his totality. His intention is always sincere, you cannot doubt his sincerity, but his intelligence is not so indubitable. And a man with strong intentions, but not a high quality of intelligence, is more dangerous than anybody, because the intention is blind. Gandhi thought that he was teaching nonviolence, but in fact he was teaching people to be violent to themselves.

This cannot happen to my way of life. Reverence for life does not exclude me. If I am full of reverence for life all around, how can I be irreverent towards my own life?

In deep silence there is no mine and no thine. Life is simply life; it is one flow. We are joined together by invisible threads. If I hurt you, I hurt myself. If I hurt myself, I am hurting you all.

I want the distinction to be clear. It is delicate. The man who believes in nonviolence will be very careful not to be violent to anybody — too careful! But because he has not experienced reverence for life, it is only an ideology. Rationally he has concluded that this is good, that this is the right path, and he is going to be very violent to himself. In fact his violence towards others will turn upon himself but the proportion will remain the same.

I have experienced it in people, for example hunters, who are violent people, killers. Just near my university, two hundred miles away, was a forest reserve — one of the most beautiful forests in India, Kanha Keshali. For hundreds of miles, all kinds of wild life — you could find every kind possible, imaginable. Hunting was prohibited except for special guests of the viceroy, of the governor, and later on, of the prime minister, the president, and the chief minister. For special guests hunting was allowed, otherwise it was completely prohibited.

Whenever I had time I used to drive to Kanha Keshali. The rest house in Kanha Keshali was in such a beautiful place, on a vast lake, surrounded by greenery as far as you could see. And for days you would not come across or see a man, but you would see thousands of deer passing in the night. And in the night the deer's eyes become almost flames. A thousand or two thousand deer passing in the night, if it was a full-moon night you could see thousands of small lights moving in line. And they had to come to the lake in the night to drink water. All the animals would come in the night; you only had to sit in the rest house and you would be able to see lions and tigers.

Once in a while I would meet a group of hunters, special people. I was surprised to know one thing, that these hunters were violent people, but very loving, very friendly. I have lived with nonviolent people who are never loving, never friendly. The contrast was such that I started to look deeper into it: what was the matter? I made friends with great hunters of India, kings, princes — and in India there were so many maharajas and so many princes, and they were all hunters. If you go into a maharaja's palace you will find out how many lions he has killed; they are all on exhibition. The whole house is full of dead animals, preserved, stuffed. And that is their pride.

I started making friends with these people and what I found was that they were all very nice, very loving, very simple and very innocent people. The man may have killed one hundred lions, but he himself is very childlike. He has not that arrogant, egoistic attitude of a non-violent Jaina or a non-violent Gandhian. He is a simple man, a simple human being. He knows he is not a saint. But these people who believe in nonviolence automatically start believing they are saints, superior beings, higher than everybody else. In their egoistic attitude there is more violence than there may be in the whole life of a hunter who has killed many animals.

The nonviolent believer does no violence to you physically, but psychologically he is very violent. Psychologically he will try to prove his superiority in every possible way. And one thing more: whatsoever violence he has prevented reaching others has not simply disappeared; things don't disappear like that. The violent mind is inside. If you don't allow it to express its violence on others, it is going to turn upon itself

So, nonviolent people have been torturing themselves in every possible way. They are very inventive in finding new methods of torturing themselves. The violence has not disappeared; it has only taken a roundabout turn. Gandhi was very violent to himself — just any excuse and he would go on a fast. Fasting is violence. If you keep somebody else starving it is violence. And if you keep yourself starving, isn't it violence? Do you have double standards?

Whether I keep you starving or I keep myself starving, it is the same; the same principle and the same standard should be applied: I am a violent man, if not to your body, then to my own body. And in being violent with you, there was a possibility that you may have retaliated — you may have stopped me being violent to you. But to be violent with your own body is the easiest thing in the world. What can your body do? It cannot retaliate, it cannot prevent you. It has no defense against you. So the person who is violent to others, at least is violent to someone who has the right to defend himself and can be violent in return. But the person who is violent with himself is really cunning, very cunning. He has found the most innocent victim in the world, defenseless. You can do anything you want to your own body.

There have been monks who have been beating their body every morning, till the blood starts oozing all over the body. And they were thought to be great saints! There was one Christian saint in Alexandria who remained on a sixty-foot-high pillar — on top of it there was space enough just to sit. For thirty years he remained sitting on that pillar. He was sleeping there; people were sending food and he was pulling the food up on ropes. He was defecating, urinating from the pillar ... but this was thought to be great austerity. And from hundreds of miles people would come to pay respect to this madman. He had no other quality, but even kings came to pay him respect. What was he doing? — just torturing himself.

I have seen in India so many people torturing themselves in so many ways that it became absolutely clear to me that all the religions up to now have been dominated by sado-masochists. There is no question about it. These religions give enough evidence that the people who founded the religions and the people who followed the religions were sado-masochists.

I came across a man who was standing for many years. Now, you cannot stand very long; he was standing for many years. All his body had shrunk. His whole weight had gone into the legs; the legs had become elephant legs. Now even if he wanted to sit, it was impossible. He had to sleep standing. Just in front of him there was a wooden support hanging from the ceiling. He would put his hands on the support and sleep that way, and the whole day also he was standing. And thousands of people were worshipping him.

I asked them, "What quality is there that you are worshipping? Is it just because he is standing, just because he is an idiot? What has he gained by standing? Just look at his face. Has he ever said a single thing which has any meaning?" He was a very ordinary man. But he managed, just by standing, to become a great sage. Now, this man is nonviolent to everybody but himself; this is sheer violence. And I cannot conceive, if you have reverence for life, how you can destroy your own life in this way.

Jainism is the only religion which allows a monk, if he wills it, to fast unto death. They don't call it suicide, they have a very beautiful name for it: santhara. Santhara means one who has dropped the lust for life, who has gone beyond the lust for living. Many Jaina monks die every year by santhara. The government cannot do anything because it is their religious practice. The secular government is not supposed to interfere in anybody's religion. And they don't commit suicide by taking poison or killing themselves with a sword — no, they have a very torturous method. An electric chair would be far more nonviolent — you just sit on it and you are gone, you may not even feel it. Or you can be put under chloroform, so you don't even feel when you are and when you are not.

But the Jaina monk will fast for two months, three months. There have been cases which have lasted up to ninety days: three months of not eating. He goes on becoming a skeleton; as more and more days pass, more crowds go on coming and he cannot even open his eyes. People are singing and chanting in his praise, and I don't think he can hear anything — for two months he has been on the fast; he is just bones. You can say he is alive because he is still breathing, but except for the breathing and the pulse and the heartbeat, there is no sign of life. For three months he may hang on in this limbo, between death and life. And these people are non-violent people!

Gandhi learned his nonviolence from these idiots. He recognized as one of his gurus, his masters, a Jaina monk, Shrimad Rajchandra, who tortured himself and taught people the same — because what else are you going to teach people? Whatever you are doing, you are going to teach people the same. Hence I call them sado-masochists; these people are both. Ordinarily, in psychiatric hospitals you will find somebody is a sadist, somebody is a masochist; it is very rarely you find one man having both diseases, the sado-masochist.

The sadist enjoys torturing others. Adolf Hitler, Joseph Stalin, Mussolini, Mao Zedong, Tamerlane, Nadirshar, Alexander, Napoleon — these are the people who are sadists, who enjoy others being tortured. And there are masochists who enjoy torturing themselves. The masochists offer themselves to be tortured. They are in search of a sadist.

Somebody was asking me what kind of a man and woman would be the best couple. I said, "One should be a sadist and one should be a masochist. That will be the best-fitting couple in the world. They are never going to divorce. One enjoys torturing; the other enjoys being tortured. They are immensely fulfilled." And there are couples who you may think are ideal couples, for the simple reason that one is a sadist and the other is a masochist. They fit.

The masochist finds strange ways, philosophies, rationalizations. One woman is here... When she first came to see me, fifteen years ago, she brought a young man; she had come with that young man. The young man was in search of a master who could teach him to live only on water. She had brought that masochist. But he did not think he was a masochist. He thought he was in search of the most natural way of living. Of course he could not stay with me. The woman had brought him; he escaped and she was left with me.

That kind of man you will find in many places. Somebody becomes a naturalist, and he lives according to the ideals naturopathy gives him. One of my aunts was a naturopathy freak. I told her many times, "You will simply kill yourself doing these stupid things." And that's what happened. She was perfectly okay, but the naturopath goes on finding something wrong. And if you search you will find; the body is a complex phenomenon. Just a slight headache, and that's enough to go on a fast; you are just feeling tired, that's enough to take an enema. Anything ... and you know what to do because you go on reading. Books are available with simple treatments, and there are not many of them, so every patient becomes a doctor in naturopathy. Just any small book you can read, and that's all, it is not much.

I told her again and again ... I was living with her for four years, and I was preventing her in every possible way. I would throw out her enemas, and throw away her bath tub — she had many sizes of sitz baths, and I don't know what. She had such a collection of strange instruments, and I would simply throw them out. The moment I found anything I would throw it away. And she was continually putting mud packs on her stomach, on her head, on her back. I said, "What is going on? Continually — twenty-four hours a day? Millions of people are moving around but nobody is doing these things that you go on doing." So while I was in the house I would take away her mud packs, ice packs, hot packs — but the moment I would leave the house, because I had to go to the university, she would immediately try to do her thing.

For two years I had to go out of Jabalpur for my MA degree. In those two years she killed herself — not even two years, it took just one year. I had not even completed my course there; after just nine or ten months I went to see her; she could not even recognize me. And it was her own doing. I told her husband, "You see now? You were also supporting her. And you were all against me, because I was taking her instruments and things." But she was always trying to find them in different places. She had different kinds of mud from different mines. She would go miles to find a special kind of mud. I said, "You would tell me, 'You throw these things out, and this is not good.'" For just nine months I was away, and she went mad. The doctors said that she couldn't survive; she had destroyed her whole system.

In India naturopathy became associated with Yoga, naturally, because that is a traditional thing. So to clean yourself... Now what uncleanliness is there? And if you are really going to clean yourself, you are going to die because everything is unclean. Inside there is blood and mucus and meat, flesh, this and that; everything is unclean — so clean yourself!?

She was continually cleaning herself. You can clean your lower intestines with an enema, but you cannot clean the upper part with an enema. Yoga has a method for it: you swallow a thirty-foot-long cloth just like a thin rope. You go on swallowing it so it goes inside you — it is thirty foot long so it is going to go right inside — and then leave it as long as you can. Then take it out so it brings all the mucus and anything that is impure from inside. I was preventing her from doing this, but once I was gone she was completely free, so she cleaned herself — and died. Then I told her husband, "Now you clean yourself and follow her."

Other people will just eat rice; they say that rice is the only right thing. These people are basically finding some way they can convince themselves that they are doing something good to themselves.

So, people like Adolf Hitler are sadists. Then there are masochists. Masochists don't do much harm, they only do harm to themselves. Sadists do tremendous harm because their joy is in torturing others. But the greatest harm is done by sado-masochists.

Mahatma Gandhi is a sado-masochist. First he tortures himself; that self-torture gives him the authority to torture you. He knows the path, he knows the way; he has done it all. He was also a faddist about naturopathy, mud packs and enemas, and only eating this and not eating that. And this had to be followed by everybody. Of course he was far ahead of the disciples, so he had the authority. The disciples knew that they had limitations, but they would do the best they could. The master of course is the master.

I have no philosophy of nonviolence, but I have a way of life, which you can call reverence for life. And this is a totally different perspective.

Non-violence simply says don't kill others. Do you think that is enough? It is only a negative statement: don't kill others, don't harm others. Is that enough? Reverence for life says share, give your joy, your love, your peace, your bliss. Whatsoever you can share, share.

.

If you are reverent towards life then it becomes worship.

Then everywhere you feel existence alive. Then watering a tree becomes worship. Then feeding a guest becomes worship. And you are not obliging anybody, you are not doing a service; you are simply enjoying yourself. The same way those people are enjoying torturing, you are enjoying sharing.

So I want it to be remembered by you once and for all that reverence for life is my approach. Then nonviolence comes automatically, there is no need to bother about it. And when it comes of its own accord it is never ugly.

And you ask me: What do I say about the Christian philosophy, the Christian attitude of turning the other cheek? Jesus learned that idea from India. There was no other way for him to learn it, because Jewish scriptures have no ideas about nonviolence. Even the Jewish God is not nonviolent. He clearly declares, "I am an angry god. And those who are not with me are against me. I am not nice," he says, "I am not your uncle."

Certainly he is your father, not your uncle. With an uncle you can have some nice relationship, friendship. Mostly uncles are nice. But your father ... So he makes it clear: "Don't try to make me your uncle. I am not your uncle." Actually declaring this: "I am not your uncle, remember it, and I am not nice; I am a very angry and jealous god." When Adolf Hitler said, "Those who are not with me are against me," perhaps he was not aware that he was being very Jewish! That is the attitude of the Jewish God.

From where did Jesus get the idea of nonviolence? It had never existed anywhere except in India. And particularly at the time when Jesus moved from Egypt to India, it was very much in the air because Mahavira had passed away just five hundred years before, Buddha had passed away just five hundred years before. Sanjay Viletthiputta who was a very significant master, Ajit Keshkambal who was also a very charismatic figure, Makhkhali Gosal — all these people had turned the whole climate of India toward nonviolence. Everybody was talking about nonviolence.

Brahmins became ashamed of their scriptures; they started changing the commentaries on their scriptures. They started changing their rituals. You will be surprised: now if you go into a Hindu temple, you are supposed to offer a coconut. This coconut was originally not a coconut but the head of a man. But a coconut resembles the head of a man: it has two eyes, beard, and a skull. They started interpreting their scriptures to say that it was not actually a man's head; it was only a coconut you had to offer. You will see in India the statues of Hanumana covered with a red color. Once it was blood, but they had to change it, otherwise they would look very foolish.

The whole country was impressed by these great teachers; they were all of tremendous importance, and they were logically mostly on solid ground. They stopped all kinds of sacrifices. But what will you do without blood? Some red color substitute will do. A few very orthodox places continued in their old ways. For example in Kolkatta, in the temple of Kali, animals are still killed every year and the blood is poured over Kali. In very orthodox places it remained; otherwise it disappeared and substitutes came in.

When Jesus reached India, he must have reached at the time when the whole country was agog with the philosophy of nonviolence. He got the idea from India, and that is one of the reasons why Jews could not accept him. He got many ideas from India and from Egypt. When he came back he was thirty years old. From age thirteen to thirty, seventeen years are completely missing from all Christian accounts. Those seventeen years he spent in Egypt, in India, in Kashmir, in Ladakh, and perhaps Tibet too. The vibe of Buddha and Mahavira was still very alive, so it was not his own vision. But he became tremendously impressed by the idea of nonviolence.

And the idea was rational: to harm somebody must be against God, because it is God's creation — you should not be destructive. But the question was, if others harm you, then ... ? That's where turning the other cheek comes in; that was his invention. It is mentioned nowhere in Indian scriptures that you turn the other cheek. The question was not raised, it seems. Nonviolence was preached so rationally that nobody asked, "If somebody harms you, then what?"

Mahavira and Buddha would be perfectly ready: "Let him harm you, he will be punished by his karmas. Do not bother about it; go on your way."

Yes, once Buddha was asked, "If somebody hits me," a bhikkhu, a monk asked him, "what am I supposed to do?"

Buddha said, "You are walking and a branch of a tree falls on you, hits you. What are you going to do?"

The man said, "What can I do? It was just an accident, a mere coincidence that I was under the tree and the branch fell down."

Buddha said, "So do the same. Somebody was crazy, mad, angry; he hit you. It is just like a branch falling on you. Don't be disturbed by this, don't be distracted by this. Just go on your way as if nothing has happened."

But when Jesus came back to Jerusalem and started saying this — people must have been asking him again and again because it was so new to the Jewish tradition. It was bringing in a very foreign idea which did not fit with the Jewish structure at all.

Jesus said that if somebody hits you on one cheek, turn the other cheek. You are asking me what I have to say about it. This will be the attitude of a man who believes in the idea of nonviolence, the philosopher of nonviolence. But when you are hit by somebody and you give him the other cheek, you are encouraging violence in the world. It is not nonviolence.

And you are assuming something which is absolutely your imagination. If somebody hits me, according to Jesus I have to give him my other cheek. But his tastes may be different. He may have enjoyed the first hit, he may enjoy the second even more: he may be a sadist. Then you are encouraging a sadist to torture people; you are encouraging violence. Even to allow your own body to be tortured by somebody is to encourage violence.

No, this stupid ideology has been the downfall of the whole of India. After Buddha and Mahavira, India never again became the same golden bird it was. After Buddha and Mahavira the downfall began. Buddha and Mahavira are absolutely responsible for twenty-five centuries of slavery in India, because they taught people to be nonviolent. They completely forgot that the other people surrounding the country are not nonviolent. You are encouraging those people, inviting them: "Come and be violent to us."

That's actually what happened in Indian history for twenty-five centuries. Anybody who wanted riches, women, slaves, invaded India. There was no trouble; India was nonviolent. Most probably they would pass through kingdoms and there would be no fight at all, no resistance even.

If you look at your nonviolence and it has provoked violence, then what kind of nonviolence is it? It has brought more violence in the world than there was before. Before Buddha and Mahavira, India was never invaded. There had never been any violence because people knew that to invade India was to just invite your death. But after Buddha and Mahavira's teachings people became just like butter — you just cut into them with your knife, and there would be no noise at all. And millions of people were killed, burned, without any resistance because resistance would be violence.

But you go on missing the point that you are provoking the violence in the other person. Who is responsible for it? Now turning the other cheek means you are telling the other person, "Please hit me a little more, it is not enough; I am not satisfied. Hit me a little more so that I can become a little more saintly." And you have only two cheeks. What are you going to do when he has hit you on your second cheek? What Jesus is saying looks like a beautiful statement but it is not at all practical, pragmatic or scientific.

Reverence for life approaches the whole problem from a different angle. I will say respect life, yours included. In fact, you have to be respectful towards yourself first, only then can you be respectful towards anybody else. Be loving towards yourself, then you will be able to love others too.

Reverence for life will not allow any provocation to violence. It will not start violence, but if anybody starts it, it will stop it immediately.

Jesus says, "If somebody hits you on one of your cheeks, turn the other cheek." I say, "Okay, turn his other cheek — and hit him harder! Teach him a lesson. Make it clear to him that it is not so easy to hit somebody on the cheek; it comes back, and comes back harder. And if you are capable, hit both his cheeks at the same time. Why give him the chance to turn the other cheek and become a saint? Hit him and tell him simultaneously, 'I do not believe in violence, hence I have to stop it at the first chance. And remember that you cannot just be violent without being prevented.'"

You have to prevent violence if you respect life.

And in another way too, it is respectful to hit the man, not to give him your other cheek, because that is very disrespectful. This may seem a little difficult for you: you hit me, and I don't hit you, but show my other cheek to you, and say, "Please be kind enough to hit me." I am trying to be superhuman and reduce you below humanity. I am humiliating you far more than I can humiliate you by hitting you. By hitting you I simply declare you are human, I am human, and I speak the same language that you speak. We are both on the same ground.

This is more respectful because you are not raising yourself higher; you are keeping yourself on the same level as the other man. You are telling him, "You are my brother; if you hit me you are going to get a bigger hit. Be watchful and be careful, because somewhere you may get into real trouble."

I am not in favor of your being superior to the other man. That's what Jesus is saying: "Be meek, be humble, turn the other cheek, because then you will inherit the kingdom of God."

I am not promising you any kingdom of God. You are not going to inherit anything. You have already inherited it — that is your life. Be loving and respectful to it. Be loving and respectful to others. But don't try to be superior and higher and above others. Don't put the other man down.

You don't find it in that sentence of Jesus, but it is there: you are humiliating the other. You are creating guilt in the other. He will think it over at home: "What did I do? What kind of man was he? I hit him, and he gave me the other cheek. How cruel and how animal I am that I again hit him on the other cheek." The man will not be able to sleep the whole night. He will come back tomorrow. The first thing he will want is to be forgiven. But to forgive him is again to put him down. No, I will say if he hits you, just be a sportsman. Don't try to be a superman, just a sportsman. Hit him really hard and tell him, "Whenever you need a good hit, you can always depend on me."

Never do any harm to anybody, but never allow anybody to do any harm to you either; only then can we create a human world. We have tried the other way in India, and the experiment has completely failed. Twenty-five centuries of slavery, slaughter, rape, and still nobody raises a finger to say that Buddha and Mahavira are responsible for it. They created this impotence in the whole country, this weakness in the whole country. No, I am not in favor of creating impotence, slavery, and provoking people to do violence to you.

Never do violence of your own accord, but never allow anybody else to do it to you either. Only then is there a possibility of creating a human world.

Chapter 3
Politics and the will-to-power

? *Oregon Senator Bob Smith has quoted you as saying that all Oregonians are idiots. Please comment.*

I am not disappointed. He has proved my point. I have never said what he is telling people that I have said. What I have said is so clear that even an idiot would be able to understand it, but poor Bob Smith has missed even that.

I had said, "I have seen all kinds of idiots, and I was thinking that this was it, there are no other kinds of idiots. But after coming to Oregon I came to know that I was mistaken. The Oregonian idiot is a class unto itself."

In this statement, where am I saying that all the Oregonians are idiots? I am only talking about the Oregonian idiot as a special class. I am a generous man, but not that generous. I cannot make the whole of Oregon so special in the world. It will become a unique place if all the Oregonians are idiots. Then there will be no other place comparable to it, it will be simply extraordinary.

Bob Smith has simply proved my point. I was waiting ... Somebody was going to prove my point, and now Senator Bob Smith is the first of that special class of idiots in Oregon. He should be happy that he tops them all! Now anybody else will come second. Bob Smith has won the Nobel Prize.

He has also said that we should not be allowed to remain here. We have not committed any crime, we have not been in any way harmful to anybody. We are minding our own business. But why are these politicians so shaken, worried? And just one and a half years back the same man had said, "These people are absolutely legal and I have nothing to say against them." Now, within one and a half years everything has changed.

We are the same people; but his political situation has changed, and now anybody who wants to make his political status solid can cash in on us. All the politicians are doing it. We are doing them such a great favor; they should be obliged to us for it. Any politician wanting to win an election has only to do one thing: he has to talk nonsense against us — that's enough, and he is going to win. All the politicians are doing it. Now his political situation is not so solid, it is shaky.

We can help him; there is no problem in it. He can condemn us, he can make the threat that we should be thrown out; he can do anything if it will make his position solid. We will be happy that we supported one drowning man, we saved his status. He may not be thankful to us, but we don't wait for anybody's thankfulness, we simply do anything that seems to be humanitarian.

And remember, these senators can become street people any day. Politicians are either in power or on the streets; there is no midway point. Even a powerful politician like Indira

Gandhi once sent me a message: "I am persuading my son Rajiv to come to you because he is not willing to leave, to resign from his service as a pilot in the Indian airlines."

And Rajiv's argument was solid. He said to her, "The day you are not in power, then how are we going to support the family? We don't have our own house to live in. I am the only member of the family earning money — and in your old age, have I to see you on the streets?" She could not persuade him to resign. And his argument was absolutely clear, "Where will you be?" In the three years when she was not in power and Morarji Desai became the prime minister, it was Rajiv who pulled her through. At least she did not have to beg.

Politics is a strange career. A few things are worth understanding about it, because they will throw light on the human mind. First: only a certain type of man becomes attracted towards politics, just as a certain kind of man becomes attracted towards science, poetry, painting, music, dance. You cannot think of Winston Churchill dancing; that would be simply unimaginable. Nor can you think of Nijinsky as a prime minister. Nijinsky was a dancer, and perhaps the best dancer the world has ever known; his dance was almost magic. He was born to dance.

It was not some talent that he learned; it was some instinct in him, a born quality. The magic was such that no other dancer has been able to imitate it. Once in a while, dancing, he would jump so high that it was against the law of gravitation. Physics cannot explain it. It is not possible with that weight to jump that high. And the most miraculous thing was his coming down: he came so slowly, just like a dry leaf falling in the fall, slowly, with no hurry to reach the ground. That is absolutely against the law of gravitation.

Gravitation is such a pull, it is a magnet. It simply pulls you forcibly; you are not able to manage, or do anything about it. It is not in your hands to come down slowly or to come down fast. Everything falling towards the earth is absolutely helpless — the earth's gravitation will decide its rate of fall. And the earth is so vast, its power of gravitation is so vast, and we are not even light like a leaf. Even Nijinsky was surprised, always surprised. He could see himself coming down slowly, not falling — as if gliding.

People asked him again and again, "What is the technique, the strategy, the method?"

He said, "I am as surprised as you are. I don't know. And whenever I try to do it, it never happens. It happens only once in a while, when I have completely forgotten about it. When the dancer disappears, when there is no Nijinsky, it happens. I am just a watcher, just as you are a watcher. I see my body falling down. I have tried it in private, tried it in every possible way. Neither can I jump that high, nor can I fall that slow. I have tried in front of friends, my lovers, but whenever I have tried, it has simply escaped from my hands.

"So I have learned one thing: there are things which you cannot try. There are things which are not possible through any method, any technique, any strategy. There are things which happen; you only have to allow them to happen. And the way to allow them is not to interfere — so much so that you are not even present, because your presence will also be an interference.

You know it. Now physics has come to discover a strange fact. We have known it about human beings. You are in your bathroom making faces in the mirror, knowing perfectly well that there is nobody watching you. But suddenly you become aware that somebody is watching through the keyhole. Everything changes. You stop making faces, you start arranging things and start doing something relevant, rational. You have been caught red-handed. You start looking busy — and just a moment before you were not busy at all.

Modern physics has come to discover that it is very difficult in the first place to observe the behavior of electrons, how they behave. But now we have instruments through which you can observe the behavior of the electron. But the trouble is, the moment you watch, the behavior changes — exactly the same keyhole story. The electron starts behaving in a different way. Just now when you were not observing, it was behaving differently. Physics has not come to any conclusion — what to conclude about it? But the fact is so clear that the electron is as conscious as you are conscious. There is no other way; otherwise, how can the electron become aware of your being aware of it?

Nijinsky said, "The moment I am not, not present at all, suddenly it happens. And while it is happening I am only a watcher. At that moment if I even start looking around to see how it is happening, things get disturbed. I have fallen in the middle of a jump so fast that I have broken my legs. Because I came in, the happening disappeared, and the gravitational pull was so much that I fell with a thump on the ground." Otherwise he used to come down like a feather. He would not even make a sound when he came to the ground.

There are born poets, there are born dancers. In fact, everybody is born to be something. There are those who somehow happen to find what they are born to are the most blissful people on the earth. But those who start moving into directions which are not for them, they are the most miserable.

The politician is a certain type. It is the same type as the criminal. The criminal is one who could not succeed in being a politician. Both are power-seekers, both are dominated by the will-to-power. The politician moves legally, constitutionally towards power, and once he has the power in his hands, then he can manipulate the law, the constitution and everything, in a thousand and one ways. He can corrupt and prostitute everything once he has power. But until he has power he moves very legally, constitutionally, morally.

The criminal is also after power, but he does not know how to move legally, constitutionally, morally. He is wilder, not so tamed as the politician. He is less cultured, not so cultured as the politician who uses culture as a stepping-stone. He is not so articulate as the politician. The politician's basic art is to be articulate, to be able to express your hopes, transforming them into his promises. He is so articulate that he goes on finding your conscious and your unconscious dreams and hopes, and translates them into promises for the future: that if you give him power, he is going to fulfill all these things. It is a bargain: you give him power, and he will give you the promised land.

Once you have given him power, who cares about you? The man who had promised you was powerless. This is a totally different man; he is powerful. Lord Acton's saying I have been quoting again and again in my life: "Power corrupts, and absolute power corrupts absolutely." And Lord Acton is saying it through his own experience; he is not just philosophizing. He has known power, he has known its corruption, and because of its corrupting influence he dropped out of it.

Once you have power, then all the corrupting forces that have been hidden in your unconscious start raising their heads. Who cares about others? Those promises were not given with an honest mind, they were given by you knowing perfectly well that they are not going to be fulfilled. It was just a policy to gain power, and you have gained power. Now you have your own unconscious desires to be fulfilled.

The politician can turn at any time into a criminal. We see it happening throughout history, and still we don't become aware. Joseph Stalin, before he came to power, was not a criminal. He had not killed a single human being, he was not a murderer. But what happened when he came to power? The first thing he did was to destroy the whole twelve-member committee, the communist presidium, which ruled over the whole Communist Party, the topmost leaders. He started killing them one by one.

He killed Kamenev, then he killed Zinovyev, then he killed Trotsky. He went on killing them one by one, and while he was killing one, he took the support of all the others. And they all were happy that there was one less; the power was coming into fewer and fewer hands, and that was better. From twelve, there were only nine people; then there were only six people. He poisoned Lenin who was the topmost man of the revolution. The second man was Trotsky. Once he succeeded in killing Trotsky — Trotsky was killed here in America, in Mexico, because he had escaped. Seeing Zinovyev and Kamenev being killed, he escaped.

You will not believe that when he escaped in disguise — he had to escape in disguise — and in such a hurry because Stalin was just getting ready to finish him ... It was a question of two or three days, not more than that. And he was a minister, the defense minister of Russia. All the military, all the forces were under him. The moment he became aware of it, that same night he escaped. And he could not bring his dog, whom he loved very much. Stalin even killed the dog — it was Trotsky's dog. Such criminal minds! He sent a hired murderer to kill Trotsky in Mexico.

Trotsky was writing Joseph Stalin's biography, which is one of the most profound biographies ever written because he knew Stalin as nobody else knew him: Trotsky was the second most important man in the revolution. Stalin was nowhere; he was somewhere around eleventh or twelfth. But Trotsky was alert that this man was dangerous — because he never spoke; he was always keeping quiet, everything about him was secret. His friends — who are his friends? His enemies — who are his enemies? Nothing was ever revealed. Trotsky was concerned about this man — he seemed to be a dangerous type. So he started collecting facts about him.

And when Stalin started murdering, the procedure that was adopted was a beautiful conspiracy: Lenin was given daily poison in the name of medicine. The doctor was a hired man of Stalin. The poison was to be given in such small doses that it would kill him over a long period of time. While he remains alive, he remains the leader because the masses still know him. He should not die right now, because if he dies right now Trotsky will be the man to control the country. Before Lenin dies Stalin should make his base solid, and all others should be removed, so after Lenin, Stalin will be the second man. So he had to be kept alive but almost in a coma. He became paralyzed and slowly, slowly was dying. He was confined to his bed; his eyesight was disappearing, and whatsoever Stalin was bringing him, he was signing it — he could not read it. Stalin killed everybody necessary to his cause, and then he killed Lenin: the last dose was given to Lenin.

The time that Trotsky remained in Mexico he devoted to writing the biography of Stalin. It is a rare book because never has an enemy written a biography with such great insight, with such profundity, with no hatred — just factual, no fiction. He was killed when he was completing the last page. It remains incomplete — the last page. It is a big biography, nearabout twelve hundred pages. He was writing the last page when he was killed with a hammer from behind. The hammer hit his head many times. His head fell on the book and splashed his blood onto the last page. In a way, that made the book an absolutely authoritative biography of what he had been saying all along about how people had been killed. He was killed on the last page; he died on the book, and the first edition was printed with the blood marks.

Stalin had never killed a single man before; he had never committed a single crime. In fact, his education had happened in a Catholic monastery — he was a Christian — and the monks had raised him. He lived in the monastery because his village was far away in the Caucasus, and the monastery was the only place where education was possible, so his father — he was a poor man — had left him there. The monks at the monastery, out of compassion, accepted the boy, trained him, educated him — and this is what he turned out to be. After gaining power he must have killed millions of people. There is no way to count them; he simply went on killing. Anybody, who was not for him, had to be killed. There was no other punishment. He made it very simple: "Either you are for me, or you are no longer."

The politician is basically a criminal. He is trying to find power through legal methods, that is the difference. The criminal does not bother about the legal methods, and gets caught. The politician never gets caught — or once in a while, like Nixon got caught in Watergate. And do you know what Mao Zedong said when Nixon was caught? "What is this? So much fuss about nothing. Every politician is doing it!" In fact every politician is doing it. Watergate was not something exceptional that Nixon was doing. All over the world, all the politicians who are in power are doing the same kinds of things; they are just not getting caught. It was a misfortune that he got caught, and couldn't manage ...

In fact I have a certain respect for Nixon. A man like Stalin in Nixon's place, or Mao Zedong, or Adolf Hitler, or Mussolini in Nixon's place would have done something that you cannot imagine — and the idea must have crossed Nixon's mind too. That is a simple method: when things were getting so hot, the best way would have been to drag the world into a war. Watergate would have gone down the drain; then who would have cared about Watergate? All that would have been needed was to divert people's attention. That's what those leaders would have done — immediately started a world war. Nixon would have remained the president and would have become the greatest president of America. If he had passed through the war and proved himself victorious, he would have proved himself the greatest man in the whole of history.

I have a certain respect for the man, that he avoided the criminal idea that was bound to have come into his mind. I can guarantee it; it is so simple. I don't know much politics; although I have been a student of politics I know nothing about active politics. But just being a student of politics, I know with absolute certainty that this idea was bound to have crossed his mind: just put the world into such chaos that Watergate becomes a small thing compared to the chaos that arises out of a world war. Then everybody would have forgotten about it.

But the man seems to be much more moral than people have thought him to be. That's why I say I have a certain respect for him. He decided rather to go down as the first president in American history to come out of the White House with such condemnation. But he accepted the condemnation, the worldwide notoriety, and did not drag the world into a war. He proved more a man than a politician, more human than any other politician would have proved.

The criminal mind wants power because without power you cannot do anything. Just as the painter needs paints, and the poet needs a great vocabulary, language, the feel of different words and their nuances, the subtle undercurrents that run through words, so the politician knows perfectly well, deep inside, why he is after power. If you are not going to paint and you go on collecting paints, then you are crazy. If you are not going to play music and you go on collecting all kinds of musical instruments, you are mad.

Why power? Just the other day I told you that Jawaharlal Nehru had invited me to come to see him, and I went. He listened to me. I was very young, and he was a great statesman, but he listened to me as silently, as intensly as if I knew much about politics and what had to be done in the country. He told me, "Why don't you come into politics? Whatsoever you are saying, if you really want to do these things, then you will have to come into politics. Nobody else is going to do it for you, only you can do it. I can understand your ideas, but who is going to implement them? Join!"

I said, "No, because I don't have any interest in gaining power. Whatever I have said to you was just exposing my heart because you have the capacity, the power to do things, the understanding to do things. I simply exposed my heart. I have finished. I am not going to run after power. And I am not asking anybody else, I am asking you. If you feel I am right, then prove it by doing something."

He said, "You are right, but I cannot do these things, because the people through whose support I am standing here will not support any of the ideas which you are giving to me. If they come to know that I am going to implement these ideas, I will simply be thrown out. Politics is a pyramid. It goes on becoming thinner and thinner: at the top there is one man. So, you see that one man at the top, but underneath him are three men; those three men have nine men underneath them; those nine men have ninety ... And they are all depending on those who are lower than them. They are standing on their shoulders; they can be thrown off at any moment."

And in politics, once you have the power which you have got from so many people's support you have to fulfill all those people's desires. Somebody has supported you in order to get licenses, somebody has supported you to have an industry started; somebody has supported you for something else. Now you have to fulfill their desires. Otherwise, while you are standing on their shoulders, they can move away. The topmost man is a very weak person in a way; he has nothing above him to hold on to. Underneath are people who would not miss a single chance to throw him out, because if they can throw out this man, then one of those three who are under him will come to the top. So he has to fulfill all kinds of criminal things.

I know, because that's how Indira Gandhi came to power — because she was living with her father. She was a born politician; her husband was not. While studying in England they fell in love. The husband was not even a Hindu, not a brahmin. Indira was a brahmin, a very high-caste brahmin, a Kashmiri brahmin. The man she fell in love with, Feroz Gandhi, was a Parsi. The whole family was against it — nobody had ever heard of a brahmin girl marrying a Parsi, a man who was not even a Hindu. It is a totally different religion.

But she was the only daughter of Jawaharlal, and after Jawaharlal's wife died — she died very early — Indira was the only person close to him. He stood by her and told her, "Don't be worried about your grandfather and your grandmother. I will manage them. First get married. If you wait for their permission, it will be impossible; even I cannot manage to persuade them. And they will be hurt. It is better that you first get married, and when you come home, married, I will persuade them: 'Nothing can be done now; the marriage has happened.'" That's how they got married in the court.

But Feroz Gandhi had no interest in politics. Just because he was the son-in-law of Jawaharlal he became a member of parliament, but he had no interest in it at all; that was not his thing. But for Indira that was the only thing. They started quarreling immediately, and fighting, and soon Indira moved to Jawaharlal's house, the prime minister's house, and left Feroz Gandhi. They lived separated, not divorced, but for years they were not seeing each other. All those years she was a watcher of all the politicians, and she was collecting information about each politician: his weakness, his crimes against the society, his exploitation of others, his corruption — and yet on the outside that man would go on keeping a pure Gandhian face.

She was collecting a file — she showed me the file — against every leader, and that was her power. When Jawaharlal died all these politicians were afraid of Indira because she had the key. She could expose anybody before the public, before the court. She had all the evidence, she had all the letters. They were afraid of her for the simple reason that only she could save them; otherwise they would be exposed. That file was her power.

I have looked into the file. All those people were exploiting that poor country. They all had bank balances in foreign countries, in Switzerland, in America. They all had connections outside India, from where they would get bribes and money and everything, for giving secrets. They were all connected to one country or other; they were agents. They had one face before the masses, the poor masses; and their reality was something totally different. And they were also afraid because Indira was absolutely incorruptible. That was one thing she had learned from Jawaharlal. He was incorruptible because he was not a politician; he was more a poet. He would have loved to be a painter or a sculptor; any art would have been closer to his nature.

Politics was just accidental to him, it was almost forced on him — it sometimes happens. Because he was interested in the independence of India, he fought against the British government, but with no idea that he was going to become the prime minister when the country became free. He had never thought about it. He was just a soldier of the freedom movement, as were many thousands of others. He might have been shot, he might have been killed, he might have been sentenced to death — anything could have happened. There was no question of power.

When the fight for freedom was over, then the question arose of who was to be in power? Till then there was no question of power at all. The question was how to remove the invaders. He became interested because he was so sensitive a man that he loved the idea of freedom. It had nothing to do with politics; he loved the idea of freedom — as a poet. But when freedom came there was a great struggle for who should be the prime minister. There were people like Sardar Vallabhbhai Patel, who was a real politician, a solid politician who could commit any crime. He did commit them when he became deputy prime minister. Even Jawaharlal could not stop him.

And there were others, because in the freedom fight there were thousands of people of caliber. Jawaharlal was the only one who was not interested in politics, not interested in power. That's why Gandhi chose him, because to choose those people who were really interested in power... In fact their fight for freedom was not a fight for freedom but just a step to reach power. It was a shock to all the politicians because none of them had been chosen by Gandhi to be the prime minister; and Gandhi had total control of the Indian mind.

Sardar Patel was shocked because he was very close to Gandhi and he was also a Gujarati — Gandhi was a Gujarati — and he had served Gandhi his whole life with total trust. And at the last moment Gandhi simply said to Sardar, "Step down. Don't fight with Jawaharlal. I will make you deputy prime minister but let Jawaharlal be the prime minister.

"Why?" Patel asked.

And the reason that Gandhi gave was right. He said, "He is the only one who is not interested in power. You will all be fighting with each other; he is the only one who is above all of you."

Because Gandhi said, "Be the prime minister," Jawaharlal said okay. When Gandhi had said, in 1942, "Be the second soldier in the freedom fight" — the first was Vinoba Bhave — he said okay.

Vinoba Bhave was not known at all in India up to that time. He was just an inmate in Gandhi's ashram. He massaged Gandhi, bathed Gandhi, read scriptures to Gandhi, and because he was a Sanskrit scholar, explained to Gandhi what those scriptures meant. But as far as the country was concerned, he was an unknown person. Gandhi chose an anonymous person to be the first freedom fighter — that he would go to jail first -- and the second would be Jawaharlal.

Jawaharlal didn't say, "This looks disrespectful towards me. This man, nobody knows" — and particularly Jawaharlal never liked Vinoba. Jawaharlal was almost a western man, educated in the West, brought up in the West; his lifestyle was western. In every possible way he was not an Indian, except that he was born in India. He was a meat-eater — because he lived in England and grew up in England there was no question of his being a vegetarian. He had every reason to dislike Vinoba, but there was no problem because Vinoba was doing different work. I have talked with both Vinoba and Jawaharlal, and both have confirmed that they had a dislike for each other.

For example, Vinoba's beard: Jawaharlal did not like it. He himself shaved twice a day, and a beard was not the right thing for him. He was very intolerant, impatient: the dress that Vinoba used was not the "right" dress; in the twentieth century you have to be a twentieth century man. Vinoba's education was an orthodox brahmin education. He studied in Varanasi, in a Sanskrit college, and lived like an old Sanskrit scholar. He was not educated in western subjects, western languages, so there was nothing in common between the two. And to put this man first ... Jawaharlal must have felt hurt but his devotion to Gandhi was unquestionable: if Gandhi chose Vinoba to be the first, then it had to be that way.

If Gandhi had chosen Sardar Vallabhbhai Patel to be the prime minister, Jawaharlal was not going to dispute it or say anything. He had actually offered to Gandhi, "Why create so much misery in these people? I can withdraw; they can choose anybody they want. I am not interested, I have never thought about it. I was fighting for freedom and freedom has come, I am happy." So he was not corrupted by his prime ministership. He was the second man to Gandhi, and after Gandhi's death he had the whole monopoly over the Indian mind.

But Indira was a politician, a born politician. She dropped her husband and forgot about him; politics was more important than the husband. The whole love affair was finished when it became a question of choosing between them. And Feroz became insistent: "Either be with me or be with your father, the prime minister. I don't care, but this cannot go on. The whole day you are there and you come here for a few minutes, just to say hello, and again you escape and you are in the prime minister's house. You go on his travels with him but you never go anywhere with me." He made it clear that the choice had to be made.

Indira simply moved out. She said, "There is no question of choice; I belong to politics, and I am going into politics." From her father she learned one thing: that no politician can pull you down if you are incorruptible. Let all of them be corruptible but you keep an eye out and go on collecting all the data about them. And that was her whole power; they could not discredit her because she had never done anything wrong, and she could discredit all of them. Politicians are legal constitutional criminals.

Now this man, Senator Bob Smith, wants to throw me and my commune absolutely out from Oregon. The way these people talk — they are senators — is the way of a fascist, communist, nazi. They talk about democracy, they talk about freedom of speech, they talk about respect for the individual, but I don't think they belong to Washington, Jefferson, Lincoln; they belong to Joseph Stalin, Khrushchev, Brezhnev. These people should put themselves in their proper line.

But they are cashing in on us. Now, by telling the Oregonians that I have called all of them idiots, this man is trying to cash in on us. I have not said that at all. But now I say that the first idiot, I have found. He himself has declared it. And I will wait for the second, because Oregon has two senators, so the second will be just around the corner. He is already late. Senator Bob Smith has come first in the race.

My statement is so simple that even a child can understand it. I said the Oregonian idiot is a class in itself. How does he manage to understand from this statement that all Oregonians are idiots? Then what about me? Then what about you? We are all Oregonians, and we are going to remain Oregonians.

These people can do, can say, anything. Our sannyasins were present in a hearing where he spoke. He had called the hearing and two or three of our sannyasins were present, but they never participated because what is the point of participating in all these nonsensical things? It was so absurd a hearing — one cannot imagine how people go on tolerating such things.

On our property we have a few small pieces of land which belong to the government, the federal government. They are leased for fifty years, and when we purchased the land, the lease also came to us. This hearing was about a concern that we were not allowing people to approach the government land — a charge that was absolutely false, because even the officers who look after the government land said that we had never done anything illegal, we had never prevented anybody. And there is no reason for anybody to go to the bare land or hills.

So we never participated and argued at the hearing, for the simple reason that the government office itself was arguing for us, saying that we had never done anything illegal and everything was absolutely as it should be — so there was no case at all. But all the bigots who have been against us since we came here were all present there, giving their evidence against us.

And this senator, this Don Quixote, was telling the commissioners how they could manage to destroy the commune, the city. He was giving instructions to these people — in front of our people who were sitting there — for how they could get around the law, how they could make our life impossible so that we had to leave.

This is democracy. These are democratic people. They are the people who are looking after people's needs. This is the democracy that has been described as "for the people, of the people, by the people." I don't know who these people are — certainly we are not the people.

> **?** *Since each of us is born alone and dies alone, and aloneness is the state of our being, what is the function of a commune?*

The function of the commune is exactly that: to make you aware of your absolute aloneness.

The family does not allow you that. The family gives you the fallacy that you have a mother, you have a father, you have a husband, you have a brother, you have a sister — that you are not alone.

The society gives you the idea that you are a member of the Rotary Club, the Lions Club; that you belong to this church, to that temple, to this congregation or that congregation — that you are not alone. The society provides you with all kinds of crowds to mingle with. You are republican, you are democrat, you are liberal, but you are not alone, all the republicans are with you.

The function of the commune basically is to destroy all these fictions. Nobody is with you. You are alone, and you have to understand that this aloneness is so precious that you should not lose it.

It does not mean that you cannot relate. It only means that you don't believe in relationships. Try to see the distinction between the two.

Relating is a flowing river. You can relate, and you can relate only because you are alone, because you are an individual — there is somebody who can relate from your side. And you can relate only to the person who understands his aloneness, otherwise you cannot relate.

If you know your aloneness, and you fall in love with a woman who does not know her aloneness, this love is not going to go anywhere. This is going to be finished sooner that you can imagine, because the woman is asking for a relationship. The person who is lonely is asking for a relationship: "Fill the gap, I am lonely. Be part of my being."

But a person who is alone knows that neither you can fill anybody's gap, nor can anybody else fill your gap. You can meet, but you will remain two alonenesses.

And it is beautiful that two alonenesses can meet, two individuals can meet, but the meeting cannot be made solid, concrete. It cannot be reduced to a relationship, it will remain a relating. It will always remain a changing flux, a movement, because the other person is changing and you are changing. You are not static — though that's what people expect.

When two persons get married, both are getting married to a certain image which is going to change tomorrow. The woman you have married is not going to be the same tomorrow. She is alive, she is growing, she is moving — tomorrow will be tomorrow. But if you expect her to remain stuck here, in that moment when you signed the register in the court, you were trying to stop the clock.

But even if you stop the clock, your clock is not running the time. Both will carry the image stuck in their minds, and they would like you to go on fulfilling that image. If, in some way, you differ from that image, then you are deceiving, cheating. Nobody can fulfill that image, it is impossible, it is against nature.

The function of the commune is to give you the opportunity to be together, without any relationship. It gives you the opportunity to relate to people without getting fettered to people. It gives you the opportunity to know others, feel others, but without any bargain, without any bondage, without any imprisonment. You remain you; the other remains the other.

It is good if we meet today, it is a joy to be together, but if it is not going to happen tomorrow then there is no need to go on weeping for spilled milk. It is pointless. Perhaps this meeting was meant to be only for this time. You remain a stranger, the other remains a stranger, and you don't reduce each other into acquaintances.

The strangeness is absolute, indestructible.

So the commune is not another society. It is not providing you with a society, a club, a congregation, a party. No, it is simply providing you a space, and an understanding that all these people are lonely, just as you are. But don't try to fill it, because if you try to fill it, you are trying to do something against nature and you will be miserable. Hence, don't think in terms of loneliness; better to think in terms of aloneness.

And to be alone is so beautiful; untrespassed, nobody trampling on you, you are left to be yourself and you leave others to be themselves. Yes, once in a while you meet ...

India has produced a few great geniuses in this century; one of them was Rabindranath Tagore. I love one of his novels — The Last Poem is the name of the novel:

There are two persons: one, a young man, a poet, a philosopher, actually says what Rabindranath would like to say — he represents Rabindranath — and a woman who is in need of relationship. She is continually harassing him about marriage. And particularly in India, if a woman and a man are even seen walking together, that is enough for a scandal. They might not be doing anything, but just walking together and it is enough for a scandal; the whole town will be agog, and so many stories will start springing up from nowhere. And of course the woman suffers more because everywhere people start pointing at her.

So she was desperate. She was saying, "Why do you go on postponing? You love me, you want to be with me. If you don't love me, I will not force you."

And the man says, "I love you, that's why I am not going to marry you." Now, this is very difficult for the woman. If she had been from my commune she would have understood. But what kind of statement is this: because I love you I cannot marry you? But she goes on and on, so he says, "I will marry you on one condition."

They are sitting on the bank of a lake. He says, "I will make my house on this side of the lake and you make your house on the other side of the lake. Once in a while, walking, perhaps we may meet. Once in a while, perhaps I may knock on your door or you may knock on my door. Once in a while, perhaps I am in a boat and you are also in a boat, and we meet on the lake.

But it always has to be without any prearrangement. It has not to be a dating. I will never inform you that I am coming; you will never inform me that you are coming. I will marry you on this condition only. For a few days we may not be able to see each other. You will never ask me, 'Where have you been?' I will never ask you where you have been. We will never interfere in each other's freedom. We will remain as strangers, as we are now."

The woman said, "Then what is the purpose of marriage?" Naturally she cannot understand what the purpose of the marriage is.

The purpose of marriage is to be in each other's head twenty-four hours a day. The purpose of marriage is to destroy each other in the name of love: to nag, harass, fight. The man is suggesting exactly the right thing: "It will be a great joy suddenly seeing you on the lake. I will not be expecting it. Unexpectedly, I will find you in the jungle by the side of the lake." Just to think of that unexpected moment, is relating. There is no relationship.

He cannot send a message: "You have to come tonight because you are my wife, otherwise I am going to court." In fact the husband cannot say to the wife, "Sleep in the other room." That is enough to create trouble. The wife cannot say to the husband, "You cannot sleep in my bed." That is enough for trouble, because we have completely forgotten a simple thing: our aloneness. And we are trying to forget it as much as possible — the very idea should be dropped. Aloneness is a natural phenomenon. And there is nothing painful about it. When you know it, it is the greatest bliss.

The function of the commune is to give you the space, to give you the understanding, to give you the feel of aloneness, and the experience of relating without getting into relationship.

Chapter 4

Danger — Truth at Work

? *Why are the common masses against you, when what you say appears to be the very truth?*

That's precisely why: because it appears to be the very truth. Truth is dangerous, dangerous to all those people who have been living in fictions, beautiful lies, nice dreams, utopias.

Truth is bound to be looked upon as an enemy by all these people, because it is going to shatter all that they have believed and lived for. Truth is just the death of all kinds of lies, howsoever consoling they may have been.

Why were the common people against Socrates? Why were the masses so antagonistic to Al-Hillaj Mansoor? Why were the orthodox, the religious, the respectable, against Jesus? Their only crime was they were saying something which was tremendously disturbing to people's sleep. Nobody wants to be disturbed when he is having a beautiful dream. And people don't have anything else except dreams.

All around there have been dream merchants who have been selling dreams to people and exploiting people, and in return they were not giving anything. All the religions, up to now have been dream sellers, exploiters of people's weaknesses. Yes, there are weaknesses. Every man who is born is going to die. You cannot hide the truth of death.

How long can you make the cemeteries beautiful? Gardens, lawns, flowers, marble graves ... but you cannot hide the fact of death. You can see that in every country the cemetery is outside the city. It should really be exactly in the middle of the city, so everybody passing by comes to be reminded of death again and again — because that is the only thing that is certain. Everything else is just probable; may happen, may not happen. But death is not a probability.

Death is the only certainty in your whole life.

Whatsoever happens, death is going to be there. You cannot escape from it. You cannot go anywhere away from it. Death will meet you wherever you go.

I am reminded of an ancient parable. A very great king dreamed that death was standing before him — a dark figure. He became frightened even in his dream. But he was a brave man; somehow he gathered his courage together and asked this strange figure, "Who are you and what do you want?"

The figure said, "I am your death, and I have come to warn you: Don't forget the right place, and the right time to meet me." Only this much he said, "Don't forget the right place and the right time to meet me tomorrow." And the shock of his statement was such that the dream was shattered, the king woke up. It was in the middle of the night but he immediately called his wise advisers, astrologers, dream-interpreters, future-predictors, all sorts of people; and he told his dream.

They all started quarreling and discussing and arguing about what the dream meant. The old servant of the king, who had been almost like a father to him — he had raised him from his very childhood... The king's mother died early, and his father was constantly going on faraway journeys, invading countries, conquering, expanding the empire. So he was left with this trustworthy servant and he treated him almost like a father.

The old man was standing by his side. He whispered into the king's ear, "Don't waste time! These people can quarrel for centuries; they have been quarreling for centuries. These philosophers, these astrologers, these prophets — they have never agreed on anything. And it is going to be morning; tomorrow is just going to begin and there is not much time. My suggestion is: take your fastest horse and escape from this place." The advice appeared to be solid: "And let these people argue. They are not going to come to any conclusion at all. The evening will come soon — they will take centuries — and there will be no conclusion. If you depend on them, you will repent; just escape! Leave these people here, let them argue and I will listen to their arguments."

The king simply slipped away, took his fastest horse and rushed as fast as it was possible, away from the palace where the dream had happened. By the evening he had gone hundreds of miles, and he was very happy that he had come so far away: "Now it will be difficult for death to find me at the place, at the fixed time."

The sun was setting. He had reached the outskirts of the city of Damishk. Just to rest ... because the whole day he had not eaten, he had not even taken a cup of water. Time was so precious. Thirst is not going to kill you in just one day; hunger is not going to kill you in just one day. He was going to rest in a garden just outside the city. He went into the garden and was tying the horse to a tree, and was thanking the horse, because the horse was perhaps really the best horse in the world. He was thanking the horse and saying to him, "You really proved your mettle today. Even I was not aware that you could go so fast. Now rest, and I will arrange for your food and for your water."

Just then, he felt a hand on one of his shoulders. He looked back. The same black figure was standing there, laughing. The king was shocked; he said, "Why are you laughing?"

Death said, "This is the place and this is the time. I was worried whether you would be able to make it or not — but your horse certainly is the best horse in the world. I also thank him."

Where can you escape? Perhaps wherever you are going, there is the right place and the right time. In fact every place is the right place for death, and every time is the right time.

Now, facts like death... Religions have been trying to console you, giving you ideas that can help you to create a buffer between you and the fear of death — shock absorbers — so that you don't get continually shocked; otherwise life would become impossible. So, all kinds of fictions have been woven into mythologies, into theologies. Anybody saying the truth is bound to cut through all these cobwebs, these mythologies, these fictions.

And when you suddenly see the naked truth, you are going to be against the person who has brought you such a shocking gift. You would like to believe that it is not true, but you know it is. Hence the anger; otherwise there was no need to kill Socrates.

If you are right, and you know that you are right, then let this man befool himself with his "truth" — it does not matter to you. The people of Athens believed in an afterlife, as did the people of the whole earth. Everybody, except the atheists, believed in an afterlife of some kind. The Greek mythology was rich, but Socrates said, "Nothing can be said about death because nobody has ever returned. So we have to keep our minds open. We cannot accept any fiction about death and life after death, because there has not been a single eyewitness. Until I die, I cannot say whether one lives after death or not. If I die, then there is no question, no problem arises — I am simply not there.

"What about before you were born?" His argument was solid. In what trouble were you: what anxiety, what anguish, what suffering? You know that there is no question of any suffering or any anguish before you were born. Who was going to suffer, and who was going to be in anxiety and anguish? You were not there!

Socrates just simply looked at death with the same vision. If you are simply finished, as the atheists say; if you completely disappear, if nothing of you remains, then there is no problem because you are not there. All problems, all anxieties disappear. This is one possibility.

The other possibility is that perhaps the theists are right, and you survive. But then too, he said, "I don't see any problem. You are surviving right now, and somehow you are managing your misery, your anxiety, your problems; somehow you are managing. And if you are there, you will be experienced, more experienced; you will still be able to manage."

So he said, "I don't see any problem to be bothered about. Either I die, then there is no question, or I will be there, more experienced, wiser. And I can trust myself. If I could pass through life, I will pass through death too. But I cannot say anything before I have experienced it. And I cannot promise you either, that when I have experienced it I will be able to come back and tell you, because up to now nobody has come back. Perhaps there is no way to come back. Perhaps the very bridge falls as you pass, all communication becomes impossible — but nothing can be said about it."

He would not say anything definitely, and that was the problem that he was creating in people's minds. He was creating anxiety. That was one of the points raised against his being in Athens: "He should be expelled or sentenced to death, because this man has been creating anxiety and anguish in people's minds. People who were perfectly happy doing their work, comfortably ... This man meets them, and once he has met them, they are never at ease again."

And this was a routine thing for Socrates: just to go around the town, to catch hold of anybody and ask him any question. Even if the other person wanted to escape, Socrates wouldn't allow it: "You have to answer!" And then, once you had answered a question, he would hammer your answer from every possible angle and soon you were left without any answer. Then he would tell you, "You can come to my school" — he had a school — "if you want to learn, because your answer was absolutely bogus. Some idiot has sold that answer to you and cheated you. You have been living a lie."

Yes, lies can be comfortable; can be very convenient. Truth, in the beginning, is very inconvenient, is very uncomfortable, but in the end it is the ultimate blessing.

We can summarize: a lie is always sweet in the beginning, bitter in the end; the truth is bitter in the beginning, sweet in the end. But you need patience for the end. If you are impatient, then you are going to buy some lie.

The common masses have no mind of their own. For centuries they have been conditioned, hypnotized, brainwashed continuously. So when a man like me says something, it needs guts in the first place even to hear it. Then it needs tremendous courage to absorb it, because it is bitter, it goes against all your conditioning.

So only a very few people who are really seekers of truth will be ready to go through all this turmoil. Everything will go upside down: their God, their heaven, their hell, their Devil, their messiahs, their prophets.

A thick wall exists between you and truth. And all these people are standing between you and the truth. You will have to tell them, "Get lost! Go to Oregon!" That is my translation for "Go to hell," because that has become too old. We should continue to make proverbs fresh.

A Christian will have to put Christ aside; it is very difficult. It was difficult for Jews to put Moses aside when Jesus was telling them something far truer. It was difficult to put Moses aside, now the same problem arises for the Christian: it is difficult for him to put Jesus aside. And Jesus' claim is far more than Moses ever claimed. Moses never claimed that he was the only begotten son of God.

Jesus claims that he is the only begotten son of God. Can you put it aside and tell Jesus, "Go to Oregon"? It will be difficult. Rather than doing that, you would prefer me to leave Oregon. That's what your politicians are trying to do; they are telling me, "Leave Oregon." That seems to be simpler, because with me they have no ties. I have not sold them any sweet dreams. I have not promised them anything, nor am I promising them now.

My whole work is to demolish: to demolish all the lies that are surrounding you and not to replace them by anything else, but to leave you utterly naked in your aloneness. To me, only in your aloneness will you be able to know the truth — because you are the truth.

You have not to go anywhere to find truth. Neither Jesus can give it to you, nor Krishna can give it to you, nor Buddha can give it to you, nor I can give it to you. It is not a commodity that somebody can just give to you. Just think: if truth is a commodity, a thing which can be given to you, then it can be stolen, it can be taken back, it can be lost — anything can happen to it.

But nothing happens to truth. It happens to you, but nothing happens to it. It cannot be stolen; it cannot be purchased.

There is a story in Mahavira's life... One of the very famous kings, Bimbisara, had conquered the whole of India and the neighboring countries. He had made a vast empire. He was a man who, once he wanted something, would have it. He had never come across anything that he wanted and could not find a way to get. He had heard many times about Mahavira, who was just resting for the rainy season outside the city, his capital.

He inquired, "What has this man got? — because I see thousands of people going to him."

Somebody said, "He has got the truth."

Bimbisara said, "Then there is no problem. How much is he asking for it? I am ready to pay. There is no question of bargaining, simply inquire how much he wants for it."

The man could not say to the king, "You are talking like a fool." He said, "It is better, your majesty, that you go to him and you negotiate. I am a poor man; don't put me in this situation. You are a great king; he is a great tirthankara, a great soul which rarely happens. Only twenty-four persons reach that height in one cycle of existence."

He is saying that in millions and millions of years, only twenty-four ... and he is the last for this cycle. Now there is not going to be another man of his caliber again in this cycle of existence. When this whole existence burns out — when all these stars and galaxies and solar systems have gone, disappeared, and a new creation starts from scratch — then the first tirthankara will appear. "Now this man is very rare because for millions of years there is not going to be another comparable to him. So it is better you go."

Bimbisara went with all his paraphernalia, and he was respectful to Mahavira — just a formality. In India even if a king goes to a sage, he has to touch the feet of the sage; that is just a formality. And he said, "I have come for a simple thing. Give me your truth, and whatsoever you want — even if you ask for my whole empire — I will give it to you. This is my whole life's standpoint: anything that I want, I have to have it. It matters not what it is going to cost."

Mahavira laughed, he said, "You unnecessarily came this far. In your very capital lives one of my disciples. He has got the truth; and he is a very poor man — he may be ready to sell it; I am not ready to sell it. And you must know that I am also the son of a king. I was going to inherit the kingdom of my father; I renounced it to get the truth. Now, how can I sell it for a kingdom? Even if you give me the whole kingdom, how can I sell it? I have already renounced a whole kingdom to get this truth, and after forty years of struggle, I have found it. I cannot sell it."

Mahavira must have had a sense of humor that Jainas have missed completely. He sent him back to the poor man in the capital. The king had never gone to that quarter of the capital, because only the poorest, the very poor, in fact the outcasts, lived there. His golden chariot was standing there before the poor man's hut. The poor man came running, and Bimbisara said, "Rejoice! I am ready to give anything you want, just give me the truth. Your master has sent me; I have come from Mahavira."

The poor man said, "My master must have joked with you. Perhaps he did not want to hurt you before so many people because you had gone with your whole court, all your advisers, ministers, generals. He did not want to hurt you or say no to you. That's why he has sent you to me. I can give my life if you want. I am just your poor servant; I clean your streets. You can ask for my life and it is here, ready. You can cut off my head — but truth ... ? Yes, I have got it, but the very quality of truth is such that it cannot be given. Not that I don't want to give it to you; I am absolutely willing.

"If you can take it, take it. You can kill me; if you find it inside me, so far so good — I am ready. I will be happy that I had the chance to serve you so intimately and so closely. But I warn you, you will not find it there because the truth has to be authentically yours, only then is it true. If it is somebody else's, then it is no longer true. My truth cannot be your truth. The moment I say something about the truth, you only hear the words; the truth is left behind. The truth can never be squeezed into words, there is no way."

Words have been reaching the common people and they have believed that those words are the truth — somebody believing in the words of Jesus, somebody in the words of Buddha, somebody in the words of Mohammed — but they are not the truth.

No book contains truth; no word can ever contain it. But you become satisfied, and whenever somebody disturbs your satisfied state, you are angry. And of course you have the majority of people with you. That helps you tremendously — so many people cannot be wrong. But truth never happens to crowds, it happens only to individuals. Whenever truth comes, it comes in the vibe of an individual, so that individual is always standing against the whole crowd.

Otherwise, the whole crowd is with you, because they have also been fed with the same kind of stuff. The Catholics: how many are they? — perhaps six hundred million. Now, any Catholic has a great consolation, that six hundred million people are with him. Six hundred million people cannot be wrong. And against one person ... Naturally they feel that this person is a disturbance. It is better to finish with this person and go to sleep, back to their dreams.

It is not new to me. From my very childhood I have been in the same position.... .

My father would take me with him if he went to some ceremony, some marriage, some birthday party, anywhere. He would take me on the condition that I should remain absolutely silent: "Otherwise, please remain at home."

I would say, "But why? Everybody is allowed to talk, except me!"

He said, "You know, I know, and everybody knows why you are not allowed to talk: because you are a disturbance."

"But," I said, "in things which concern me, you promise me that you will not interfere with me, and I will promise you that I will remain silent."

And many times it happened that he had to interfere. For example, if some elderly man was there — a faraway relative, but in India it doesn't matter — my father would touch his feet, and would say, "Touch his feet."

I would say, "You are interfering with me, and our contract is finished. Why should I touch this old man's feet? If you want to touch them, you can touch them twice, thrice; I will not interfere, but why should I touch his feet? Why not his head?"

And that was enough of a disturbance. Everybody would explain to me that he was old. I said, "I have seen many old people. Just in front of my house there is an old elephant; I never touch his feet. That elephant belongs to a priest; it is a very old elephant. I never touch his feet, and he is very wise — I think wiser than this old man. Old age does not just give him any quality.

"A fool remains a fool — perhaps becomes more foolish as he grows old. An idiot becomes more idiotic as he grows old, because you cannot remain the same, you are going to grow. And the idiot, when he becomes senile, his idiocy is multiplied. And that is the time when he becomes very respectable. I am not going to touch the feet of this old man unless it is proved to me why I should."

Once I went to a funeral; one of my teachers had died. He was my Sanskrit teacher — a very fat man, funny looking, and funnily dressed in the way of old brahmins, ancient brahmins, with a very big turban. He was a laughingstock in the whole school, but he was very innocent too. The Hindi word for innocent is *bhole*, so we used to call him Bhole. As he entered the class, the whole class would recite loudly, "Jai Bhole" — long live Bhole. And of course he could not punish all the students; otherwise, how was he going to teach, whom was he going to teach?

He died. So naturally, thinking that as he was my teacher I would behave, my father didn't ask for the contract. But I could not, because what happened there I had not expected — nobody had expected it. His dead body was lying there when we arrived. His wife came out running and fell upon him and said, "Oh my Bhole!"

Everybody remained silent but I could not. I tried hard, but the harder I tried, the more difficult it was. I burst out laughing and I said, "This is great."

My father said, "I had not made a contract with you thinking that as he was your teacher you would be respectful."

I said, "I am not disrespectful, but I am surprised by the coincidence. Bhole was his nickname and he used to get angry about it. Now the poor fellow is dead and his wife is calling him Bhole, and he cannot do anything. I am just feeling sorry for him."

Every place I used to go with him he always made the contract; and he was the first party to break it, because something or other would happen and he would have to say something. And that was enough, because that was the condition: that he was not to interfere with me.

One Jaina monk was in the town. Jaina monks sit on a very high pedestal, so that even standing you can touch their feet with your head — at least a five-foot, six-foot-high pedestal, and they sit on it. Jaina monks move in a group, they are not allowed to move alone: five Jaina monks move together. That is a strategy so that the four keep an eye on the fifth to see that nobody tries to get a Coca-Cola — unless they all conspire. And I have seen them conspiring and getting Coca-Cola, that's why I remember it.

They are not even allowed to drink in the night and I have seen them drinking Coca-Cola in the night. In fact, in the day it was dangerous to drink Coca-Cola — what if somebody saw it — so only in the night ... And I had supplied it myself, so there was no problem about it. Who else would supply them? No Jaina would be ready to do it, but they knew me, and they knew that any outrageous thing, and I would be ready to do it.

So five pedestals were there. But one monk was sick, so when I went there with my father, I went to the fifth pedestal and sat on it. I can still remember my father and the way he looked at me — he could not even find words: "What to say to you?" And he could not interfere with me, because I had not done any wrong to anybody. Just sitting on a pedestal, a wooden pedestal, I was not hurting anybody or anything. He came close to me and he said, "It seems, contract or no contract, you are going to do whatsoever you intend, so from now on we will not make the contract, because it is absolutely pointless."

And those four monks were in such uneasiness and they also could not say anything — what to say? One of them finally said, "This is not right. No one who is not a monk should sit on an equal level." So they told my father, "Bring him down."

I said, "Think twice. Remember the bottle!" I had supplied the Coca-Cola.

They said, "Yes, that's right, we remember the bottle. Sit on the pedestal as long as you please."

My father said, "What bottle?"

I said, "You ask these people. I have a double contract: one with you and one with them, and nobody can prevent me. All four of you agree that I can sit here, or I will start saying the name of the bottle."

They said, "We are perfectly satisfied. You can sit here, there is no harm — but please keep silent about the bottle."

Now, many people were there, and they all became interested — what bottle? When I came out of the temple everybody gathered; they all said, "What is this bottle?"

I said, "This is a secret. And this is my power over these fools whose feet you go on touching. If I want, I can manage to tell them to touch my feet, otherwise — the bottle. ..." These fools!

My father, on the way home, asked me, "You can just tell me; I will not tell anybody. What is this bottle? Do they drink wine?"

I said, "No. Things have not gone that far, but if they remain here a few days more, I will manage that too. I can force them to drink wine; otherwise I will name the bottle."

The whole town was discussing the bottle, what the bottle was, and why they had become afraid: "We have always thought that they were such spiritual sages, and this boy made them afraid. And they all agreed that he could sit there, which is against the scriptures." Everybody was after me. They were ready to bribe me: "Ask whatsoever — you just tell us what is the secret of the bottle."

I said, "It is a very great secret, and I am not going to tell you anything about it. Why don't you go and ask your monks what the bottle is? I can be there, so they cannot lie — and then you will know what kind of people you are worshipping. And these are the people who are conditioning your mind."

In the university there used to be a professor who wanted to resign because of me. He was a very old, senior professor, and very much honored. Perhaps he is still alive. His name was Doctor S.N.L. Shrivastava; he was a PhD, DLitt. In philosophy he was a well known name — and he threatened to resign because of me.

His condition to the university was that if I was not expelled from the university, then this was his resignation: only one could live in the university, either I or he. And I was just a student, only a first-year student. I had just matriculated from my village and had come to the bigger town. And within three months he became such a mess that when he saw me he would get out of the class.

I would run after him and ask him, "What is the matter? Why are you going away? I pay the fee. You are supposed to teach, I am supposed to learn, and all that I do is learning. If I ask a question, it is just to learn."

"But," he said, "you ask questions which always put me in such a dilemma. If I say yes, then I am caught; if I say no, then I am caught. Each question is just to provoke other questions, and there is no end to it. Three months have passed; you don't allow me to go any further than the first day. We are still stuck there; and I know that there is not going to be anything else for the two years you are going to be here with me. You won't let that first day be finished. So it is better ... "

"But," I said, "you are so learned, with so many degrees, honorary degrees, and thirty years' teaching experience, you must have passed so many students — why are you so disturbed? If you don't know, you can simply say 'I don't know.' Your only trouble is that you cannot say 'I don't know.' I am not your trouble. You want to keep the pretension that you know everything, and the fact is nobody knows everything, not even you know everything."

He was teaching us Aristotelian logic; he was the professor of logic and philosophy. And in India, for the first two years you have to learn logic, so those two years, the first two years, are devoted to Aristotle and his logic. And I said to him that even Aristotle was not all-knowing; he was as ignorant as anybody else. He writes in his book that women have one tooth less than men.

Now look at the fool. He had two wives; he could have told Mrs. Aristotle One or Mrs. Aristotle Two, "Just open your mouth." And in fact women are always keeping their mouths open; there was no need to say it. If he was afraid he could have counted them in the night when they were asleep. But no, in Greece it was believed, traditionally believed, that a woman had to be, in everything, smaller than man, lower than man. How could she have exactly the same number of teeth as a man? So he never bothered to check.

I asked Shrivastava, "This man, you say, is a logician, the father of logic? It is such a simple thing that even a very mediocre man would think that the first thing was to count the teeth; then he could have written it. And what was he doing with two wives anyway?

Without counting their teeth he just believed public opinion. And for thousands of years in Greece, this was the opinion — nobody bothered to count them. But it is simply strange that neither any man nor any woman bothered to. At least some woman should have counted them, and said that this was absolutely absurd nonsense.

But he said, "It is enough and I don't want to listen any more. I am going to the vice-chancellor to give my resignation. Either he expels you or I resign."

He didn't come for three days, so the vice-chancellor called me. I asked him, "What is my misdeed? Expel me — there is no problem with that — but please tell me what I have done wrong? Have I asked any single question which was not related to logic? And if I have come to learn logic, I have to ask questions because my doubts should be satisfied. Otherwise the man should say that he does not know, and I am allowing that. Once he says, 'I don't know,' I will not raise that question again. He is not courageous enough even to say, 'I don't know.' And now there is the threat that he will resign.

"He knows that he is a valuable professor. If he resigns in the middle of the term, where are you going to get a man of the same caliber? He knows that against a student who has been in the college only three months, it is going to be decided in his favor. But," I said, "it is not going to be easy. Then my fight, which was going on with Shrivastava, will start with you. I will be here in your office every day. You will have to give me in writing what the reasons are that I have been expelled."

He was a really nice and intelligent man. He said, "I don't see that there is any reason for you to be thrown out and I would be the last person to expel you. But please understand my situation: we cannot lose that professor. So do one thing ... I will not expel you; I will make arrangements with another college. You have not to do anything, but just do me a favor: I will make arrangements in another college, and you move to that other college. Jabalpur University has at least twenty colleges, so you can choose any college you want."

I said, "It is not a question of my choosing any college. Phone all these principals to see if anybody is ready to accept me, because now everybody knows about this S.N.L. Shrivastava thing: that the best professor of philosophy in the university is ready to resign. Then who is going to take me? You try; I am ready."

Out of twenty colleges, only one principal was ready to accept me — on the condition that I would never go to the class. He would give me the percentage needed, but I should never go to the class.

I said, "That is a perfect arrangement. I myself don't like unnecessarily bothering to go and then finding idiots there who don't know what they are doing, what they are teaching. So this is a good arrangement; you can make it. But remember, I am not going to pay the fees. I am doing you a favor, so you arrange for the fees for two years. I will never go to that college; you arrange for the fees, and you take care of everything. After two years I will come to you. If anything goes wrong, then you will be responsible."

He said, "I will take every responsibility" — and he took every responsibility.

After two years I went to him and said, "Give me my permission card to enter the examination. I have not been going to that college; I have not even seen that college."

This is the common mass — even educated people belong to the common mass — they don't have integrity, intelligence or even the courage to say, "I don't know." Now this condition, I know, had come from the professor. The principal had asked the professor, "Can we accept this student? This is the trouble ... "

And the professor said, "I don't want any trouble in my class. You can accept him only on the condition that he never comes to the class."

Not long ago I read an article by the same professor, Soleri is his name, proudly declaring that I was his student. I have not seen his face, he has not seen my face; I have never been in his class or on his college campus or around there. And now he is proud that I have been his student and that he always knew that I was going to be somebody special. These fools! They can lie so easily. But their whole lives are full of lies.

The common masses are, in a way, innocent. But the pedagogues, the priests, the politicians — these are the people who go on poisoning the common masses and keep them at the level of a mob.

What we call democracy has not yet come to the point of being a democracy. It is still, everywhere, only a mobocracy, because the mass that elects the people is a mob; it is not yet alert or aware.

Just a few days ago there was an election here. What I heard was that before the election on the sixth of November, on the night of the fifth of November, in front of the Wasco County Court, all the Christian congregations gathered. All the priests — who are enemies of each other, continually fighting, arguing about who is right, who is wrong and who is closer to Christ and God and who is not closer, and who is really orthodox and who has just gone astray — they all gathered there together: all the priests, with all their congregations before the county courthouse — for what? — to pray against the Antichrist, to save Wasco County.

Now who is the Antichrist in Wasco County? And Wasco County needs to be saved from the Antichrist? I really enjoyed it, that they are all praying for me — because I don't think there is anybody else who can claim to be the Antichrist. But I am a little crazy. They say I am anti-Christ, anti-Buddha, anti-Mahavira, anti-Krishna, anti-Semite. Anything — just put anti before it and it refers to me. And in reality I am just for myself and not against anybody. I don't care a bit about Christ, so why should I be anti-Christ? I don't care about anybody. They never cared about me, why should I care about them?

These people go on... The journalists asked the priests, "Who is the Antichrist?" and they were not even courageous enough to utter my name. They just went round and round answering, "We are just praying so that the county is saved from evil forces." Why only Wasco County? Are all the evil forces gathered here in Wasco County? They should have gone to the White House in Washington and prayed there, because if all the evil forces are gathered anywhere, there are two places: the Kremlin and the White House.

And if the world is going to suffer, it is going to suffer from the Kremlin and the White House.

But the strangest thing about these priests is: in the Second World War in England they were praying to God, the Christian God, for England's victory, for Winston Churchill's safety. And the Christians in Rome, where the pope is, in the Vatican, were praying for Mussolini's safety and his victory — to the same Christian God. Not only that, Adolf Hitler was being blessed by the Christian bishops, and they were praying for his victory — to the same Christian God. Now what happened to that Christian God? He must have committed suicide! How to decide? — all are his people, and his agents are praying. In whose favor is he going to decide?

And Christians don't see the point that when Adolf Hitler is in power, then the Christian priest prays for Adolf Hitler. He is just a coward. He could not say, "I will not pray for you and the ideology you stand for. I am going to pray that you should be defeated." But no, brave people don't become priests; they have other, better things to do. These are cowards. And these cowards go on poisoning other people's minds; they make other people cowards. They have destroyed the whole of humanity and made it into a madhouse.

So if the masses are against me, it is expected. It cannot be otherwise, it is natural.

What is unexpected is that there are a few people all around the world who are able to stand with me, who are courageous enough to put their prejudices aside and listen to me, who are intelligent enough to recognize the truth when they come across it — whatsoever the cost and whatsoever the consequence.

In fact, nobody before me had such intelligent people as I have around the world, people of such caliber, so receptive, so willing to go through the fire test.

Yes, it is walking on fire when you go towards truth.

It is going to burn you; it is going to burn you completely. And then that which remains unburned, alive, is your reality. Everything else, which got burned, was rubbish poured over you by others. Nobody can burn the truth, but to attain the truth you will have to drop so many things, so many burdens.

But I am fortunate that at least one percent of humanity is almost ready to jump and create the first real religion of the world: a religion of truth, consciousness — with no lies about God, heaven, hell, the Devil — just the purest twenty-four-carat truth.

Even one percent around the earth is a tremendous force. You should not think that it is only one percent against ninety-nine percent. No, those ninety-nine percent are nothing because they don't have any fire of their own. They are dead before death; they are just walking corpses.

This one percent is tremendously powerful because it is alive.

The fire in it is going to transform the whole world. And those ninety-nine percent don't count at all.

So I am not concerned with what the masses think about me. I am concerned only about the one percent of intelligent people in the world — what they think about me.

Chapter 5
Ecstasy is now — why wait?

? *What is renunciation? What is its place in your vision of religiousness?*

The idea of renunciation is one of the fundamentals of all pseudo-religions. Its phenomenology has to be understood very deeply.

All the religions have been preaching a division between this world and that world which is beyond death — between the soul and the body. The body belongs to this world, the soul belongs to that world; hence if you want to achieve the world beyond death, which is eternal, and the happiness there is unending, then the happiness here is not worth calling happiness; it is momentary, it is dream stuff. It comes, and even before you have been able to grasp it, it is gone. It is illusory; it is a kind of mirage in the desert.

When you are far away you see a lake of water. You are thirsty and great hope arises in you. And the lake is absolutely real as far as you can see, because the proof of its reality, that water is there, is that the trees are being reflected in the water. If there is a mountain by the side, the mountain is reflected in the lake, the sun is reflected in the lake. What more proof do you need? Without water these reflections cannot happen. You rush with great hope, but as you come nearer, you find the lake is receding; the distance between you and the lake remains the same.

It was just an illusion created by sunrays reflected back from the hot desert sand. When sunrays are reflected back, they move like waves, and their movement from far away creates the illusion of water. And in their wave-like movement they attain the quality of reflecting things; they become just like a mirror. That is one half of the mirage.

The other half is in your thirst. If you were not thirsty, perhaps you would have been able to detect, to find out that it was a mirage. You have seen mirages before; you know that mirages can appear almost as if they are real — but your thirst is there. The physical phenomenon of the returning rays of the sun gives half the reality to the mirage. The other, and the far more important half, is contributed by you and your thirst. You want to believe that it is true. Even if somebody was there trying to prove that it was not real, you would feel angry with this man: you are thirsty and the water is there and he is trying to prove that the water is illusory. He does not know what thirst means — perhaps he is not thirsty. There is no way to convince a thirsty man that what he is seeing is not the real thing. All that you see is not necessarily real. Appearance does not mean reality.

The religions have been saying to people for millions of years, that the happiness in this world is of the same nature as a mirage in the desert. That's why you are never capable of catching hold of it. You never get hold of happiness in your fist; it comes and goes. You can feel it like a breeze, but by the time you become aware that it is here, it is already gone. Perhaps it is more unreal than the mirage. A mirage at least has some reality — the reflected sunrays contribute half, and your thirst, the other half. But in your so-called happiness of this world, you are contributing one hundred percent; there is nothing else there which contributes anything.

And you know it. Today a woman is so beautiful to you that you can say Cleopatra was nothing before her. She seems to be the most beautiful woman in the world. Not only today — you cannot conceive that there could have been any woman more beautiful ever, or could be in the future. You are projecting, because the same woman to others is nothing; and the same woman tomorrow will be nothing to you too. And then you will be surprised, shocked — what happened? What happened to the woman? Nothing has happened to the woman, she is the same person — something has happened to you.

Yesterday you were thirsty; lust was being projected. Today the lust is fulfilled; now there is no biological projection. The woman is an ordinary woman and the happiness that you got was just from your projection — you created the whole game. The woman, at the most, played the part of an inactive participant; she allowed you to project yourself upon her. Perhaps she was also projecting her mind upon you so it was a projection from both sides. Sooner or later it is going to disappear because projections cannot last once their basic cause is missing.

The basic cause is in your biology; and biology doesn't bother about love and poetry and romance, or anything — biology means business! Biology is not interested in fore-play and afterplay: a sheer wastage. Biology is interested in reproduction. Once biology has done its work, it withdraws; the projection disappears. Then you are standing there, the same woman is standing there — but nothing is any longer the same. Where has the happiness disappeared to?

You were feeling like you were on the top of Everest, and you have fallen to the depths of the Pacific. The woman deceived you and the woman thinks you deceived her; and you both try to dump on each other. Nobody has deceived; both have been deceived by biology. But biology is not somebody outside you; it is intrinsic to your body. You are a projection of two other biologies, those of your father, your mother, and they were a projection of two other biologies. It is a continuum, a river-like flow.

The religions tried to exploit this fundamental truth. It is true that romance and poetry ... And the so-called love affair is just a shadow of biology. So it is not very difficult: a certain injection with certain hormones can create all the poetry right now, all the romance. Another injection — and you fall into the Pacific! Now we know a man can become a woman, a woman can become a man; just a little change of hormones, just a little change of chemistry.

Religions exploited this simple truth. It is true, but rather than explaining it to you, they exploited it. They said, "This is momentary happiness. Don't run after it; you are wasting your time. The real world is beyond death." Why beyond death? Because death will destroy all your biology, physiology, chemistry; everything that is material, death will take away. Only the spiritual will be left behind and the spiritual knows the eternal. The material, the physical, knows only the momentary.

It appeared very logical; the first part is true, the second part is fictitious. Yes, it is true that moments of happiness in this life are very fleeting, but that does not mean that there is another life beyond death where these moments become eternal. There is no evidence for it. At least these moments are there, are experienced by everyone. Howsoever small and fleeting, they exist. Nobody can deny their existence. You can say they are made of the same stuff as dreams are made of — but still they are there. Even dreams have a reality of their own. They are there, and they affect you; and when something affects you it becomes real.

For example, you are hungry. The whole day you have not been able to eat anything; you are tired, you fall asleep. Now, the body is hungry and wants food. The mind creates a beautiful dream that you are a guest in a great feast. The mind is serving you because if the mind is not going to create the dream, your sleep will be disturbed — the hunger is there. Somehow you have to be convinced that you are eating, that you are not hungry. Your sleep remains undisturbed. The dream is doing something real. How can something unreal do something real? It is not possible — but a dream has its own existence. Yes, it is different from a rock, but so is a roseflower different from a rock. The dream is even more different; but it affects you, it affects your life, it affects your lifestyle — and those changes are real.

So, one thing to be remembered: in this life there are momentary pleasures, fleeting experiences of happiness, sudden explosions of joy — but you cannot catch hold of them.

You cannot keep them in your safe deposit. You cannot make them permanent. Just because you cannot make them permanent, religions have exploited you. It was a very cunning strategy. You want to make them permanent; your deepest desire is to remain happy for ever, not to know pain, sadness, anguish — ever. Just to be always in paradise — that is your desire.

The religions exploited this. They said, "There is such a place, but you cannot get anything without paying for it." It looks perfectly mathematical, economical. The religions started teaching that you sacrifice this life if you want to attain the permanent world of paradise that is beyond death. And it is very cheap, because what you are sacrificing are just momentary, once in a while, fleeting experiences.

If you collect all the moments of happiness in seventy years of your life, perhaps you may not get even seven moments which you can be absolutely certain were of the nature of ecstasy.

In seventy years of life, not even seven moments? Then what have you been doing here — torturing yourself and others? Yes, you cannot find even seven moments, because the nature of those moments is such that when they are there, they take you over totally, they possess you — yes, that is the right word — they possess you completely. But when they are gone, they dispossess you as completely as they had possessed you, so only a memory is left. And how long can you live on the memory which proved so deceptive?

After a few days you start doubting whether it happened or: "Was I just imagining?" Because in your whole life's experience that moment is so contradictory: years pass, then one moment perhaps... And that too is not in your hands; when and where it is going to happen, you cannot decide. So, years of dragging, and a certain moment which has remained just a memory... Slowly, slowly, even the smoke of memory starts disappearing.

So even if you ask a man seventy years old, he cannot say that there were even seven moments. And as you become older, there is less and less possibility of those moments. There is more and more disillusionment, more and more disappointment. In the future there is only death and darkness, and in the past nothing but deception.

The religions had a beautiful space through which to exploit you — and they did well all over the world. For thousands of years they have found the greatest business — greater than anybody else's: they have been selling you paradise, and almost for nothing.

All they ask is: "Renounce this momentary life and the eternal world of ecstasy is yours." Hence renunciation became a foundational belief: the more you renounce, the more you become worthy, and the more you can be certain that you are coming closer. So people have tried to renounce everything.

Mahavira was going to be the king. His father was old, and he was continually asking Mahavira, "Now let me retire. I am tired; and you are ready, young, well-educated — I am perfectly satisfied. Where can I find a better son than you? Just be ready to relieve me."

But Mahavira had other ideas. While he was being educated by the priests and the monks, they had poisoned his mind. They had told him that if he could renounce the kingdom, "Then the kingdom of God is yours." The greater the renunciation, the greater, of course, will be the reward. That's why the twenty-four great masters of the Jainas were all kings.

I have been asking the Jaina monks, "What is the secret of this? Was there nobody else in the country who could attain, become a great master — a warrior, a brahmin, a scholar, anybody — why only kings?" They don't have any answer. I used to tell them, "I am not asking you for the answer because I have the answer. I am just asking you the question so that you start thinking about it."

The answer is simple: because they renounced the kingdom, the greatest reward had to be theirs. A poor man can renounce whatsoever he has — but what has he? He cannot become a *tirthankara*, the supreme-most master. Even in paradise he will be living somewhere outside the town. He won't get in because they will ask, "What have you renounced? In the first place what have you got to renounce?"

So of course the kings will be very close to the palace of God; then will come the richest, the super-rich people; then the middle class people; then the lowest strata and then will come those who had nothing to renounce — they were already without anything. In fact they should be by the side of God already because they don't have anything. But they will be outside the boundary lines of paradise; they will not be able to show what their bank balance is in the other world.

All the Hindu avataras are kings: Rama, Krishna … Buddha is also a king. It is strange that these people are drawn only from kings, but if you understand the structure, the strategy of the priest, it is clear: they have renounced the most, naturally they are promised the most. Nobody knows whether they get anything after death or not, but the idea became so ingrained for the simple reason that it has a grain of truth in it: in this life everything is momentary.

To me, nothing is wrong if it is momentary. In fact, because it is momentary it is so exciting, so ecstatic. Make it permanent, and it will be dead.

In the morning, the roseflower opens up, so fresh, with fresh dewdrops still on its petals, so fragrant. You cannot conceive that just by the evening these petals will be falling into dust, and the rose will disappear. You would like it to remain permanent, but then you need a plastic flower; a real flower won't do. A real flower has to be momentary. To be real it has to be momentary; only plastic things can be permanent.

Plastic is a new discovery. It was not known to Buddha, Mahavira, Mohammed, Jesus, but I can say to you that paradise must be made of plastic. If there is any paradise, it cannot be anything but plastic, because plastic has the quality of not dying, it is deathless.

Now scientists are worried — particularly the environmentalists are very worried — because plastic is so cheap that you go on disposing of it. Glass was not so cheap; you were saving the bottles or returning the bottles and getting your deposit back. Plastic is so cheap that everything made of plastic is disposable: use it once and dispose of it. But you don't know where it is going. It is getting collected in the oceans, in the riverbeds, in the lakes under the earth, and there is no way for nature to dissolve it because nature is not prepared, was not made to absorb plastic.

If God has made this world, he certainly is not all-knowing. At least one thing he did not know: that plastic was going to happen one day. He has not made anything in nature, any chemicals, which can dissolve plastic, so plastic goes on accumulating. Soon it will have accumulated so much that it will destroy the fertility of the earth, it will poison the waters. Nothing can destroy it; it will destroy everything.

In the Hindu paradise, the *apsaras* — how to translate the word *apsara*? They are call girls for those great sages who live in paradise. Of course, they need call girls. Those call girls, those *apsaras*, are the most beautiful; it has to be so. They remain always young — that gives me the clue that they are plastic. They are stuck at the age of sixteen; for millions of years they remain just sixteen. In the Indian mind sixteen is the most mature age for a woman, so they remain at sixteen.

Apsaras don't perspire; neither Mahavira nor Buddha nor Jesus nor Mohammed had any idea of deodorants, so the only thing they could conceive of was that those girls who serve the sages should not perspire. But only if your body is made of plastic will you not perspire; otherwise, perspiration is absolutely necessary. And those girls will not get old, will not die.

Nothing dies in paradise, nothing gets old, nothing changes; it must be an utterly boring place. Can you imagine the boredom — where everything remains the same every day? There is no need for any newspaper there. I have heard that only once was one newspaper published — one edition, on one day — and it flopped because after that nothing happened! It described everything in the first edition; that was the last edition also.

This desire for permanency is somehow sick; but it was there, so the religious firms — yes, I call them firms — Christian, Hindus, Mohammedans, for centuries did great business. They are still doing it, and their business can never end, for the simple reason that they sell invisible commodities. They take visible things from you and they give you invisible things which you have to believe in.

I am reminded of a story. A king had conquered the whole world and he was very restless — now, what to do? He was thinking that once he had conquered the whole world he would rest. He had never thought that he would be so restless; he had never been so restless. While fighting, continuously invading, going on and on — because there is always some place to go, some enemy to destroy, some country to conquer — there was no space, no time to be restless; he was so occupied. But now he had conquered the whole world, he was utterly restless — what to do now?

A con man heard about this situation. He came to the palace, asked for an audience with the king, and said, "I have the remedy for restlessness."

Immediately he was taken inside, because all the physicians had failed. The king could not sleep, could not sit, was walking back and forth and was worried continually. He was asking, "What to do now? Isn't there another world? Find out! We will conquer it."

This con man came into the court before the king, and he said, "Don't be worried. You are the first man who has conquered the whole world. You are worthy to receive the clothes of God himself — and I can manage it."

This was a great idea. The king became immediately interested. He said, "Start working! God's own clothes... have they ever before appeared on the earth?"

The man said, "Never, because nobody has been worthy of them. You are the first man. So for the first time, from paradise, I will bring the clothes for you."

The king said, "Every preparation should be made, and how much will the cost be?"

The man said, "They are beyond cost; still, millions of rupees will be needed — but it is nothing."

The king said, "Don't be worried, money is not a problem at all. But don't try to deceive me."

The man said, "There is no question of deception. I will be staying in your palace and you can put your army around the palace. I will be working here; of course, my room has not to be opened until I give a knock from the inside. You can lock it from the outside so you can be completely satisfied that I cannot escape. But whatever money I ask, you have to go on sending to the person whose name I give you. It will take not more than three weeks." And in three weeks he withdrew millions of rupees. He was sending a name every day: morning, afternoon, night ... immediately! Urgent!

The king knew that the work was such... And the man could not deceive him. Where could he go? He was locked in. And certainly he didn't escape. After three weeks he knocked on the door, the door was opened. He came out with a huge beautiful box. He had gone into the room with the box, saying, "I will have to take the box with me for the clothes I have to bring you." Not to be deceived, the king had opened the box to see whether he was carrying some clothes in it. It was empty, there was no deception; the box was given back to him.

And now the con man came out and said, "The box will be opened in the court before all the wise, the learned, the generals, the queen, the king, the prince, the princess — everybody has to be present because this is a unique occasion."

The man must have been really courageous — con men always are. He called the king, "Come close, here. I will open the box. Give me your turban. I will put it in the box, because this is how I have been instructed: first, I put your turban in, then take out the turban which God has given, and give it to you. You put it on yourself. One thing more," he declared to the court, "these clothes are divine, so only those who are born really from their own fathers will be able to see them. Those who are bastards will miss out. I cannot do anything. This is the condition."

But everybody said, "There is no problem with it. We are born of our fathers."

The king's turban went in, and the con man's empty hand came out, and he said to the king, "Look at the beauty of the turban!" His hand was empty but the whole court started clapping, and everybody was trying to outdo the other, shouting that such a beautiful thing had never been seen.

Now the king thought, "If I say his hand is empty then I am the only bastard and all these bastards are really born of their fathers. So it is better to keep quiet." In fact, this was the situation with everybody. They all saw his hand was empty, but who would come out and be condemned when everybody else was seeing something there? They started suspecting, "Perhaps I am a bastard, so better keep quiet. What is the point of becoming unnecessarily condemned by all the people?" So they started shouting more loudly in praise of its beauty.

The king put the turban, which was not there, on his head. But it was not only the turban; by and by, other clothes started disappearing. At last, only his underwear was left. The king thought for a moment: "Now what to do?" But it was too late to turn back. "If I have seen the turban and I have seen the coat and I have seen the shirt, then why can't I see the underwear? Now it is better to see it. There is no way to go back. This man ..."

The man was holding the invisible underwear in his hands, and was showing them: "Look how many diamonds are on the underwear!" The whole court was applauding, saying, "Such an experience has never happened in the whole history of man."

The king's underwear also went in. But that con man was something! He said, "When I was coming, God said to me, 'These clothes are going into the world for the first time, so tell the king from me that when he wears these clothes he has to go in a procession round the whole capital, so all the people can see. Otherwise, those poor people will never be able to see them.' The chariot is ready, please come on."

Now, with each step it was difficult to go back. The king started thinking, "It would have been better if I had stopped the whole thing with the turban — but now it is too late. If I say I am naked ... but the whole court is applauding."

And they started saying, "Yes sir, this is right; if God has asked, it has to be done. And that is the right welcome for the clothes."

The streets were packed with people because the rumor had gone far and wide that God's clothes were coming. And the king agreed. Naked, he stood on his chariot, and before him the man was announcing, "These clothes will be seen only by those who are born of their own fathers."

So everybody saw them, except a small child who had come with his father. Sitting on his father's shoulders, he said, "Da" — Da means daddy — "the king appears to be naked."

His father said, "You idiot, keep quiet! When you grow up, then you will be able to see those clothes. It needs a certain maturity; just a child like you cannot see the clothes. Keep quiet if you want to see. I was not willing from the very beginning to bring you here."

But the child could not resist; again and again he said, "But I see him clearly, naked." The father had to escape with the child out of the crowd, because if others heard him, it would have meant that the child, was not his but somebody else's.

With invisible commodities it is very easy to exploit people, to force them to do things against themselves — and that's what renunciation is. It is con-manship, done by the priest in the name of God, truth, *moksha*, nirvana.

Their names may be different, but the priest is the greatest con man in the world. Other conmen are just small criminals. Of what can they cheat you? But the priest, the prophet, the messiah, the avatar, the tirthankara — these are the super conmen.

They have sold things which nobody has seen, which nobody is ever going to see. Not a single witness exists. Nobody has returned from death and said, "Yes, there is eternal beauty, eternal joy, eternal silence, eternal peace." The business goes on because nobody can contradict it. If you contradict it you are wrong, because the whole world believes in it.

But there was a certain truth which they tried to fix into their strategy of exploitation: in life everything is momentary. But nothing is wrong in it; it has to be so. If it were otherwise, life would have been intolerable.

Things change, and it is good that they change, otherwise they would be dead. Change keeps them alive.

You are changing continuously. Do you remember on what day you jumped from childhood and became a young man, or when from youth you became an old man? You cannot draw the line between when you were a child, when you were adolescent, when you became a young man, when you became middle-aged, when you became old. Can you draw the line? No, every moment you are changing; it is an ongoing process.

Since you were conceived, you have been changing. In the mother's womb, in those nine months you changed so much; in ninety years of your life you will not change so much. If you are shown pictures of the nine months' life in your mother's womb you will not recognize that they are your pictures. Or do you think that you can recognize them? You have changed completely, and you are changing every moment — and not only you, everything around you is changing. All the stars are moving and changing. Every day some star dies and disappears — it may have been here for millions of years — another star is born. Every day that is going on.

Life is a flux, a movement, a continuum.

There is nothing wrong in it. Enjoy that moment which comes and goes. Drink out of it as much as you can because it is fleeting — so don't waste time thinking. Don't start thinking that it is fleeting. Don't be bothered about what will happen tomorrow, whether this will be with you or not; and don't think of yesterdays.

While it lasts, squeeze the whole juice out of it, drink of it completely. Then who cares whether it goes away or if it remains? If it remains we will be drinking it. If it goes, good, we will be drinking some other moment.

Why should you insist that this moment remain permanent? How do you know that better moments are not coming? Just a moment before you would not have thought of this moment. And who knows — when this moment goes, something better may be on the way. In fact, it is on the way, because if you have drowned yourself in this moment totally, you have learned something of tremendous importance. You will be using that in the coming moment. Each moment your maturity is growing.

Each moment you are becoming more and more centered, more and more in the moment, more and more aware, more and more alert, more and more capable of living.

So who cares about death? We will enjoy it when we die. Death will also be a moment in life. Death is not the end of life, but only a moment of transformation, because nothing can die. You cannot destroy anything; it only changes shapes, forms.

Now science is capable of destroying Hiroshima, Nagasaki, the whole world ... But not really. It cannot destroy a single piece of stone. It cannot destroy it totally, it cannot annihilate it; it will still be there. You can break it into pieces but those pieces will be there. You can heat it as much as if you have brought the sun itself under it; it will melt, but it will be there. Yes, you can change the form, but there is no way to throw it out of existence.

Nothing dies, nothing is born.

Birth simply means that the form that you were was not this form, but some other form, so you cannot recognize it. You cannot recognize even pictures of you in your mother's womb. If I show you a picture of your past life, are you going to recognize it? Forget about the mother's womb, you may not be able to recognize the picture of when you were three months old, six months old, nine months old. Continuously, everything goes on changing.

Death is a great transformation.

You ask about the place of renunciation in my vision of religiousness. Before I answer you, there is one thing more to be noted: this idea of renunciation became so deep-rooted in the whole of humanity that even the people who have denied the existence of life after death have also used the same logic. The logic became almost universal.

For example, in India there was a school of atheists called Charvakas. The word *charvaka* is worth understanding. Their enemies — and all the religions are enemies of Charvakas — have burned all the books, so not a single book of the Charvakas is available. All that we know is from the scriptures of Hindus, Jainas and Buddhists criticizing Charvakas. So we can guess something of what those people were saying, but we cannot be absolutely certain. And these are all religious people, and they destroyed the Charvakas' scriptures. Perhaps they have killed many of them also, because today there is not a single Charvaka in India. And all the scriptures are so much against the Charvakas, that it seems they must have once been a tremendous force. Otherwise why criticize them when there is nobody who follows the philosophy?

All three religions were continually hammering and arguing against the Charvakas. It must have been a very popular philosophy. And in fact, it is still a powerful philosophy all over the world, but because people are hypocrites, they don't recognize it. Just listen to their philosophy and you will see that out of one hundred people, ninety-nine point nine percent are Charvakas. They may be Christians, they may be Hindus, they may be Mohammedans, it doesn't matter; these are just masks.

So the enemy scriptures describe the meaning of the word charvaka: eat, drink, and be merry. Charvaka means one who believes in eating, eating, eating — through all the senses. I cannot say that any Charvakas have said it, but it is possible. The enemy scriptures quote Charvakas as saying, "Even if you have to borrow money, don't be worried, but drink, eat, be merry. Go on borrowing money, because after death neither are you there to pay, nor is there anybody else to ask you, 'What about my money?' Everything is finished with death, so don't be bothered by these priests telling you that you will suffer for your karmas. Enjoy yourself in every possible way. Don't miss enjoyment. This is the only world."

This is the meaning given by the enemies, but in one enemy scripture — it must have been a very liberal person who wrote it — it says that this is the meaning given by the enemies, by us. But Charvakas themselves have a different meaning of their name. It means one who has a sweet philosophy — that meaning is possible from the same word — one who speaks words of honey. And certainly they do speak words of honey. But they also are trapped in the same logic.

The religious people say, "Renounce this world if you want to enjoy that world." And Charvakas say, "Renounce that world if you want to rejoice in this one." But the logic is the same. They have taken it from different angles, but both are asking you to renounce one for the other. Charvakas say renounce the other world; there is no God, no nirvana, no paradise — renounce it. This is all there is, so enjoy it.

In Greece, Epicurus had the same philosophy and got caught up in the same logic. Even Karl Marx was caught up in the same logic: there is no other world. The first effort is to deny the other world, only then can you enjoy this world. So first demolish the other world: there is no God, no paradise, no heaven, nothing. There is no soul to survive; with your body everything dies. You are nothing but your body, your chemistry, your biology, your physiology, all together — a byproduct of all these things. It is just like a clock that goes on working — it does not mean there is a soul which is moving the hands. Just take the pieces apart and you won't find any soul, just a certain arrangement of the parts. Arrange it again, and it starts ticking.

Karl Marx says, "Consciousness is only a byproduct, it has no independent existence." So when the body dies, consciousness disappears. Why this insistence on denying the other world? — for the simple reason that unless you deny the other, you will not be able to enjoy this.

But please see my point of view which is totally different from all these people — the religious, the anti-religious, the theist, the atheist. I don't belong to any of them. I say to you that life continues to exist, but there is no need to call it the other world. It is the same world, the same continuity.

The Ganges arises in the Himalayas; it is just a small rivulet. As it descends, other waterfalls, other rivulets go on joining it; it goes on becoming bigger and bigger and bigger. When it comes out of the Himalayas it is a vast river. You cannot conceive that it is the same river. You can see from where it arises. Because Hindus love the cow as the mother, they have made the origin of the Ganges a stone cow's face. The Ganges falls through the face; it is so small, so tiny.

By the time the Ganges reaches Benares, you cannot believe its size. And when it reaches near Kolkatta to meet the ocean, it becomes almost oceanic itself. Standing there, you cannot decide which is the ocean; it is so vast. It falls into the ocean; then too it remains. Where can it go? Yes, it is no longer a river — perhaps some water may evaporate into the clouds, some water may become ice and move towards the arctic — but it will remain, nothing is lost.

So I don't say that you have to renounce anything: this world for that, or that world for this. You have not to renounce at all.

You have to live! You have to live intensely and totally, wherever you are, whatever you are.

And if you enjoy this time, this space, this opportunity that is available to you, in its totality, you will certainly be moving to a higher consciousness. You will be gaining, learning, understanding, becoming more aware. Life will continue. It will depend on your awareness what form it takes, higher or lower, whether it moves towards more anguish or more ecstasy — but it depends on this moment. So I am not saying to renounce this world.

I am a strange man in a way, because I am against the religions. Religious people in India have been writing against me in books and articles — and communists have been writing books and articles against me too.

Once I was traveling, and the president of India's communist party, S.A. Dange, was also with me in the compartment. His son-in-law had just written a book against me. He asked me, "Have you seen the book my son-in-law has written against you?"

I said, "I am so much involved in living that I don't care who is writing what about me. And anybody who is writing about me must be a fool because he is wasting his time writing about me. He should live! Or even if he wants to write, he should write something about himself. And why should I read his crap? He may be your son-in-law — so you can read it, I'm not interested."

He was ready to give me the book. I said, "Throw it out of the window, because so many books have been written against me, I cannot waste my time." I told him, "Just for your information, it is strange but religious people write against me and anti-religious people, communists, also write against me. This has never happened before."

But the reason is that I am trying to give you a totally new viewpoint, which goes against all the old logic. They are both partners in the same game, and I am trying to destroy their whole game, the whole logic.

They both believe that one world has to be renounced; which one is another matter. But on one point they agree: one world has to be renounced. The religions say this for that; the communists say that for this — that is the only disagreement between them. But the basic logic is similar: you can have only one world. And I say: why can't we have both? I don't see any conflict; I am having both. And my experience is that the more you have of this, the more you will have of that, because you will become more experienced.

If there is a paradise, then one thing is certain: your monks will not be able to enjoy it. What will they enjoy? The whole of their life they were denouncing women, condemning women, and there they will find beautiful call girls. They will be so nervous; many of them will have heart attacks. Here they are renouncing: you should not eat food with taste, taste is an attachment to food — and there they will be served the most tasteful food; they will be vomiting. Their whole life experience will be against it.

Only my people can enjoy paradise fully.

Neither the religious people can enjoy it, because they have destroyed and crippled themselves and their capacity to enjoy, nor the communists, because they will not open their eyes. They have denied the existence of anything after death. They will keep their eyes closed to remain convinced that there is nothing; otherwise their whole life's philosophy is proved wrong. It is better to keep your eyes closed. That's what people do: if anything goes against you, any fact, you try to avoid that fact; it is disturbing. Communists will go blind; they cannot accept the idea that Karl Marx is wrong and *Das Kapital* is wrong.

And the religious people will be the most troubled people in paradise, everywhere they will find difficulty. Perhaps there are divisions in paradise, as it seems. Mohammedans' paradise seems to be different from the Hindus, from the Christians, from the Jainas — perhaps different zones are allotted to different kinds of people.

In the Mohammedan paradise there are rivers of wine. You drink as much as you want: swim, jump, and drown yourself — whatsoever you want to do. But here — don't touch wine. Now, this seems to be very illogical. Here these people should be trained for such a great experience or they will simply die. Sitting on the bank of a river where champagne is flowing, they cannot drink because of their past habits, their whole life's training and discipline. And there is no description of any river which has water; in Mohammedan paradise all the rivers are wine. Why? When you can drink wine, why bother about water? They will either die of thirst, or they will start drinking in spite of themselves. They will really be in a mess. Many of them will go mad: that what kind of reward is this? This is punishment!

Only my people will be able to swim in any zone. In the Mohammedan zone they will not be worried; they will enjoy it. They will fit anywhere because they haven't any fixed routine of living, a fixed style of living.

All that I am teaching is to remain flexible, free, open, available to new experiences, to new explorations. So my people are not going to remain in one zone. They are going to use all the zones and enjoy all the sights of paradise; nobody can prevent them.

You can have both worlds — so why cripple people? Make this life an experience, a school, a learning, a discipline, because something unknown is going to open up after death and you have to be ready in every possible way. Don't miss any opportunity of living. Who knows what kind of life you are going to have after death?

I do not give you a fixed idea, because if I give you a fixed idea, I am your enemy; I make you a fixed person, inflexible, rigid, dead. Be flexible, so you can move in any dimension that becomes available.

In my vision there is no place for renunciation.

The Sanskrit word for renunciation is *sannyas*, because renunciation became so important that the very word *sannyas* was used for it. But I have given it a new meaning. The people who have called *sannyas* renunciation, meant by *sannyas* "the right way of renouncing life." By *sannyas*, I mean "the right way of living life.

The word *sannyas* can mean both. When it can mean the right way of living, why cripple people, cut off their life, destroy their naturalness, their spontaneity? Why not help them to have as many aspects to their life as possible, as many dimensions open to them as possible?

My vision is multidimensional. The whole of life is yours. Love it, live it to the fullest. That's the only way to get ready for death.

Then you can live death too, to its fullest; and it is one of the most beautiful experiences. There is nothing comparable to the death experience in life, except deep meditation.

So those who know meditation know something of death — that's the only way to know before dying.

If I am saying there is no more significant experience in life than death, I am saying it, not because I have died and come back to tell you, but because I know that in meditation you move into the same space as death — because in meditation you are no longer your physiology, no longer your biology, no longer your chemistry, no longer your psychology. All these are left far away.

You come to your innermost center where there is only pure awareness. That pure awareness will be with you when you die because that cannot be taken away. All those things which can be taken away, we take away with our own hands in meditation.

So meditation is an experience of death in life.

And it is so beautiful, so indescribably beautiful that only one thing can be said about death: it must be that experience multiplied by millions. The experience of meditation multiplied by millions is the experience of death.

And when you pass on you simply leave your form behind. You are absolutely intact, and for the first time out of the prison of physiology, biology, psychology.

All the walls are broken and you are free. For the first time you can open your wings to the existential.

Chapter 6
Transformation, not renunciation

? *Is there really absolutely no place for renunciation in your vision?
The question arises because since I came in contact with you, many
things in my life have dropped away. I cannot even relate to my old
self.*

There is really absolutely no place for renunciation in my vision. I can understand the question and the difficulty of the questioner. He has not been able to make a distinction between dropping things, and things dropping by themselves.

Renunciation is the enforced dropping of things. And whenever you do anything with force, nothing really drops away. It simply goes deeper into your unconscious. It becomes more of a problem than it was before. Now it will try to come up in different ways, garbs, masks, and you may not even be able to recognize it. But it is going to assert itself, and with force. You have given it that force by forcing it deep down into the unconscious.

When you force something, you are giving force to it. You are making it stronger, and you are making the enemy hide within you, in the darkness, from where you become more vulnerable. When it was in the conscious, it was in the light; you were less vulnerable.

Renunciation is repression. That is the right psychological word for it: repression. How can you renounce sex, except by repressing it? And repressed sex becomes perverted.

It is easier to understand sex, to become more aware of it and let it drop by itself, than to understand it when it is perverted, because then it comes in an unnatural form. First it is difficult to recognize it — that it is sex. A person too greedy for money — can you think that this greed for money can have anything to do with suppressed sex? It is so far-fetched it needs a Sigmund Freud to see it. An ordinary person will not be able to connect them at all. How? Money and sex seem to be so far away; they are not so far away.

If you repress sex, it comes as ambition. It can become politics. The politician can completely forget about sex, because all his sexuality, his sex energy is now converted into his political ambition. He will have the same kind of enjoyment by reaching higher and higher in the hierarchy. The higher he reaches, the more he will feel a kind of sexual pleasure, which you cannot understand.

I used to live with a very rich man. He was a bachelor and he had no interest in women at all. His only interest was money — day in, day out he was working for money — but because I was living in his house, somehow he became interested in my ideas. He had a big house and he was alone; his father and mother were dead. He was unmarried with no children, just servants. I liked the place because there was no disturbance, no children, no old people in the house, and no fighting because he had no wife. It was really quiet, the servants would go away at night, and it was such a big house that we two were almost alone.

He was not interested in anything except money. So he would close the doors of his room — there was nobody except me, but he would lock his room from inside — and start working: counting how much he had gained, how much he had lost; how much was in this business and how much was in that business. Before he went to sleep, he would be perfectly clear where he was financially. Only then would he go to sleep — sometimes at two o'clock or three o'clock. By the time I was waking up, at three o'clock, he was going to sleep, and I would go for a walk.

I once asked him, "Do you ever think of what you are going to do with this money? You are not extravagant; you are a miser. You don't have any children to whom you are going to leave the money. You are not so generous that you give it to your friends or to those who are in need. You are not in any way parting with a single pai. What are you going to do? Are you going to take it with you when you die? What is the purpose of this money?"

Because money really is meaningless if you don't use it, its whole meaning is in its use. You may have the same amount of money as I have but you can use it in such a way that you are richer than me. The value of the money is in its use. Certainly those who know how to use money use it a thousandfold more than those who don't know. They have the same amount of money, but they are poor.

Now this man was a poor man. Money was in the safe, money was in the banks, money was in shares — but he was a poor man.

I said to him, "There seems to be no reason for you now to go on earning; you have enough. Even if you live two hundred years, it will do. The miserly way you are living, it will do for two thousand years. Two hundred, I am saying if you live like me; otherwise two thousand, and still you may not be able to spend it all. You may go on living just on the interest from it forever. Why are you so worried? You cannot sleep well, you don't have any time for anything — and have you ever thought about how this disease happened to you, where you got this cancer?"

He said, "I have never thought about it, but you are right. I have enough money, and I can live … Certainly I am not going to live for two thousand years — just seventy or eighty will be enough. My father died at seventy, his father died at seventy, so I cannot live more than seventy or perhaps eighty years. Yes," he said, "this makes sense. But can you tell me why I am doing this?"

I said, "For a simple reason: you have avoided women in your life."

He said, "But what have women and money to do with each other?"

I told him, "That we will discuss later on, first tell me why you avoid women."

The reason was very simple. He had seen his grandfather being harassed, nagged continually, tortured by his grandmother. He had seen his father in the same position, he had seen his uncles in the same position. They were all miserable, and he thought that their misery was caused by the women. He became a woman-hater from his very childhood. And then he came under the influence of the Jaina monks, because his father was a very religious man.

People who are tortured by their wives become religious. Except for religion, there is no other shelter for them. Only religion can give them some consolation: "Don't be worried, it is only a question of a few years. Next life, don't commit the same mistake; and start withdrawing yourself even in this life. The woman is powerful over you because you are sexually interested in women. It is your weakness that she is exploiting." And that's what he heard from the Jaina monks. In Jainism, sex is the first thing to be renounced, because with it many other things are renounced automatically, you need not work at them separately; sex seems to be the main problem.

Seeing the situation of his grandfather, uncle, father, neighbors and then listening to the Jaina monks, it became a decided thing in his mind that he was not going to get involved in this constant headache.

I told him, "That's from where your interest in money arises. The energy needs some object, some infatuation." And I told him, "You may feel hurt, but I have to say it: I have seen you counting notes, and the way you touch the notes looks as if you are touching your beloved."

He looked at me, shocked. For a moment there was silence, and then he said, "Perhaps you are right. I really enjoy touching those notes. I count them again and again. Although I have counted them, even in the night I count them again. Just touching them gives some strange satisfaction to me — even the notes of other people."

For example, sometimes he would come into my room and if there was some money on the table — because that was the only place for me to keep it — the first thing he would do was count it, and I would tell him, "This is simply foolish. It is not your money, why are you counting it?"

He said, "I simply enjoy it; it is not so important to whom it belongs."

Can you see the point? If you become interested in somebody else's wife, do you think of whom she belongs to? There is no question of whom she belongs to — she looks beautiful, that's all, so you are interested. Whomsoever she belongs to is not your business. This was exactly the case with him: money is money; it is nobody's really. And just to touch it, to count it, to play with it ...

I told him, "If you want to get rid of this infatuation with money, which is absolutely idiotic ... "

I am not against money; I am against the infatuation. The man who is infatuated with money cannot use it. He is really destroying the money, its very purpose. In every language, in all the languages of the world, money's other name is currency — that is significant. Money needs to be a current, river-like, flowing, moving fast. The faster it moves, the richer is the society.

If I have a one-hundred-dollar note with me and I simply keep it in my pocket and never use it, then whether I have it or not, does it make any difference? I could have kept any piece of paper; that would have served the same purpose. But if I use this hundred-dollar note and it circulates in here, and everybody who gets it immediately uses it — so it passes through one hundred hands — then it is one hundred dollars multiplied by one hundred; then that much money is here in this room.

The miser is really anti-money. He is destroying its utility because he is stopping it being a currency.

I told him, "Do one thing: become interested in a woman."

He said, "What!"

I said, "Just try. I can arrange for a few women to be introduced to you" — because so many women used to come from the university. There were many women professors from the colleges who came to visit me, to ask about meditation and things. I said, "There is no problem. Just indicate in whom you are interested, I will introduce you; and any woman is going to be interested in you."

He said, "Why?"

I said, "Because of all the money. She is not going to be interested in you; she is going to be interested in your money. And once you become interested in the woman, you will start spending money; you will relax. The energy that has become perverted will start moving in the natural way. And you can't find anybody better than a woman to finish your money. You will not need to live two thousand years; long before that the money will be gone. And once you become interested in a woman, your infatuation with money will drop to its natural state."

He said, "I will have to think it over."

I said, "You can think it over, but don't waste too much time because right now you are almost forty-five. Once you are over sixty, then it will be difficult even for me to make an arrangement. So don't waste fifteen years. Think about it tonight and tomorrow morning when we meet, tell me."

He could not sleep the whole night. He thought about it again and again, and slowly the thing became clear to him: "Yes, deep down it is women, and I am constantly keeping myself occupied with money in order to avoid women, because if there is no space, no time, then from where can the woman enter? And why I am so infatuated now makes sense. It is a substitute woman."

So this greed for money, this greed for power, this greed for fame — sex can take any form — will depend on the type of person. You will be aware of the fact that although poets continually write poetry about women, most of the poets have stayed away from women. Most of the great novelists were not interested in women. Most of the great painters were afraid of women for the simple reason that either you can paint or you can be married. You can't have two wives — together they will kill you.

There is an ancient parable in India: a man was caught as a thief in a house. He was presented in court and the magistrate said, "Do you accept your guilt?"

He said, "I accept it absolutely but I want to say one thing. You can give me any punishment, but don't tell me to be married to two women."

The magistrate said, "I have never heard of any punishment like that. My whole life I have been punishing people, but I have never punished anybody that way."

He said, "Then you are a really good man. You can sentence me to death, but not ... "

The magistrate said, "But I would like to know why this condition?"

He said, "This is the reason why I was caught. I entered a house where a man lives with two wives. One wife lives on the ground floor, the other wife lives on the floor above. And they were both pulling at the man — one was pulling him to the upper floor, the other was pulling him to the ground floor. I became so interested that I forgot why I had gone there. I became interested to know what was going to be the result, ultimately who would win. Certainly the man had no chance of winning — he was getting beaten from both sides.

"That's why I got caught — otherwise, in the whole of my life, have you ever seen me in court? I am a born thief; my father was a thief, my father's father was a thief — this is our inherited profession. And this is the first time anybody from my family has been caught. I am ashamed. My father's soul, my grandfather's soul — they will all be ashamed of me. And there was no problem, I could have stolen things and escaped, but the story with those two women and that one man... And a crowd gathered; that is why I got caught. They said, 'Who is this man? And what is he doing here? He doesn't seem to be from this neighborhood.' So you can sentence me to death or life imprisonment, whatsoever you want, but please don't order me to get married to two women."

This has been the situation for the poet, for the painter, for the musician, for the dancer — any creative artist finds it easier not to get involved with women, or to get involved only casually, perhaps with strangers. Perhaps traveling on a train he may become interested in a woman because there is no fear — at the next station he is going to get off. Artists have told me that they get interested only in strangers; they don't know their name, they don't want to know their name. The strangers don't know the artist's name nor does he want them to know it — they remain strangers.

The fear is deep-rooted, and it has a reality of its own. And perhaps that is one of the reasons why women in the past have never been creative: they could not afford to live alone in a society which is absolutely man-made. A woman living alone is continually in danger. Only recently in human history a few women have started careers -- as a novelist, as a poet, as a painter. This is because for the first time, just in these last few years — and that too only in a very few advanced, progressive, avant-garde places — a woman has been able to live independently, just like a man. Then they start painting; they start composing poetry, music.

Women have all the talents but for millions of years their sex was their only creativity, and when the whole sexual energy was involved in producing children... You can't imagine a woman having a dozen children and composing music — or can you imagine it? Those twelve children all around doing everything that is not right ... and the woman can compose music or poetry, or can paint? Do you think those twelve will sit silently? They will be painting before she paints!

It looks strange that poets are the least experienced people with women. Perhaps that's why they write about women; it is a perversion. Otherwise, why should poets write about women? They don't have much experience; they are almost monks. Why do painters go on painting nude women? Why do sculptors go on making marble statues of nude women, for what? It is all perversion: better than collecting money or going into politics, but still it is a perversion. They are satisfying their natural instinct in an unnatural way. So on the one hand they go on doing their painting, music, poetry, and on the other hand they go on feeling that life is meaningless.

Artists feel the meaninglessness of life the most. It is strange; they write such beautiful poetry, they paint such beautiful paintings, yet life is meaningless. Life is not meaningless for a clerk, and it is meaningless for Jean-Paul Sartre, who wins the Nobel Prize! It is not meaningless for a schoolmaster who must be the most miserable person in the world — thirty children against one poor man — but he is not feeling life to be meaningless.

In fact, the people who feel that life is meaningless are the people who have not moved naturally; their natural energies have taken an artificial, arbitrary route. They will never feel meaningful. They have moved away from life's source.

Similarly, monks are strangely the most articulate against women, and they have no experience with women at all. I have asked Hindu monks, Buddhist monks, Jaina monks, Christian monks, "What experience do you have of women? You speak against them, but more experience is needed to speak against than in favor. What experience do you have?" And none of them could say that they had any experience. I said, "Then why do you go on speaking against them?"

Yes, the monks have one experience: the woman in their unconscious is continuously pulling them down from their holier-than-thou pedestal. They are projecting their antagonism against that woman — they don't know about it, it is deep in the dark — on any woman that they can find outside. All women are evil, agents of evil.

These people have no experience at all. In fact, if they stop condemning women, there is a fear that the infatuation for women may come back — it is just knocking on the door continuously. They have to keep themselves occupied, condemning them as loudly as possible so they cannot hear the knock: that the woman is there. If they stop condemning, they will hear the knock and it will be irresistible for them to open the door, and that will be their fall.

I told this friend, "Just try — there is no harm. The women who come to me are not poor and they will not ask for money or any costly present from you. And I will be introducing you only as a friend, just so that you can have a little acquaintance with women."

Next morning he said, "I am ready. And perhaps you are right; I will lose my interest in money. The whole night I thought about it, weighed it up: what should I do? But finally I thought that perhaps it is right, that what I am gathering is rubbish."

I introduced him to a woman to whom he got married within six months — and I finished his career!. He was thinking of becoming the richest man in the city, but then the woman started using his money. Every day he would see me, and he would say, "You have got me into trouble, there is no end to her demands. And I have lost interest in money, so I am no longer after it as madly as you have known me to be. If it comes it is okay, if it doesn't come I don't bother; but she is continually spending. Now, two hundred years or eighty years ... I think she will finish me nearabout sixty or before. But you were right."

I said, "Now there is a possibility; before that, there was no possibility. If you had renounced money, you would have been renouncing something which is not at all a natural instinct in you. You would have been renouncing only a path of perversion without knowing that it was a perversion, and the perversion would have taken another path. You may not have been after money, you may have got involved in politics; then power would have become the same problem. But now you are on natural ground. Any transformation can happen only when you are a natural human being."

The philosophy of renunciation is that you renounce money. I know, because money is an artificial thing, man-made, that even renouncing it is not going to lead you anywhere. These people will say, "Renounce the house," but what does it matter? You will be staying in the temple; you will become a burden on the society. These people say to you, "Renounce earning your own livelihood," then you will start begging.

In India you see so many beggars but you will never come across a beggar who feels guilty that he is begging. I have never come across one. Traveling for thirty years continually, I have never come across a single beggar who thinks he is doing anything wrong. If you don't give to him, you are guilty.

One day it happened, at a station, Khandwa, a junction station. I was coming from Indore, and from Khandwa I had to take a train for Mumbai. I was alone in the compartment, and the train was to leave from Khandwa in one hour's time. So I was just sitting looking out through the window. A beggar came and told me that his mother had just died and he needed some money for her funeral rituals, so I gave him one rupee.

He could not believe it, because he must have been begging his whole life and nobody gives one rupee. He looked at me. I said, "I have given it to you knowingly. Your mother is dead. Go home and do something."

The man thought, "This man seems to be either mad or a simpleton." He was wearing a coat, but he came back after fifteen minutes without the coat and, pretending to be somebody else told me, "My father is very sick."

I said, "It is bound to be so." I gave him one rupee and I said, "Go and help your father. Just a few minutes before, somebody's mother had died. Your father may die; you just go and help."

Now, it was very difficult for the man to go and leave me alone. After fifteen minutes he removed his cap also, and he came again.

I said, "Some family trouble?"

He said, "How did you guess? Yes, my wife is pregnant; any moment she is going to give birth to a child and I have not a single pai."

I said, "Take one rupee and go fast. Today there are so many things happening. One man's wife has died — he was wearing a coat and a cap. Another man's father is almost dying — he was not wearing a coat, but wearing a hat. You don't have a coat or a cap, and your wife is in danger. Just run!"

After fifteen minutes he came back. I said, "Some family trouble?"

He said, "No. I was thinking that I am cheating you, and now I feel guilty."

I said, "For what? You are a different man — those people were different."

He said, "No, I'm the same man."

Then I said, "Don't be worried; then I must be a different man."

He said, "How is it possible?"

I said, "Don't be worried — I must be a different man. Somebody else must have been sitting here before; otherwise an innocent person like you could not do that."

He said, "Now, this is too much. Please take these four rupees you have given to me."

I said, "No. You take one more, so you need not come naked next time, because if you get rid of any more clothes... And from where will you find more family? Your whole family will be dying, finished!"

But what he said, I have not forgotten. He said, "You are the first man who has made me feel guilty; otherwise, whenever people give to us we feel they are fools. If they don't give to us, we say they are sinners; we never think about ourselves."

No beggar does. He is simply giving you an opportunity to be virtuous; you should be obliged to him. He is putting a ladder before you; you can go to paradise. No beggars, although they are begging, ever feel inferior.

The mind is so cunning; it can take you in any direction and distort your simple, natural being.

Now, nobody naturally would ever like to beg, nobody is a born beggar. But the sexual instinct can take any form — it can become the greed of a rich man, it can become the greed of a beggar.

When I was a professor, one student of mine, studying in the post-graduate philosophy department, was always coming with costly clothes and looked rich. One day it happened, I was coming out of the station — because I was continually moving from Jabalpur all over India, twenty days per month I was out of town. I would come back after three days for a few hours, just to show myself in the university, that I was there, because they could not give me that much leave nor could I take that much leave; otherwise from where would I get money?

So this was the arrangement: one of my students used to take my car and park it in the same place where I would normally park it. The car was always parked there; that was a symbol that I was in the university. I told him, "So park the car there at two o'clock and at four o'clock take it away — just two hours. Everybody will know it is there because that is the rush hour, when everybody is there, and everybody knows that I never come before two; from twelve to two I sleep. So there is no problem."

So every third or fourth day I was coming and going: coming in the morning and going in the evening. And there was this beggar who was continually getting one rupee, fixed — whether I came or went, he would get it. One day, just by coincidence, I saw this student of mine with that old man, just behind the shed where my car was parked. I went closer: What was this rich man's son doing with the beggar? And the beggar was giving him rupees.

So I went outside and called them both. Both of them started trembling. The old man said, "Don't tell anybody — he is my son."

I said, "How much do you manage to earn? This boy lives the best in the university, so you must be earning nearly thirty, forty or fifty rupees."

He said, "You are right."

I said, "How much have you got in the bank?"

He said, "Now I cannot hide anything from you." He had fifty thousand rupees in the bank.

I told him, "Then why are you begging? You could do some business."

He said, "This is business. And with no investment — in what business can you earn fifty rupees a day in India?"

I said, "That is true."

He said, "And I am leaving enough for my son; he can live a rich life. I am not going to die for a few years yet, so I will leave enough for him; and he is now well educated. But please don't tell anybody, otherwise his career may be affected."

Now, this man is a beggar but he does not think there is anything wrong in begging. It is a business, without investment and with good earnings. All that you have to do is just befool people.

The sexual instinct can take many paths. It can become greed. It can become a will-to-power. It can become a subtle ego trip: holier-than-thou.

That's what the monks are doing; otherwise they have no other enjoyment. They are torturing themselves, and have renounced everything you think of as pleasure, as joy. Then what keeps them ticking, going tick-tock? What keeps them ticking? From where do they get the energy? The energy is from a holier-than-thou attitude: you are all sinners, we are the only people who are not sinners; we are saints. And they will look down from heaven and find you there, burning in hellfire.

Renunciation can teach you to drop sex, to drop tasteful food, to drop clothes, to be naked, to drop all possessions — but in a strange way you will remain attached to all those things.

When I was in Mumbai, a Hindu monk came to see me; he had a disciple with him and he wanted to know what kind of meditation would be suitable for him.

I told him, "Tomorrow morning we are meeting near the beach and we will be doing the meditation. It is better that you come there because it is a question of practical experience."

He said, "It will be very difficult for me to come tomorrow. The day after tomorrow I can come."

I said, "What is the problem with tomorrow?"

He said, "The problem is that my disciple has some work tomorrow morning, he cannot come."

But I said, "Let him do his work — there is no need for him to come."

He said, "You don't understand — I have renounced money."

I said, "You are making it more and more of a puzzle. You have renounced money, perfectly good, but what has that to do with this man and his engagement tomorrow morning, and your coming to my meditation group?"

He said, "Are you not aware of a simple thing: "I cannot touch money, so he keeps the money for me. And in Mumbai you have to go in a taxi — then who will pay? I cannot touch money; I have renounced it. He keeps the money; he pays out the money and if somebody donates money to me, he receives it. I am completely out of it, I have nothing to do with money."

I said, "Good arrangement! You have nothing to do with money; then what have you to do with this man? You will go to heaven and this man will go to hell; and he, poor man, is simply serving you continually, following you everywhere — and yet he is going to hell. If you have renounced money, then live without money, then suffer without money. Why send this man to hell? You will be responsible for sending this man to hell. You will fall into a deeper hell than this man."

People can find strange ways because they have not understood what they are doing; they are simply following a dead creed, a dead dogma. They are renouncing it because for centuries money has been condemned by the religious people. I said, "But it is becoming more complicated. It would have been simple to put your hand in your own pocket; now you have to put it in somebody else's pocket. That is pick-pocketing." I said, "You are also a thief. What are you doing? And you are a bigger pickpocket than others because at least they use their hand; you use his hand, picking up money from his pocket. His pocket, his hand, and you are completely above it, superior."

I said to the disciple, "Escape right now, leave this man here. I will not allow him to go with you. Just escape as far as you can, where he cannot find you again, because he is managing and arranging for your hell. And whatever money you have, it is yours, because he has renounced money. He cannot claim it."

He said, "Is it so — all the money?"

I said, "What do you mean by 'all the money'?"

He said, "Right now when we go somewhere, I keep just two or three hundred rupees in my pocket, but at our temple we have thousands."

I said, "All that money is yours. Simply go there. I will keep this man here, so take all that money and escape. And if this man leaves here I will give him to the police because he has renounced money. He cannot even report to the police that his money is stolen."

The monk said, "What! I came here to learn meditation."

I said, "I am teaching you what renunciation means. And what you are doing is just cheating yourself, cheating this poor man, cheating God — cheating everybody."

Renounce anything and you will become more attached to it than when you had not renounced it. Your mind will move around and around it.

An ancient parable: A man continually wanted to learn the secret of miracles. He had heard so much about it: that there are sages in Tibet, in the high peaks of the Himalayas who can teach you, who know all kinds of miracles. So he was always serving any kind of sage. In India there are so many sages — just as here there are so many sage bushes. When I first came here and I came to know that there are so many sages here also, I said, "These people are not going to leave me alone."

He found a very old, ancient sage and he was continually massaging his feet, bringing him food and doing whatsoever he could do. The old sage knew, the whole town knew, why he served such people. The old sage said again and again, "I am a simple man, and I don't know any miracles."

The man said, "That's the true sign of a sage: those who claim are worthless; you are the person who knows the secret."

He said, "It is very difficult. If I say I know then there is difficulty — you say, 'Teach me.' And I am telling you the truth, that I don't know any miracle and I don't think that anybody does except people like you, who go on creating myths around somebody; otherwise there is no miracle."

But the man would not leave; day and night he was serving the sage. One night the old man wanted to sleep but the man was massaging him. So he said, "Stop!"

The man said, "I am not going to stop until you tell me. If you want to sleep tonight, just tell me a simple secret so that I can do miracles."

The sage said, "Okay, I am going to tell you. It is very simple. Go home, take a shower, sit down in the lotus posture — and this is the mantra: Om mani padme hum, the Tibetan mantra. Just say it five times and in the morning you will be able to do any kind of miracle that you want to do."

Hearing this, the man simply jumped up and out of the room. The old man said, "Wait! You have not heard the condition."

He said, "In the morning I can come again."

The old man said, "No, the condition has to be followed, otherwise the mantra won't work."

The man said, "What is the condition?"

The sage said, "The condition is, while you are repeating the mantra five times, you should not think of a monkey.

The man said, "Don't be worried. In my whole life I have never thought of a monkey. I always think of sages and saints, so this condition is nothing."

But as he was coming down the steps of the temple, wherever he looked he started finding monkeys in the trees, they were hiding in the bushes.

He said, "My God! So many monkeys tonight." They were always there, it was just that he had not renounced them, but today he had renounced them. By the time he reached his house, he could not believe whether it was true or untrue: a crowd of monkeys all around him, making faces. But he said, "First let me take a bath, perhaps that will help."

Nothing was going to help. While he was taking a bath, the monkeys were inside the bathroom. He sat in padmasana, closed his eyes, and just ... the monkey — not one, a whole crowd! He could not even repeat Om mani padme hum, just a small mantra, even once. The monkeys were continuously there. He tried the whole night: again a bath, again the posture, but those monkeys ...

Before the morning he rushed to the temple. The sage was laughing but the man was really angry; he said, "This is no time to laugh. Is it funny?"

The old man said, "I have always told you that I don't know any miracles, secrets, mantras, or anything, but you wouldn't listen to me, hence I had to lie.

The man said, "If you had to lie, you could have at least kept your mouth shut about the monkeys.

The old man said, "But without the monkeys, the mantra is incomplete. Did the monkeys trouble you?"

The man said, "Trouble me! You are an old sage and I have accepted you as my master, otherwise I would have killed you."

Once you renounce something forcibly — and the very word renunciation means that you are forcing yourself against yourself — you are dividing yourself. All renunciation creates a schizophrenic condition in you: one part renouncing, another part becoming more infatuated — you are being split.

All these religions are criminal because they have made the whole of humanity split. You can be one only if you are natural.

And I can understand the difficulty of the questioner. But the difficulty is that he has not understood a very clear-cut distinction. Yes, my sannyasins find that many things, many habits, which they had long tried to drop, have simply disappeared on their own. They have not even made an effort. In fact, if they want to revive those habits, it is impossible to revive them.

But this is not renunciation; this is transformation

As you become more aware, more natural, more silent, more at ease with yourself — not fighting, in a deep let-go — you start seeing habits which are meaningless; and it simply becomes impossible to continue to do them. It is not that you stop doing them, just the opposite: you simply find, one day ... What happened? A certain habit which used to be with you twenty-four hours a day, has not been there for many days, you have not even remembered it.

There was one professor at my colleague in the university, who was a chain-smoker. The doctors were against it, his wife, his children and all his colleagues were against it because he was burning his lungs, destroying his health.

The doctors said, "If it continues, no medicine is going to help. The moment you wake up, the first thing is a cigarette, and the last thing at night is a cigarette, continuously." You would never find him without a cigarette. When one cigarette was finished, another cigarette was lit from the one that he was finishing. He never carried a lighter with him, there was no need; he only carried cigarettes, in all his pockets.

One day I was sitting in the common room. One chair had become, without any effort, my chair. Somehow, it was just accidental that the first day I entered, that chair was empty and I sat on it. Slowly it became known that it was my chair. In the common room there was nobody's personal chair. It was a common room and all the professors could use any chair they wanted, and were using them.

Just that chair was mine, because people were somehow afraid of me, because I was not interested in their gossips, I was not interested in the movies, I was not interested in their politics, not interested in who was going to win the election for dean or who was going to win the election for vice-chancellor, and this and that. And they were completely clear that I thought it was all crap. So not only that chair — two chairs on this side and two chairs on that side — I had five reserved chairs. Only once in a while would somebody come, very afraid, and ask, "Can I sit?" And I would say, "There is no problem."

This man came one day and almost shaking, with his cigarette in his hand, trembling. I can still visualize him; his fingers were burned, his lips were burned. I said, "Yes, you can sit. Can I be of any help? Nobody comes unless he feels I can be of some help."

He said, "Only one thing: I want to drop smoking. My doctors are after me, my family is after me, my friends are after me; everybody is angry. And it is not that I don't want to stop — I have tried in every possible way, but I cannot exist without cigarettes. Even for a few moments I cannot sit without cigarettes. And it is sure that I am going to die from them. Can you help me?"

I said, "Yes, I can help you. The first thing is, tell all your friends, doctors, your wife, your parents, your children, 'I'm going to smoke and you have to stop telling me not to. I have heard enough, and if you don't stop, I will disappear from the house.'"

And, I said, "you can come to my house. That will do, that threat will be enough: 'I will never come back to this house if anyone mentions cigarettes.'" And I told him, "Tell them, 'If it is possible, now I am going to start smoking even in my sleep' — but make it absolutely clear."

"But," he said, "How am I going to stop?"

I said, "You don't have to stop, just do what I say. Stop the very idea of stopping it; this is the first step. The second step is: smoke, but be conscious."

He said, "What do you mean?"

I said, "When you take the packet, take it from your pocket consciously." I told him, "Show me how you do it."

He simply took it out. I said, "That is unconscious. You were not alert that you were doing a certain action. Your hand, the packet, the weight of the packet, the feel of the packet, the texture of the packet — you have to be alert to it. Try it in front of me."

He tried. He said, "It seems to be different."

I said, "That's okay. Now take a cigarette out — not the way you usually do. Be alert. And not the way you go on tapping it on the packet, but consciously. If you usually tap it three times, tap it six times, there is no harm — but be conscious. Put it in your mouth, wait a little, there is no hurry. And start carrying a lighter with you. Wait, be alert, then do the same with the lighter. Light the cigarette, but continue to be alert.

"Start smoking. Take the smoke in, but be alert that the smoke is going in, that the smoke is going out — be alert. This is what Buddha was doing, without a cigarette," I told him. "He was just doing it with pure air. You are a modern man, you are doing it with impure air, that's all, there is no harm, but the consciousness will be the same. Whether you do it with pure morning-fresh air or with dirty cigarette smoke; it doesn't matter.

"And whether you die two years earlier or two years later, what does it matter? What will you do if you live two years longer? You will smoke more — so don't be worried. And these people will torture you more, so forget about it. Smoking has not to be renounced, it has to be watchfully understood what is happening."

He was really a very intelligent man, because within only 24 hours he reported to me, "I am feeling completely different. I can do the same thing just by breathing."

I said, "There is no harm. Try it just by breathing. Don't use cigarettes, but keep the cigarettes with you. Any moment you feel uneasy, bring out the cigarette, but in the new way, the new style."

In just seven days the man was doing Vipassana with his breathing. I asked him, "Did you have to drop the cigarettes?"

He said, "No, they have dropped on their own. And this awareness has not only helped me drop cigarettes, it has helped me in many other ways of which I was not aware."

A meditator will find many habits dropping from him, but he is not dropping them. So I repeat categorically, that in my vision of religiousness there is no place for renunciation. But that does not mean that you will remain the same.

I am giving you a potential methodology of transformation, which will take away all that is meaningless, all that is unnecessary, all that is stupid, all that you are doing just out of habit, all that you are doing because others have said not to do it and just to retaliate, as a reaction, you are doing it.

Yes, out of you will be born a new man who will find it difficult to relate to the old self — naturally, obviously, because the old self was nothing but a bundle of all the old habits which you have forgotten somewhere on the way. Where you have left it, you don't know.

And the new self is sharpened by your awareness, cleaned by your awareness, is continually rejuvenated by your awareness.

Only one thing I want you to learn, and that is awareness. It will take care of all your problems. Without awareness, whatsoever you do you will create more and more problems; they will be farther and farther away from your nature, and it will be very difficult to solve them, because they are phony.

Even if you succeed in solving them you have not solved anything; your perversion will start moving in another direction, it will take another shape. It may not come in from the same door; it will find another door — your house has many doors, of which many are not even known to you.

But with the light, with the flame of awareness inside you, you know your house for the first time, with all its doors and with all its windows. And when the house is lighted, then I don't say, "Do this, do not do that." There is no need; you will do only whatsoever is right.

People ask me continually, "What is right, and what is wrong? My answer is: that which comes out of awareness is right, that which comes out of unawareness is wrong. Actions are not right and wrong. It is the source from where they come which is.

Chapter 7
Nature is all there is

❓ *Why have all the religions used repression as a basic strategy?*

Religion has passed through many phases. The first phase of religion was magical; it has not died yet. The Red Indians in America are still living in the first phase of religion; in South Africa, amongst the aborigines of India, religion is a magic ritual of sacrifice to God. It is a kind of bribery so that he helps you, protects you. So whatsoever you think valuable in food, in clothes, ornaments, whatsoever you think valuable, you go on giving to the god.

Of course there is no God to receive it; the priest receives it — he is the mediator, he profits by it. And the strangest thing is that for at least ten thousand years this magical, ritualistic religion has kept man's mind captured.

There are so many failures; ninety-nine percent are failures. For example, the rains are not coming at the right time. Then the magical religion will have a ritual sacrifice and will believe that God is happy now: the rains will come. Once in a while they do come — but they come also to those people who are not doing the ritual and praising God. They come even to the enemies of the people who have prayed to God. Those rains have nothing to do with their ritual, but it becomes proof that their ritual has succeeded.

Ninety-nine times the ritual fails; it is bound to fail because it has nothing to do with the weather. There is no scientific cause-and-effect relationship between the ritual, your fire ceremony, your mantras, and the clouds and the rain. The priest is certainly more cunning than the people he is exploiting; he knows perfectly well what is really happening.

Priests have never believed in God, remember. They cannot, but they pretend to believe more than anybody else. They have to, that is their profession. The stronger their faith, the more crowds they can attract, so they pretend. But I have never come across any priest who believes that there is a God. How can he believe? He goes on seeing every day that it is only rarely, by a coincidence, that sometimes the ritual succeeds. Ninety-nine times out of a hundred it fails. But he has explanations for the poor people: that your ritual was not done rightly, that while doing it you were not full of pure thoughts. Now, who is full of pure thoughts, and what is a pure thought?

It is very natural.... . For example, in a Jaina ritual people must be fasting. And while they are doing the ritual, they are thinking of food; that is an impure thought. Now, a hungry person thinking of food — I don't see how it is impure. It is exactly the right thought. In fact, he is doing a wrong act at that moment doing the ritual; he should run to a restaurant!

But the priest has a very simple explanation why your ritual failed: "God never fails, he is always ready to protect you. He is the provider, the creator, the maintainer; he will never let you down. But you fail him while saying the prayer or doing the ritual: you are full of impure thoughts." And the people know that the priest is right. They were thinking of food, or a beautiful woman had passed and the idea had arisen that she is beautiful, and the desire to get her... They threw away the thoughts but it was too late; it had already occurred.

So everybody knows that their thoughts are impure. Now, I don't see that there is anything impure. If a beautiful woman passes by a mirror, it will also reflect the beautiful woman. Is the mirror impure? Your mind is a mirror, it simply reflects. And your mind is conscious of everything that is happening around you. It comments, it is continuously making a commentary. If you watch, you will be surprised — you cannot find a better commentator.

The mind says the woman is beautiful, and if you feel a desire for beauty I don't see that there is anything wrong in it. If you feel a desire for ugliness, then something is wrong, then you are sick. Beauty has to be appreciated. When you see a beautiful painting, you would like to possess it. When you see anything beautiful, just by the side of it the idea comes as a shadow: "If this beautiful thing could be mine... " Now, these are all natural thoughts.

But the priest will say, "The rains have not come because of your impure thoughts," and you are absolutely without defenses. You know it; you are ashamed of yourself. God is always right. But when rains came, then too these thoughts were passing through your head; you were exactly the same person. If you were hungry, you were thinking of food; if you were thirsty, you were thinking of water.

These ideas were coming to you when the rains came; but then, nobody bothers about the bad thoughts. The priest starts praising you, your great austerity, your deep prayer: "God has heard you." And your ego feels so satisfied that you don't say, "But what about the impure thoughts?" Who wants to mention impure thoughts when you have succeeded and God has heard? But ninety-nine times nobody hears; the sky remains empty, no answer comes. But magical religion goes on and on.

Magical religion is the most primitive religion, but fragments of it remain in the second phase, there is not a very clear-cut demarcation. The second phase is the pseudo-religion: Hinduism, Christianity, Mohammedanism, Judaism, Jainism, Buddhism, Sikhism — and there are three hundred "isms" in all. These are pseudo-religions. They have come a little further than magical religion.

Magical religion is simply ritualistic. It is an effort to persuade God to help you. The enemy is going to invade the country; the rain is not coming, or too much rain has come and the rivers are flooded, your crops are being destroyed. So whenever you find these difficulties, you ask the help of God. But the magical religion is not a discipline for you. Hence magical religions are not repressive; they are not concerned yet with your transformation, your change.

The pseudo-religions shift the attention from God to you. God remains in the center, but fades far away. For the magical-religious person God is very close by; the person can talk to him, he can persuade him. Pseudo-religions still carry the idea of God, but now God is far away — far, far away. Now the only way to reach him is not through rituals but through a significant change in your lifestyle. They start molding and changing you.

The magical religions leave people as they are, so the people who believe in magical religions are more natural, less phony, but more primitive, more unsophisticated, more uncultured. The people who belong to pseudo-religions are more sophisticated, more cultured, more educated. Religion to them is not just ritual; it is their whole life's philosophy.

Your question comes here, at the second phase of religion. You ask why all the religions have used repression as a basic strategy, for what? The phenomenon of repression is tremendously significant to understand, because all the religions differ in every other way from each other, they are against all other religions in every other aspect.

No two religions agree on anything — except repression. So repression seems to be the greatest tool in their hands. What are they doing with it? Repression is the mechanism of enslaving man, of putting humanity into psychological and spiritual slavery.

Long before Sigmund Freud discovered the phenomenon of repression, religions had already used it for five thousand years — and successfully. The methodology is simple, the methodology is to turn you against yourself — but it does miracles. Once you are turned against yourself, many things are bound to happen.

First, you will be weakened. You will never be the same strong person you were before. Before, you were one; now you are not only two but many. Before, you were a single whole entity, now you are a crowd. Your father's voice is speaking in you from one fragment, your mother's voice is speaking from another fragment; and within you they are still fighting with each other — although they may both no longer be in the world. All your teachers have their compartments in you, and all the priests you came across, all the monks, all the do-gooders, moralists have all made places in you, strongholds of their own.

Whomsoever you have been impressed with has become a fragment in you. Now you are many people — dead, alive, fictitious — from the books that you have read, from the holy books, which are just religious fiction, like science fiction. If you look inside yourself, you will find yourself lost in such a big crowd. You cannot recognize who you are amongst this whole crowd. Which is your original face? They all pretend to be you, they all have faces like you, they speak the language like you, and they are all quarrelsome with each other. You become a battlefield.

The strength of the single individual is lost. Your house is divided against itself, you cannot do anything with wholeness: some parts within you will be against it, some parts will be for it, and some parts will be absolutely indifferent. If you do it, the parts which were against will go on telling you that you have done wrong; they will make you feel guilty. The parts that remain indifferent will pretend to be holy, telling you that you are just third-rate to listen to these people who don't understand.

So whether you do something or you don't do something, in any case you are condemned. You are always in a dilemma. Wherever you move you will be defeated and major portions of your being will always be against you. You will always be doing things with minority support. That certainly means the majority is going to take revenge — and it will take revenge. It will tell you, "If you had not done this you could have done that. If you had not chosen this, you could have chosen that. But you are a fool; you won't listen. Now suffer, now repent." But the problem is you cannot do anything with wholeness, so that there is nobody later on to condemn you, to tell you that you are stupid, unintelligent.

So the first thing: the pseudo-religions have destroyed the integrity, the wholeness, the strength of man. That is very necessary if you want to enslave people — strong people cannot be enslaved. And this is a very subtle slavery, psychological and spiritual. You don't need handcuffs and chains and prison cells, no; the pseudo-religions have created much improved arrangements. And they start working from the moment you are born; they don't miss a single moment.

In Hinduism, the brahmin gets hold of the child the moment it is born, and the first thing he does is make a birth chart; and he will follow the child during the whole of its life. On every important occasion he is there to guide: about marriage he will decide, in death he will decide. After death he will be the first to be the guest of the family — because in Hinduism, after a death, on the third day there is a feast. So all the brahmins and all the relatives and all the friends come to the feast, just to give solace to the soul of the departed. The priest gets your neck in his hands, and he does not let go even when you are dead.

In Hinduism, every year after a death there is a certain festival and ceremony when you pray for the dead: your father, your forefathers, all the people that you represent in some way: the whole long line of generations. In very orthodox Hindu homes you will find a family tree, a map of the generations.

One used to be in my family but I burned it. My father was very angry. I said, "You burn these people completely and nobody is angry, and I have burned just the map. And what is the point of keeping it hanging on the wall?"

"But," he asked, "how were they troubling you?"

I said, "They were troubling me — just to think of all these dead people every day. I have to pass through this room two or three times a day and this whole tree — generations!"

Now there was nothing else he could do so he started to write down again whatsoever he remembered. When he came to Pune to live with me he said, "I don't remember much — you destroyed the whole tree — I just remember my father's father and his father, just four generations back."

I said, "That is enough, even that is not needed. What are we going to do with these people and their names? And if you want I can make the tree and put any names — it will be just as valid."

But he was begging me, "Please don't destroy this paper — at least there are four generations. You are the fifth generation, and then my brothers are there, and their children and their children; my sisters are there and their children." He was making the tree again.

I said, "You are unnecessarily wasting your time because once I get hold of this, I am going to burn it. What is the point of it all?"

But the brahmins use it. If you go to Allahabad or Benares, there are brahmin families, and you can go to the same family that your father had gone to. They have written in their books that your father went there on such and such a date, and he gave so much donation, and he did such and such ritual, and that your father's father went there. They have generations of it, because for generations people have been going there from your family. And now you sign your name and become part of it. They will show you records of thousands of years, because their family has always been doing that work. And you feel really thrilled to know that so many people from your family have gone there — you are not the only one.

The whole stream of your forefathers has been going, and this family of brahmins has been serving them as their priest. And they have written down and exaggerated everything — because that is how they are going to exploit you: your father's father gave a ten-thousand-rupee donation — that donation goes to their family — and his father had given twenty thousand. Now, you don't have any records, you don't have any idea, and you feel very poor if you don't give. At least you should be able to give ten thousand; your father's father gave it, and it looks shameful if you cannot even uphold the name of the family. But whatsoever you give, don't be worried; it will be written in thousands for your children — because they will be going there too.

From these people you can get your whole family tree. It was difficult for my father to get it, because Jainas don't go to brahmins in Allahabad or Benares. For certain rituals, as when your father dies, you have to go just to take his ashes to the Ganges. And you go to the family that has been doing this work for generations, which for thousands of years has taken care of the ashes of everybody who has preceded you. That family will take care of you, will take you in a boat on the Ganges and in the middle of the Ganges they will do the whole ritual; there they will drown the ashes.

But because Jainas don't believe in the Ganges and this type of ritual, my father was at a loss; he could not find a way. Jainas have to make their tree themselves or go to the brahmin, because they have to depend on brahmins for certain things. Although Jainism is a religion in revolt against Hinduism and is basically against Brahminism, finally they had to make the compromise, because there were a thousand and one things they could not figure out without the brahmins.

Now, who is going to make the birth chart? Jainas had no idea of astronomy, astrology, palmistry, so they finally had to negotiate. In marriage, who is going to do the rituals? The brahmin does it. And the mantras have to be recited; the brahmin has to do it. In death, who is going to recite the mantras when the fire is burning the body? The brahmin has to do it.

So finally the whole rebellion disappeared, and Jainism became just a sub-caste, a sub-religion, a branch of Hinduism — but philosophically they are enemies. Deep down, Jainas think that they are higher and they are simply hiring these brahmins for certain works as they hire other servants. Brahmins think that they are higher: "Because without us you cannot even be born, you cannot die."

These pseudo-religions have created a chaos in you — that is very necessary.

I have heard:

One politician, one advocate, and one priest — three old friends — all had passed their seventieth year, but they used to go every morning for a walk and sit on a bench in the park and gossip about things which only they knew: the good old days. And many times arguments and discussions would start. One morning they started discussing whose profession was the first.

The advocate said, "There is no problem about it, my profession was the first profession in the world, because people were fighting and somebody was needed to mediate, to negotiate, to do justice, to be fair to both parties. So of course my profession came first."

The priest said, "But do you know who started the fight? Without the priest, why would they be fighting? It is the priest who gives the basic ideas and creates antagonism in people's minds. And once they get attached, infatuated with an idea, then they are ready to fight; otherwise why should they fight?"

The politician laughed, he said, "You both are right in a way, but you are not aware of the real situation. Why in the first place did people accept your ideas, your philosophies, theologies? — because of us. We created the will-to-power. Of course, the right idea is going to succeed, but we created the whole idea of success, power, of reaching somewhere, of attaining something, being victorious."

Only when there is a will-to-power do you start getting interested in the "right" kind of philosophy, the "right" kind of theology, the "right" kind of religion, so that you can reach the goal. And there are always many others who are saying, "We are right — where are you going?" All the religions are saying, "Except us, everybody is wrong."

The pseudo-religions disturbed man, his inner integrity. They disturbed the society by creating so many fictitious ideologies. You will be surprised if you look into their ideologies and their theologies. You will laugh: "How was it possible that great thinkers were concerned about these things?" In the Middle Ages people like Thomas Aquinas, a great theologian — perhaps the most important theologian among Christian theologians — was much too concerned about the problem of how many angels can stand on the point of a needle. Angels don't have weight and they do not have physical bodies, but still there must be a limit — how many can stand there?

Thomas Aquinas wasted many pages discussing how many angels can manage to stand there — and he was not alone. The whole Middle Ages remained concerned about the question. It was a great religious problem, of great urgency. I don't know what urgency there could have been. Perhaps they were thinking that after they die, they would become angels and they would have to stand on the point of a pin or the point of a needle. What was the trouble? But that is the situation with all the theologies.

Mahavira believed in seven hells and seven heavens. He was old by the time Gautam Buddha started moving around, teaching and impressing people. They had all heard Mahavira, and they would ask Buddha, "Mahavira says so, what do you say?" Somebody asked, "Mahavira says there are seven hells and seven heavens. What do you say?"

Buddha said, "He knows nothing. There are seventy-seven hells and seventy-seven heavens." Now, there is nothing to prove and nothing to disprove it. It is up to you whom you want to believe.

The same question was asked of Ajit Keshkambal, who was even younger than Buddha and was just entering the field of controversy. He said, "These people are perfectly right. Up to the seventh, Mahavira is right; up to the seventy-seventh Buddha is right, but there are really seven hundred and seventy-seven hells and seven hundred and seventy-seven heavens — because I have explored them all. Those poor people — about whatsoever they have explored they are not wrong, but if they insist that this is the end and that they have come to the very end, then they are wrong. If they say, 'This is the point up to where we have reached,' there is no problem."

Now Ajit Keshkambal was really a man with a tremendous sense of humor; he was just joking. But what was Buddha doing? He was very serious; but to me that too seems to be a joke. What was Mahavira doing? He was even more serious, but to be serious about such things... You cannot give any proof, but you can create conflict in people. Now a few became Jainas, a few became Buddhists, and a few followed Ajit Keshkambal, but because he was a man with a great sense of humor, his religion disappeared; people wanted something serious and soon they realized that this man was not serious.

How can you believe a man who is not serious? And in fact my own understanding is that Ajit Keshkambal was more sincere than the other two. He was simply making this theological business a laughing matter. He was saying, "Get rid of all this nonsense! What business is it of yours to be bothered with?"

So the pseudo-religions created chaos in individuals, they created chaos in society, and they exploited both.

If there are Mohammedans, then Hindus remain united, then Christians remain united. It is just like Russia and America — nobody can stop making nuclear weapons, although both go on talking about peace. Nobody wants a Third World War because everybody understands that it is going to finish everybody. It will be an absolutely idiotic war, if it ever happens, because a war only has any meaning if somebody is going to win and somebody is going to be defeated. But in a Third World War nobody is going to be defeated and nobody is going to be the victor — all are going to be killed. There will not be anybody left to declare, to announce, "We are victorious."

But still they both go on, continually pouring all their resources into nuclear weapons because of the fear that the other is doing it, so you have to do it. The other is also just like you, human — you are doing it, so the other has to do it. Now, where is this going to stop?

The same happened with religions. They have all helped each other unknowingly. Hindus became united against Mohammedans, Christians became united against Jews; Jews became united against Christians. And the whole world became a battlefield. Man became a battlefield inside, and the world became a battlefield outside. And the strategy used was repression.

How can repression do all these things and many more? Repression simply means: remember that your nature is your enemy — you have to fight it, you have to kill it, you have to destroy it, you have to go above it; then only are you holy.

Now, this is impossible. Nobody has ever been able to go above nature. Wherever you are, you are within nature. Yes, you can cripple yourself, you can cut your limbs to the size prescribed by your holy scripture, you can suffer, you can torture yourself as much as you want, but you cannot go beyond nature. Nature is all there is — there is no beyond. Beyond is within nature — not outside it.

So those who are fighting with nature never go beyond it. And their continual failure makes them miserable, makes them mentally unbalanced, psychologically insane. And all these things are good for the priest; he exploits you. His whole profession is to help you, but before he can help you, you must be put in a position where you need the help.

In India I came across many psychologists, psychiatrists, who had been trained in the West, and belonged to the Freudian school or the Jungian school or the Adlerian school or Assagioli's school. They had one thing in common: they were all against me. And I told them, "Can you see the point? You are all against each other, but you agree on one point: that you are all against me. Why? — because I can simply destroy your profession." And with the profession destroyed, the Freudian will suffer just as much as the Adlerian, just as much as the Jungian.

I can make man whole again. I can restore him to his integrated, centered, grounded being.

I am not a psychologist; I am not treating any psychological problems because to me those problems are created problems. They create the problem and then they come with the solution. And it is so easy to create the problem. You will be surprised how easy it is ...

One of my professors — I was a student of psychology, and he was a famous psychologist ... One day I just told him, "All the problems that psychologists deal with are created by them."

He said, "You will have to prove it."

I said, "Challenge accepted."

And next day I proved it. I went to his wife, who was very loving towards me — he himself was very loving towards me — and I told her, "You have to do one thing, just for my sake, just once."

She said, "What is it? Just tell me. If I can do it, I will."

I said, "Do one thing: when your husband gets up in the morning, just say to him, 'What happened? Your face looks pale. Couldn't you sleep the whole night? Your eyes look red.' Just put your hand on his head and ask, 'Have you a fever or anything?' And certainly he will say something. Whatsoever he says, write it down on a piece of paper — his words exactly — because I will collect it later on."

She said, "But what is this whole business about?"

I said, "I will tell you by the evening, but right now simply remember it, and do it for me tomorrow morning."

She said, "I will do it. It is done, believe me."

Just on one side lived the postmaster of the university. He was a very old man and a very good man; I went to him and chit-chatted about his garden. He was very interested in flowers but nobody used to come to praise his garden; I was the only person, so he was very happy with me. I said, "Today you have to do something for me."

He said, "What? Anything!"

I said, "When Professor Mehta goes to the university, when he comes out of his house, simply remain by the fence and say, 'What has happened? You look like a ghost! Your legs are trembling.'"

He said, "Has something gone wrong with him?"

I said, "Nothing has gone wrong. But you have to say this and you have to show by your face that actually you mean what you are saying. He will say something; write it down exactly in his words and I will collect it.

Professor Mehta used to come to the department from his house; it was almost a mile, a beautiful road, so he used to walk. On both sides were gardens and professors' houses, the professors' colony. So I made a few people ready, particularly the wives, and a few small children — anybody I thought was reliable. And they were very happy, they said, "We will do it."

And lastly, where Professor Mehta used to enter the department, was the peon who used to sit in front of the office. I said to him, "Dhyananda, I have never asked anything of you ... "

He said, "That's true. Everybody tortures me: 'Dhyananda bring this, Dhyananda bring that.' Professors torture me; students torture me. That's true; you are the only person ... In these two years, you have not even asked for a single glass of water. And I was wondering ... this is rare. So whatever is to be done I will do."

I said, "You have to do this: when Professor Mehta comes here, simply stand up and hold him saying, 'You will fall down. You are trembling. What has happened?'"

He said, "But is it true?"

I said, "No, it is not true, but you have to pretend it is true."

He said, "Okay. You have never asked anything from me — I will do my best."

The next day I collected all the pieces of paper, because I was just following the professor. He was going ahead of me, and I was just following him collecting the papers.

And Dhyananda really did a hatchet job. He really shook him so hard that he fell! I had to support him; we both took him inside. He said, "I am not even able to sit, just put me on the bench." So we put him on the bench. I ran and brought a pillow and a blanket because he was shivering, perspiring.

I asked, "What has happened?"

He said, "It seems I have some strange fever. Last night when I went to bed, everything was okay. But now my headache is such as I have never had and I feel my whole body trembling. Just call the doctor. If it had not been for Dhyananda I would have fallen and broken my leg."

And it was actually because of Dhyananda that he was going to fall. Dhyananda was an uneducated man and he did it for real! I called the doctor, and I explained to him, "You have to be very serious. Nothing is the matter, it is only to do with a challenge that I've accepted; so just be kind to me — be very serious."

He was very serious; he checked this and that, and he said, "Mr. Mehta, you need at least three months' complete rest."

Mr. Mehta said, "Three months complete rest! But what has happened?"

He said, "I cannot tell you. I will talk to your wife."

And Professor Mehta said, "But do one thing please. Take me to my house in your car because I cannot walk back again. One mile... "

He was walking every day, coming and going, because he loved walking; he enjoyed walking, but he said, "Now I cannot walk." To me he said, "Just go to the vice-chancellor and tell him that I am in a terrible mess; the doctor is saying three months ... I don't know what is going to happen, so tell him that if for a few days I don't come, not to mind but replace me with somebody."

I took him in the car with the doctor and we took him inside the house. The wife was just trying to hold herself together, otherwise she might have started giggling and laughing. And really her husband was changed completely. The doctor was holding one hand, I was holding the other hand, and he was not even able to walk. We put him on the bed, and he said to the doctor, "You can tell my wife."

The doctor said, "I will come in my own time. First let me go and prepare some medicines for you. It is urgent." So he left.

Professor Mehta asked me, "Has the doctor said anything to you?"

I said, "First look at these papers."

He said, "What papers? Has he given them to you?"

I said, "No, read them first. This is the statement you gave to your wife: 'I am perfectly okay, what nonsense are you talking?' That was six o'clock this morning. And at seven-thirty you told the postmaster, 'Yes, the night was a little disturbed.' And then to Professor Nand Dulare Vajpeyel you said, 'I had a terrible night.' These are your statements. Nothing has happened to you — you can get up. There is no need to rest for three months, even three minutes are not needed; you are perfectly okay."

"But," he said, "I was perspiring and I was just going to fall."

I said, "There is nothing to it. It was Dhyananda who just jumped on you and made you fall and you thought you were falling. He did it too well; I had not asked him to do that much and I had no idea that he would do it so perfectly. So get up!"

He immediately got up and he said, "Really? That's true. I was perfectly okay last night, and this morning I was perfectly okay. When my wife spoke to me I simply said, 'I am perfectly okay. What has happened to you?' But when everybody started asking, strangely I started feeling that something was wrong. A small boy said, 'Uncle your legs are wobbling,' and I felt that certainly my legs were wobbling, otherwise why was this child ... ?"

I said, "This is the note from the child. These were all my men, women, children, Dhyananda, the doctor. I had to arrange this whole lot because I had accepted your challenge. I created the sickness. I could have managed it for three months, you may have even died."

He said, "I cannot deny it. Seeing what has happened to me, it is possible that if I was in bed for three months and you went on trying your propaganda, you could have killed me."

I said, "This is how your whole religion has been functioning: create problems in people's minds and then where have they to go? They have to go to the priest. Then the priest gives the solution — and gets paid for it. What the psychologists are doing is the same. Out of a hundred cases, ninety cases are created by you people."

I am not saying that the psychologists do it intentionally — nor are the priests doing it intentionally — they are doing it sincerely; they think it is so. They believe in what they are doing, and their belief is infectious, so the other person starts believing it. And then their solutions are there; their prescriptions are there.

If you go to a Freudian, then go to a Jungian, then go to an Adlerian, then go to Assagioli, you will know what I mean. All four will diagnose your disease differently because their scriptures are different. They will all tell you that this is the real problem with you, and no one is going to agree with anybody else. And because the problem is different, naturally the solution is going to be different. The problem has to be different; otherwise what purpose does Jung have in the world? Freud has already done the work.

That was the reason why Jung separated from Freud. He saw the point: that with Freud he would at the most be a great Freudian, but he would never be an individual on his own. And what Freud was doing, he could do. And Jung started doing it, and he was perfectly successful. Adler escaped in the same way. If Freud reduced everything to sex, Adler reduced everything to ego.

Naturally their solutions are different because they have posed the problem differently. And if by chance you succeed, following their solutions, then their therapy has succeeded, not you. But if you fail, you have failed; you were not following the rules properly. And to follow the rules of psychoanalysis or any other school properly is such a long affair.

You may need three years' psychoanalysis, and by the time you finish the psychoanalysis you end up more puzzled, more messed up than you were ever before. Now you need somebody else's help. Now you will need help for your whole life. There are people who have been psychoanalyzed their whole life, going from one psychoanalyst to another psychoanalyst.

The same was true with religions. They created the problem by repression.

In fact psychology has used what the religions, the pseudo-religions, have sown; the psychologists have been reaping the crop. The psychologist is really the modern priest and he is exploiting the same ground, with the same strategy. For thousands of years the priest has prepared the ground, but people were becoming fed up with the priest, so they were very happy that a new science appeared. It is not a science at all, just scientific jargon.

So the people who used to go to the priest, if they are educated, cultured, sophisticated, now go to the psychoanalyst — the same people. If they are not educated then they still go to the priest. The priest is cheaper, and less harmful because he is not so clever with words: conscious, super-conscious, subconscious, unconscious, collective unconscious, cosmic unconscious, cosmic conscious. The poor priest cannot afford that much.

You can be hypnotized by the psychoanalyst and his jargon. He has arguments to support him, and what he is saying is in a way right: you are repressed, but that work was done by religion. Religion condemned sex, condemned your love for food — condemned everything that you can enjoy — condemned music, condemned art, condemned singing, dancing. If you look around the world, and collect together all the condemnations from all the religions, you will see that they have condemned the whole of mankind. They have not left a single inch un-condemned.

Yes, each religion has done its bit — because if you condemn the whole of mankind completely, he may simply freak out. You have to do it proportionately, so that he becomes condemned, feels guilty, wants to be freed from guilt and is ready to take your help. You should not condemn him so much that he simply escapes from you or jumps into the ocean and finishes himself. That will not be good business.

It is just like the slaves in the old days. They were given food, but not enough that they became too strong and revolted, and not too little either so that they died; otherwise you made a loss. You gave them a certain percentage: just hanging in the middle between life and death, and they went on living and working for you. Only that much food was given, not more than that; otherwise there would be energy left after work, and that energy could become revolution. They could start revolting; they could start joining together, they could start seeing what was being done to them.

The same has been done by religions. Every religion has taken a different segment of mankind and condemned it, and through it made him feel guilty. Once guilt is created in you, you are in the clutches of the priest. You cannot escape now because he is the only one who can clean all the shameful parts of you, who can make you capable of standing before God without being ashamed.

He creates the fiction of God. He creates the fiction of guilt. He creates the fiction that one day you will have to stand before God: so be clean and be pure, and be in such a state that you can stand before him without any fear, and without any shame.

The whole thing is fictitious. But this has to be remembered: it is true about the pseudo-religions. And whenever I say all religions, I mean pseudo-religions; the plural is indicative of the pseudo.

When religion becomes scientific, it is not going to be plural; then it will be simply religion, and its function will be just the opposite of the pseudo-religions. Its function will be to make you free from God, to make you free from heaven and hell, to make you free from the concept of original sin, to make you free from the very idea that you and nature are separate; to make you free from any kind of repression.

With all this freedom you will be able to learn the expression of your natural being, whatsoever it is.

There is no need to feel ashamed. The universe wants you to be this way, that's why you are this way. The universe needs you this way; otherwise it would have created somebody else, not you.

So not being yourself is the only irreligious thing according to me. Be yourself with no conditions, no strings attached — just be yourself and you are religious, because you are healthy, you are whole.

You don't need the priest, you don't need the psychoanalyst, you don't need anybody's help, because you are not sick, you are not crippled, paralyzed. All that crippled-ness and paralysis has gone with the finding of freedom.

Religion can be condensed into a single phrase: total freedom to be oneself

Express yourself in as many ways as possible without fear; there is nothing to fear, there is nobody who is going to punish you or reward you. If you express your being in its truest form, in its natural flow, you will be rewarded immediately — not tomorrow but today, herenow.

You are punished only when you go against your nature. But that punishment is of help; it is simply an indication that you have moved away from nature, that you have gone a little astray, off the road. Come back!

Punishment is not revenge. No, punishment is only an effort to wake you up: what are you doing? Something is wrong, something is going against yourself. That's why there is pain, there is anxiety, and there is anguish.

And when you are natural, expressing yourself just like the trees and the birds, who are more fortunate — because no bird has tried to be a priest, and no tree has yet got the idea of being a psychoanalyst. Just like the trees, and the birds, and the clouds, you will feel at home in existence.

And to be at home is all that religion is about.

Chapter 8
God is not a solution but a problem

? *Do you really believe that God does not exist?*

I do not believe that God does not exist, I know for sure he does not exist. And "thank God" that he does not exist — because the existence of God would have created so many problems, difficulties, that life would have been almost impossible.

You may not have looked at it from the angle from which I am going to talk to you — perhaps nobody has ever tried to look at it from this angle. The Christians say that God created the world. In fact, the hypothesis of God is needed for the creation. The world is there; somebody must have created it. Whoever created it, that creator is God. But do you see the implication? If the world was created, then there can be no evolution. Evolution means that creation continues.

Think of the Christian story: God created the world in six days, and then on the seventh day he rested, and since then he has been resting. The whole of creation was completed in six days. Now, where is the possibility for evolution? Creation means: finished! The full stop has arrived. On the sixth day, the full stop; and after that there is no possibility of evolution.

Evolution implies that creation is not complete, hence the possibility of evolving. But God cannot create an incomplete world; that will be going against God's nature. He is perfect, and whatsoever he does is perfect: neither is he evolving, nor is the world evolving; everything is at a standstill, dead. This is the reason why the popes were against Charles Darwin, because that man was bringing in an idea which was going to kill God sooner or later. Those popes were perceptive in a way; they could see the faraway implications of the idea of evolution.

Ordinarily you would not connect creation and evolution. What connection is there between God and Charles Darwin? There is a connection. Charles Darwin is saying that the creation is an ongoing process, that existence is always imperfect, that it is never going to be perfect; only then can it go on evolving, reaching new peaks, new dimensions, opening new doors, new possibilities.

God finished his work in six days and not long ago: four thousand and four years before Jesus Christ was born. It must have been the first of January, a Monday, because we manage to fit God into everything that we have created. He has to follow our calendar. If you ask me, I will say it must have been Monday, the first of April, April Fools' Day, because that day seems to be absolutely suitable for doing such an act of creating a complete ready-made existence.

If evolution becomes impossible, life loses all meaning, life loses all future: then it has only a past. It is not unnatural that religious people are constantly past-oriented; they only have the past. Everything has already been done; there is nothing to be done in the future, the future is empty, blank — and yet you have to live in that future. Everything that had to happen, happened four thousand and four years before Jesus was born. After that there has been no addition, no evolution, no development.

God created the world just as a potter creates a pot, a dead thing out of mud. But remember, the potter can destroy the pot any moment. If you give the power of creation to God, you are simultaneously giving the power of un-creation too. These are the implications that have not been looked into. God can un-create. April Fools' Day comes every year; any year on the first of April he can un-create. At the most it may take six days again.

The very idea that you have been created makes you a thing; it takes away your being. You can be a being only if there is no God. God and you as a being cannot coexist. That's why I say I am sure God does not exist, because I see beings everywhere.

The presence of beings is enough proof that God does not exist, cannot exist. Either you can exist or God can exist; you cannot both exist. The person who starts believing in God, is unknowingly losing his beinghood; he is becoming a thing. So there are Christian things, Hindu things, Mohammedan things, but not beings. They have dropped their being of their own accord; they have given their being to God.

The fiction has become alive, and the alive has become a fiction. I am simply putting things right side up. When I say God does not exist, I have no grudge against God. I don't care a bit about God, whether he exists or not — it is none of my business.

When I say God does not exist, my purpose is to give you your lost beinghood; to show you that you are not a thing created arbitrarily by somebody. Why did he decide, on a certain day, four thousand and four years before Jesus was born, to create the world? What caused the idea of creation? Was there something else that was forcing him to create? Was there some serpent seducing him to create? Why on a certain day, and not before? I want you to see the point. It is arbitrary, whimsical. If the story is true, God is insane. What was he doing for the whole of eternity? The idea of creation came so late to him.

The very idea of creation makes us arbitrary, whimsical, whereas evolution is not arbitrary or whimsical. Evolution is eternal; it has always been going on. There was not a time when existence was not; there will never be a time when existence will not be:

Existence means eternity.

God makes everything silly, small, arbitrary, meaningless, whimsical. Just that old man — and he must have been really old, really, really old — and then this idea of creation came to him, and in six days he completed it. That's why the popes were against Charles Darwin: "You are saying that it is not yet completed, it is evolving. You are against the Bible, the Holy Scriptures. You are against God, against the idea of creation."

Charles Darwin was simply saying, "I am not against any God, I don't know any God." He was a very fearful person, and he was a Christian. He used to pray; in fact he started to pray more after he wrote the theory of evolution. He became very much afraid: who knows, perhaps he was doing something against God. He had believed that God created the world, but the facts of nature were telling a different story: everything is evolving, life is never the same again.

So if anybody believes in God, he cannot believe that you are a being. Only things are created; they have a beginning and an end; beings are eternal.

Because of this fact, two religions in India, Jainism and Buddhism, dropped the idea of God — because to keep that idea simply meant you were dropping the idea of being, which is far more significant. They would have liked to keep both, but it was logically impossible.

Once you accept that you have been created, you accept the other part of it, that the same whimsical man, any day, can un-create you. So what meaning do you have? — just a toy in the hands of some whimsical old man. So whenever he wants, he plays with the toys, and whenever he wants, he destroys them? It was really a great, courageous step on the part of Mahavira and Buddha to choose being and drop the idea of God — and that too, twenty-five centuries ago. They could simply see that you cannot manage both; they are against each other. But they were not aware of evolution; that was a later development. Now we know that creation goes against the idea of evolution too.

Creation and evolution are absolutely against each other. Creation means completion; evolution means constant growth. Growth is possible only if things are imperfect and remain imperfect. Howsoever they grow there is always a possibility of growing more.

There are a few other things which have to be considered. If you are created, you can't have freedom. Have you seen any machinery having freedom, any thing having freedom? Anything that is created is in the hands of the creator, just like a puppet. He has the strings in his hands; he pulls one string ... You must have seen a puppet show. The strings are pulled, the man is behind the screen; you don't see him, you simply see the puppets, and they dance and they fight, but that is all false — the puppeteer is the reality.

These puppets cannot have freedom to fight, to love, to get married — all these things happen in a puppet show — to dance or not to dance; or when they don't want to dance, to say, "No, I am not going to dance." The puppet cannot say no. And all the religions have been teaching you not to say no: don't say no to God, to his messiah, to his holy book — never, never think in terms of saying no.

Why? If you cannot say no, what is the meaning of your yes? It is a corollary. Yes has meaning only when you are capable of saying no. If you have to say yes, and there is no other alternative except yes ...

I have heard that when Ford first started manufacturing cars, he himself used to go to the showroom and take an interest in the customers, talk to the customers. He would say to them, "You can choose any color provided it is black" — because at that time there were only black cars. But he used to say, "You can choose any color provided it is black."

You are free, provided your answer is yes. What kind of freedom is this? Puppets cannot have freedom. And if God has simply made you, you are a puppet. It is better to revolt against God and be a being than to submit and be a part of a puppet show, because the moment you accept yourself as a puppet, you have committed suicide.

You see puppets the whole world over, with different colors, different names, different rituals. Hindus say that without God's will, even a leaf in the tree cannot move — so what about you? Everything happens according to God. In fact, he has determined everything the moment he created; it is predestined. Now, it is so strange that intelligent people also go on believing in such garbage.

Just see the garbage: on the one hand God has created you; on the other hand, when you do something wrong you will be punished. If God has created you, and he has determined your nature and you cannot go against it, you don't have any freedom. With God there is no possibility to have freedom; then how can you commit a crime, how can you be a sinner and how can you be a saint?

Everything is determined by him, he is responsible; you are not. But people go on believing in both things together: God creating the world, God creating man, woman, everything, and then throwing all responsibility on you. If there is something wrong with you, God is responsible and should be punished. If you are a murderer, then God created a murderer; then he should be responsible for Adolf Hitlers and Joseph Stalins and Mao Zedongs. He created these people.

But no, the religious mind loses intelligence, becomes rusted, forgets completely that these are incompatible things; God and freedom are incompatible. If you are free, then there is no God.

I remind you again of Friedrich Nietzsche's statement. This man was certainly crazy, but sometimes the so-called sane people are so dumb and so dull, so idiotic, that crazy people come up with great insights — and Nietzsche had that genius. Once in a while he came up with such a great insight that you cannot believe why people had not seen it before; and Nietzsche lived just a hundred years ago.

He said, "God is dead, therefore, I declare, man from now onwards is free." This whole sentence brings freedom and God together for the first time in the whole history of mankind. It was waiting for this crazy man, Friedrich Nietzsche, to put these together: that God is dead, therefore you are free; otherwise, you are not free.

You may not have thought about it. How can you be free with a creator who is continuously watching you, who is continuously maintaining you and directing you? In the first place he has put everything into you as a fixed program. And you will follow that program; you cannot do otherwise. What you feed into the computer, the computer can only answer with that. If you start asking things which you have not fed into the computer before, the computer cannot answer them. The computer is a mechanism: first you have to feed it all the information, then whenever you need, you can ask the computer and the information will be available.

You are a computer if there is a creator! He has put certain information into you, he has programmed you, and you are doing things accordingly. If you are a saint, you are not to take the credit for it; it was the program. If you are a sinner you need not feel condemned and bad; it was the program.

In India, the life of Rama has been played every year for ten thousand years. Almost all over the country, even in the smallest village there is a drama company. Once a year the drama company starts preparing one month ahead, and big cities who can afford it can ask professional companies. There are professional companies, particularly in Ayodhya, which was the capital of Rama, and in other religious places. So, big cities that can afford to, ask the professional companies. Small villages, towns which cannot afford to, make their own company.

It happened in one of the villages: the drama begins with Sita's marriage. In those days particularly, princes used to have a certain ceremony called *swayamvar*. All the eligible young men — of course young princes, because nobody else would be allowed in the palace — from all over the country would gather together, and the girl, the princess, would take a garland in her hand and move about. It was for her to choose anybody she wanted. Or, if she was worried that on what criterion ... It was a difficult job: a hundred princes were there, and they were all beautiful and from royal families, and young and strong. It was not easy to choose just like that, and it was not something that tomorrow you could reject.

In India it is not only a life-long affair, it is going to be for many lives. It is really a great burden on the mind of the girl: how to choose? So she can take the help of God in a certain way. Some device can be managed: that whosoever solves this puzzle will be the person she will choose. Now she is leaving it to God — it is easier, in wiser hands.

In Sita's *swayamvar*, the device was a bow of the Lord Shiva, which was given to Sita's father because he was a devotee of Shiva. The bow was so heavy — of course, it was a god's bow — that even to take it up needed a superman. An ordinary man would not be able even to move it; and to use it — that was something almost impossible.

There was a fish, an artificial fish placed on the ceiling, and on the ground there was a small pond, which reflected the fish. You had to look in the pond at the reflection, and with Shiva's bow and arrow you had to shoot the fish above — a great warrior was needed. First, the problem was how to lift up the bow. Even if you managed to lift it, then the problem was how to use it; it was not an ordinary bow. And then the puzzle was that you had to look at the reflection in the water and shoot the fish, which, like the reflection, was moving; it was on a wheel.

The whole country was agog. All the great warriors and kings, they all gathered there. Ravana was one of the greatest warriors of those days. He was the king of Sri Lanka and there was every chance that he would win the contest because he was also a devotee of Shiva, perhaps a greater devotee than Sita's father. His devotion to Shiva was such, so the story says, that when Shiva was not listening to him, Ravana said, "If you don't listen to me, then I will cut off my head and put it at your feet. What more sacrifice do you want?" And he did cut off his own head and put it at Shiva's feet. Of course more sacrifice is impossible.

This is a strange story — how can you cut off your own head, and then put it at Shiva's feet? How will you manage to find where Shiva's feet are? Your head is cut off; your eyes have gone. But that's the story — he managed.

Shiva was very happy with him and said, "Because you have done something which nobody has ever done, I will give you something which has never been given to anybody: you will have ten heads. Because you have sacrificed one, I will give you ten heads. And any enemy cutting off one of your heads will not be able to kill you — immediately another head will grow. The ten heads will remain ten."

This man with his ten heads was coming to the *swayamvar*. There was every fear that ... And he must have been the ugliest man; even one head is enough, but ten heads! Everybody was afraid that he was coming and there was every chance that he would take up this bow; there seemed to be nothing to prevent him. Rama was also participating as a prince of Ayodhya. He was a young man, very young, and it was not known that he was a great warrior or anything. There was no possibility for him to win the contest.

So the sages who wanted Rama to win the contest and get married to Sita arranged a conspiracy so that when Ravana went to pick up the bow, a man came running and told him, "Your capital" — which was made all of gold — "is on fire and you are immediately needed. Without you everything will be gone." So poor Ravana had to leave the bow and rushed to Sri Lanka. Meanwhile Rama won the contest, and was married.

This is the story — the beginning. In this particular village the actors were all programmed and being prompted from the back. But when the man came saying, "Sri Lanka is on fire," the man who was playing the role of Ravana said, "Let it be! I am going to marry Sita. Enough is enough; this time I am not going to go anywhere."

The prompter was trying hard: "This is not what we have told you."

The actor said, "Stop all this prompting — I know what I am doing." In fact he was in love with the girl who was playing the role of Sita, and the girl's father was not willing for them to marry. This was the only chance to declare before the whole town... And before anybody else could do anything, Sita garlanded him.

Now, the whole town was in a shock. The story was finished before it had even started, because this was the beginning only, just the introduction; the real things were just about to happen. The actors were in such a hurry; they even forgot to pull the curtains. The whole mass was shouting and screaming and clapping, and saying, "We have seen many things but nothing like this. This is just the best drama that we have seen!"

In a drama you may go against the program, because it is acting, it is not your being; your being is still free. You may be acting the part of Ravana or Rama, but those are parts, roles; your being is still free. You can decide for or against. But if your being is created then there is no possibility of your going anywhere other than where the program says, doing anything other than what's in the program.

If there is a God who has created the world, then nobody is responsible except him. And to whom can he be responsible? There is nobody above him. You are not responsible because he has created you. He is not responsible because there is nobody else to whom he can be responsible. God means the world loses all responsibility, and responsibility is the very center of your life.

Then you can play the role, but you are not there, only promptings; whether given from the outside, from behind the curtain, or whether given from the inside through the hormones, through biology, physiology, psychology doesn't matter. You are only a collection of promptings, and you are just following them. It takes all dignity from man totally. It reduces you to a puppet.

To accept God is not to be religious, because without responsibility how can you be religious? Without freedom how can you be religious? Without an independent being of your own, how can you be religious? God is the greatest anti-religious idea.

If you look into it from every aspect, then those who believe in God are not religious, cannot be religious. So when I say there is no God, I am trying to save religiousness.

There is no danger from the Devil; the real danger comes from God. The Devil is only his shadow. If God disappears the shadow will disappear automatically. The real problem is God.

And you can see what I am saying if you look at history. Every step in evolution has been stopped by the churches out of fear that it proves creation is incomplete. Man has reached the moon, but in India I have come across Hindu shankaracharyas, Jaina acharyas — they are equivalent to the pope — who don't believe it, because their scriptures say that the moon is a goddess. The sun is a god; the moon is not a planet. You will be surprised to know that one Jaina monk has accumulated millions of rupees in donations because he is creating a lab to prove that man has not reached the moon, but has landed on some other planet!

Now, these idiots — and people believe in them because the scriptures are in their favor — collect all the quotations from all the scriptures spoken by people who are omniscient, omnipotent, omnipresent: avatars, tirthankaras, God's special messengers. And if they say this, then what can poor scientists do?

They are deceiving you, cheating you and cheating themselves. A fact that nobody can deny, a fact that all the scientists of the whole world, including India, have accepted, is not acceptable to the religious mind because it will destroy their faith in the scriptures. They are more worried about their faith than about reality.

When I say God is the greatest enemy of religiousness, it is going to shock the so-called religious people, because they think praying to God, worshipping God, surrendering to God is what religion is. They have never thought about responsibility, freedom, growth, consciousness, being; they have never bothered — and yet these are the real religious questions.

Your prayers are silly. You are simply praising God in the same way you have been praising kings and queens; in the same tone, in the same words. You are praising God and thinking that just as your queens and kings become influenced by your prayer and you can persuade them to do favors for you, so will you be able to persuade God.

The Bible's statement that God created man in his own image is absolutely wrong. Just the contrary is true: man created God in his own image, God is man's creation. Hence the Hindu God is different, the Mohammedan God is different, the Jewish God is different, because different people were trying to figure out how God looks, what language he speaks. Now, Jews cannot believe that he speaks any other language than Hebrew, and Hindus cannot believe it: "God speaking Hebrew! Have you gone mad? Do you think God is a Jew? He speaks pure Sanskrit."

I have heard that after the Second World War, a German general and a British general — just resting, taking a sunbath on the beach — started talking. The German general said, "I am simply puzzled by one thing: that we were praying to the Christian God, and you were praying to the same Christian God, but we are defeated and you have won. Is it not partial?"

The English general laughed and said, "It is not partial. Just tell me one thing: in what language were you praying — in German? That's where the fault was. God understands only English, no other language, and we were praying in English. There is no mystery in it, it is simple."

Man, imposing himself by this creation of God in man's own image, is not aware of what he is losing. He is losing all that is valuable, everything that is beautiful, everything that can become a blessing to him.

The religious person starts focusing himself upon a fiction and forgets his own reality, forgets himself and thinks of somebody there above, in the sky. That person above in the sky is non-existential, but you can focus on any non-existential thing. And you can forget yourself in that focusing.

And that is where real religion happens: within you.

Hence prayer has nothing to do with real religion. In my vision of religiousness there is no place for prayer. No true religion can have anything like prayer, which is absolutely bogus.

What are you doing in prayer? You are creating first an image of your own imagination, surrendering to your own imagination; then talking to that image. You are just performing an insane act. In all the churches, in all the synagogues, in all the temples and in all the mosques of the world, these people are doing something insane — but the whole earth is full of these insane people.

Because they have been doing this for centuries, and you have accepted them as religious, it shocks you when I say that they are not religious. They are not even normal — to be religious is far away. They are below normal. They are doing something so stupid that if they go on doing it, whatsoever little intelligence is left in them, by and by, will go down the drain. Perhaps it has already gone.

To me, real religion is a tremendous phenomenon. It is not fictitious. It is entering into the very heart of reality. It is knowing existence from its very center. But you will have to drop your fictions. Those fictions will never allow you to enter into yourself, because those fictions are projected outwards, and you get completely identified with them.

You know, you watch a movie or a television show and you know perfectly well that many times tears have come to your eyes, although you know that it is only a television screen and there is nobody there. But you forget completely that you are only a watcher. You become identified with someone, so much so, that if the other person is in great suffering, tears come to your eyes.

In Kolkatta there was a very famous scholar of Indian literature, theology, history, and all that you can conceive. He was a rare mind, Ishwar Chandra Vidyasagar. Vidyasagar means ocean of wisdom. That title was given to him by the All-India Conference of Hindu Scholars. It has not been given to anybody else, neither before nor since. He was really an ocean of what they call wisdom. I will not call it wisdom.

I will show you how wise he was: because he was so famous a scholar and carried all kinds of DLitts. from different sources, one Sanskrit university, instead of a DLitt., gave him the title Vidya Varidhi; that too means ocean of wisdom. Another gave him the title Vidya Vachaspati, master of wisdom, and the Hindu University of Benares gave him the title Mahamahopadhyaya: the greatest teacher of all.

He had all these degrees, and he was respected all over the country and particularly in Bengal; there was nobody who even came close to him. He was invited to a drama, to inaugurate it, and it was arranged by such great people that he could not refuse. Even the viceroy of India was going to be present there, because Kolkatta in those days was the capital of India. So he went to inaugurate it.

He inaugurated it and was sitting by the side of the viceroy, just in the front row. In the drama there is a very corrupted, cunning character, a villain who is continually after a very innocent woman. The story becomes so intense that at one point he finds the woman alone, far away from the village. She had come to the river to collect water. There is nobody around, the village is miles away, and he gets hold of her...

There was pin-drop silence because there was going to be a rape; that's what the man intends to do. And suddenly — the audience could not believe it — Ishwar Vidyasagar jumped onto the stage and started beating the man with one of his shoes!

For a moment nobody could think what to do or what not to do about Vidyasagar. But that actor took the shoe in his hand and he said to Vidyasagar, "This I will not return; it is the greatest prize in my life. I have been playing this role my whole life, but if a man like Ishwar Chandra Vidyasagar gets so involved and identified that he forgets himself, and forgets that it is only a drama, and I am not going to rape the woman... In the first place she is not a woman — you know it, and everybody else knows it. That chap is a young man from your own town."

Ishwar Chandra felt very ashamed, and said, "I am sorry that I disturbed the whole drama. But it is true; I forgot completely that it is a drama. I forgot completely who I am. I forgot completely that the woman is not a woman and that you are simply playing a role; you are not going to rape her. Before thousands of people and the viceroy of India, you are not going to rape her. I just forgot."

But you are also forgetting when you become emotionally involved in a film or a novel. And this is what your so-called religious people have been doing. They have become involved with imaginary gods and goddesses of all kinds and types you can imagine. And they have completely forgotten themselves. They are worshipping something which is not there, but they have been worshipping so intently that they can create the hallucination of it.

It is possible for a Christian to see Jesus with open eyes; it is possible for a Hindu to see Krishna with open eyes. But the greatest difficulty would be for Jesus to appear to a Hindu. For a Hindu, Jesus never appears — never, even by mistake — and Krishna never appears to a Christian. Once in a while it wouldn't do much harm, but they never commit that mistake. The Christian will not allow the mistake to be committed; his hallucination is of Jesus, he cannot hallucinate about Krishna. Only what you are projecting appears on the screen.

If you are projecting a film, only that appears on the screen; if you project another film then another film appears on the screen. It is not possible for you to project one film, and another film starts appearing on the screen — that is not possible. That's why it is not possible for Krishna to appear to a Christian, or a Mohammedan or a Jew. It is not possible for Jesus to appear to anybody else except Christians.

Still we go on and on strengthening, enforcing our imagination and hallucinations. And what have you got out of it? From thousands of years of hallucinations, what have you got, this humanity that you see around the world, this mess? This is the result of thousands of years of religious practices, discipline, ritual, prayer. Millions of churches, synagogues, temples, all around the earth, and this is the result: the man you see, the actual man, has come out of this whole effort.

It was bound to be so, because we have wasted all these years in sheer stupidity, calling it religion. We have wasted much time in which man could have grown to heights unknown, to depths unfathomable, to the freedom of the spirit, the compassion of the soul, integrity, individuality. If all these thousands of years had not been wasted with a bogus God, just hocus-pocus, of no worth, not a single penny ...

And you ask me, "Do you really not believe?"

It is not a question of believing or not believing — there is no one to believe in or not to believe in. There is no God!

So please remember: don't start saying that I am an unbeliever. I am neither a believer nor an unbeliever. I am simply saying that the whole thing is a mere projection of the human mind and it is time that we stopped this game against ourselves.

It is time that we said good-bye to God forever.

Chapter 9
I teach a religionless religion

> *I was shocked to hear you say that God does not exist. Then the question arose in me: how can there be any religion without God? Isn't God the center and religion the circumference?*

t is fortunate that you were shocked. It needs intelligence to be shocked. Millions of people on the earth have lost the quality of being shocked. They have been hypnotized for centuries, conditioned in such a way that no shock ever reaches them. All the religions, the so-called religions, pseudo-religions, have been doing only one work: creating shock absorbers in you.

My function is to destroy all your shock absorbers and make you vulnerable so that you doubt, you question, and inquire.

One who doubts to the very end finds the answer. One who inquires to the very end comes to know.

Those who go on believing without doubting, without questioning, without inquiring remain dull, dead, idiotic. So I congratulate you that you are shocked; it is a good beginning. The stupid person will be angry, not shocked. He will immediately become an enemy; he will not be shocked. To be shocked means that something in you is still alive, that the priests, the politicians, the pedagogues have not been completely successful with you. Perhaps a window has remained open; that's why you are shocked. And do you see the miracle of that shock?

Immediately a question of tremendous importance arises in you. Your question is not out of anger; it is not out of irritation. It is a valid, intelligent, tremendously significant question: how can there be religion without God? That's what you have been told for centuries, that God is the center and religion is its circumference. This is an absolute lie. Religion has nothing to do with God at all.

Yes, it has much to do with you, your consciousness, your being.

You ask: how can there be a religion without God? One day, if you go on inquiring, you will ask me how can there be a religion with God? And I would like you to contemplate how there can be a religion with God.

God is nothing but our idea of the ultimate dictator, the ultimate Adolf Hitler.

He created the world, just whimsically; there was no reason to create it. No religion has been able to answer why he created the world in the first place. And this world: ugly, nauseous, disgusting, this humanity which religions go on proclaiming to be the highest peak of God's creation, that God created man in his own image. What can be higher than that? And what has man been doing? In three thousand years, five thousand wars! The whole of history is a history of murder, rape, crime — and murder, rape and crime in the name of God. Millions of people have been killed, burned alive in the name of God.

And God created man in his own image. So you can think something about God too, just a little inference that if this is the image, then what will be the real thing? If Adolf Hitler and Joseph Stalin and Benito Mussolini and Mao Zedong are only carbon copies, then what will be the original? It is going to be terrible!

If God created this world, man and everything, it should show signs of divinity, signatures of God, but they are completely missing. If he cannot read and write, he can at least make a thumbprint. There seems to be no signature anywhere. It seems more probable that it was created by the Devil rather than by God, because ninety-nine percent of proof is for the Devil, not for God.

With God you cannot create religion, for the simple reason that God has already created the Bible for the Christians, the Torah for the Jews, the Vedas for the Hindus ... He has created them already; he has given you ready-made religions. He has not allowed you to seek and search and find.

And there is something of immense importance about truth: unless you find it, it never becomes truth to you. If it is somebody else's truth and you borrow it, in that very borrowing it is no longer true; it has become a lie. This is one of the reasons why the great mystics of the world have been saying again and again that truth is inexpressible, because the moment you express it, in the very process of expression it becomes a lie. All your holy scriptures are full of lies.

God has not given you the chance to discover religion, he has given you ready-made religion; and he does not allow you even to question, to doubt — that is a great sin. There are all kinds of stupidities in your religious scriptures, but you have to believe in them totally.

A man like Bertrand Russell became very puzzled, for the simple reason that there are things which anybody who has a little intelligence cannot trust — but to doubt makes you a sinner; you start feeling guilty. Finally he wrote a book: Why I am not a Christian, and collected all the points that hindered him from becoming a Christian. For example: the virgin birth of Jesus Christ. It is so unscientific that to believe it is to destroy all your intelligence. To have faith in such an idea is suicidal; you are destroying yourself, and what are you gaining? A stupid idea — virgin birth!

If Bertrand Russell could not believe in it, we cannot blame him. It was the Bible that prevented a man who could have been religious ... Russell asked, "Why in the trinity is there not a woman included? God the father, God the son, and the Holy Ghost — what kind of family is this? This holy family seems to be very idiotic. Why could they not put a woman in it? — because all the religions have been against women. To put a woman into the trinity, in the highest position of power, was impossible for them; hence they had to put the Holy Ghost.

Now, nobody knows about the Holy Ghost, whether he is man or woman or neutral. And this Holy Ghost is the person responsible for making Mary pregnant — and still he is holy! He is a rapist, because Mary was not aware of it; she was not a willing partner in it, and she was already married. But the Holy Ghost did this, perhaps he is still around in the world — and he is one third of God!

A man like Bertrand Russell was prevented from being a religious person because of the idea of God. And any idea of God will create problems. The Hindu God ... Instead of the trinity the Hindus have a parallel — Trimurti: one god with three faces, three persons joined together in one person. But all three are constantly fighting each other — so childish is their behavior. It is good that Sigmund Freud was only aware of Christian and Judaic traditions. If he had been aware of Hindu tradition he would have found immense support for his hypothesis.

In Hinduism God created the world. The first being he created was a woman, naturally, because without a woman nothing else can grow — the woman has to come first. But in creating a beautiful woman, he himself became infatuated. Now, the father becoming infatuated with his own daughter ... That's what Freud was looking for but nobody informed him that it was available. For his whole life, Freud was trying to prove that each father is infatuated with the daughter and each mother is infatuated with the son. And there is some truth in it — but God getting infatuated with his own daughter ...

Then the woman becomes afraid and she tries to escape, and the only way to escape is to change shapes, forms, disguises. She becomes a cow, but how can you deceive God? He becomes a bull. She becomes other kinds of animals, and God follows. That's how the whole creation comes into being — the woman running and the father following her and trying to rape her. He is still doing the same thing.

With such a God, what kind of religion do you think is possible? This God is a sexual maniac; he needs psychotherapy. He cannot be the center of religion; he cannot even be on the circumference of religion. He should be inside a mental asylum. But if you read Hindu scriptures you will be very disturbed by the kind of things that millions of people belonging to the oldest religion in the world are carrying.

These are the three phases of the Hindu God: Brahma is the creative phase, he creates the world; Vishnu, the second phase, maintains the world; and Shiva destroys the world when the time comes to destroy it. In a way it is perfectly balanced: all the three functions that existence needs — creation, maintenance, and one day, de-creation. But if you look into the inner life of these three persons, you cannot believe it.

One day, Vishnu and Brahma are quarreling about something. In the first place, the idea of a quarrel between two parts of God makes him schizophrenic. If your hands start fighting each other... And that's what you are doing in your mind: one part fighting against the other part. Sometimes you become so split that you are already two persons, and sometimes you are many persons. God is already three persons — he is not one whole, one piece — and all the three are constantly quarreling.

These two were quarreling and they could not find a way to settle the argument, so they both thought it would be better to look for Shiva; perhaps he might be helpful. So they went to look for Shiva. Shiva must have been American — it was morning and he was making love to his wife, Parvati. Indians don't do that; that is absolutely unheard of. I think Shiva is the first American — making love to his wife in the morning, with the doors open. Perhaps it would be better to call him Californian — doors open! Just American will not do.

Brahma and Vishnu both entered, not knowing what was happening inside, and Shiva was so much into his act of making love that he didn't bother about them. Both were very angry. In the first place, making love in the morning does not suit a god; secondly, with the doors open, anybody could come in. And thirdly, he does not even tell them to sit down; he has not even looked at them. Both the gods were very angry, so angry that they cursed Shiva, saying, "You will be known in the world by the phallic symbol." That's why in India you find no statue of Shiva, only the phallic symbol. This is the curse of those two gods: "You will be known and recognized as a phallic symbol."

You may not be aware that shivalinga, the phallic symbol for Shiva, is not alone; it is placed in a vagina. Both are in marble, and for thousands of years Hindus have been worshipping it. And still Shiva is one third of God!

You can take any other conception of God and you will find it impossible to make a religion around it. But up to now this has been the case. The fiction of God is there in the center, and around the fiction all other fictions have been created: of heaven and hell, sin and punishment, repentance and forgiveness. And this whole circus is nothing but exploitation by the cunning priests of all the religions.

Yes, without God there can be no priest. Without God there can be no concept of sin. Without God there can be no heaven and hell. Without God there can be no temple, no synagogue, no church.

If you think these are the things which make a religion, then of course you will find it difficult: how can there be a religion without God? But these things have nothing to do with religion. In fact, to me these are hindrances to finding religiousness.

And let this be another shock to you: the authentic religion is going to be Godless — and also religionless. I am teaching you a religionless religion.

You will have to go a little deep into this because the words seem to be contradictory: religionless religion. When I say religionless religion I mean that the priest, the synagogue, the rabbi, the pundit, the pope, the church, the prayer, the holy scriptures, the holy and unholy ghost — all these have to be dropped because this is what you have known as religion.

The holy scriptures are nothing but religious fiction, just as there is science fiction. And it is beautiful to write science fiction; it is art. Those religious fictions are not even artistic; they are ninety percent rubbish, crap. Nobody reads them except a few people who have some vested interest in reading them.

I have heard:

A man who was selling dictionaries house to house, rang the bell of a house. The housewife came out and asked, "What do you want?"

He said, "I have beautiful dictionaries. You must have children; they may need dictionaries, and I have all kinds for all ages."

The woman wanted to get rid of him, so she said, "But we have got a dictionary." And
far away in the corner, on a table, there was a thick book looking like a dictionary.

The salesman laughed, he said, "That's a bible."

The woman could not believe it because from that distance it was impossible to figure
out that it was a bible. She said, "You surprise me. Yes, it is a bible. I was just trying to get
rid of you, saying that we have got a dictionary. But how did you manage it? Tell me and I
will purchase a dictionary from you, but tell me the trick."

He said, "There is no trick. I just saw how much dust had gathered on it."

Only bibles, holy books, gather dust. A Playboy magazine does not gather dust. Who
wants to open the book? It has not been opened perhaps for years; perhaps it has never
been opened.

Religious fiction has to be dropped because it is hindering your way, preventing you
from reaching reality. You have to get rid of all nonsense that has been told to you by your
parents, by your society, by your teachers, by your religious elders.

Unless you clean yourself completely you cannot take the first step towards being
religious. Religiousness is a quality of your being; it has nothing to do with any ritual
outside you, it is a quality of your being.

There are a few things which are qualities of your being and are in a dormant state
because you have never thought that they are to be developed. Have you tried to develop
your consciousness? Have you tried to develop your compassion? Have you tried to
develop your intelligence?

The scientists say that even the people who are geniuses use only fifteen percent
of their intelligence; eighty-five percent remains unused. And this is about a man like
Albert Einstein or Karl Marx or Rutherford, the Nobel Prize-winners, What about the
common man, how much does he use? — not more than five percent. And that five
percent he uses because it is needed for day-to-day work: his business, his family, his
so-called religion, his political party and his club. Five percent is enough. You don't have
to be a genius to become a Rotarian. I don't think a genius would like to become a
member of the Lions Club. A man trying to become a lion seems to be falling down
rather than rising up.

If the genius himself uses only fifteen percent, then that means nobody is trying to
sharpen their intelligence. You only go on using whatsoever life, its situations and circum-
stances, forces you to use. If there is nobody, no situation forcing you to use it, you will
not use even five percent. That's why you will not find rich people's sons and daughters
getting gold medals in the universities and topping the universities. No, they don't need
to use their intelligence; their servants can do that. And now computers are available.
Soon you will not be using even five percent; people will be carrying a small computer.
They are already carrying them. Have you not seen it?

In my childhood, in my family, my father was very particular about handwriting. He would not allow a fountain pen in the house, because you cannot have the quality of an ordinary old pen with a fountain pen; the fountain pen is going to destroy your handwriting.

And you can see it. Just look back: before the press was invented, all the books were written by hand — such beautiful, artistic handwriting. What the book contains is another thing; just the handwriting itself is a work of art. But that art disappeared with the fountain pen. And when the typewriter became available to people, even the little bit that was possible with the fountain pen disappeared — people are typing. Now tell them to write and their writing looks as if they are uneducated. People are now carrying small computers to calculate: calculators — they will forget the small calculations that you can do.

There is a woman alive in India, Shakuntala, who has toured all around the world and has been exposed to the greatest mathematicians. She is only a matriculate and knows nothing of higher mathematics, but even Albert Einstein was puzzled by her. Just write any figure, howsoever big it is doesn't matter; tell her to multiply it by as big a figure as you want — and before you have finished writing the second figure down, the answer is there. Einstein said, "If I had done it, it would have taken at least three hours."

But what is happening to this woman? She knows nothing about it. She says, "Just simply looking at the figures that have to be multiplied ... " All that happens to her is a kind of silence; in that silence, figures start coming up, and she starts speaking, "Write down this figure — I don't know how it comes." It seems from birth she has had a very sharp intelligence, so that within the flicker of an eye something happens in her mind. And this is not the only case; there have been others.

A young boy, Shankaran, was so poor that he used to pull a rickshaw. Now, it is an ugly thing; it should not exist anywhere: that a man is pulling a vehicle with you sitting in it. And he was just a boy — but his father was old — and in Chennai he was just pulling the rickshaw. The mathematics department of the university became interested in him by accident. One day the professor, the head of the department, went in his rickshaw and just started talking to him. He said, "You are so young: you should be reading and studying."

The boy told him about his family. "But," the boy said, "even without reading and studying — I know that you teach mathematics — I can do mathematics. That, somehow I know." The professor tried him out, and he was amazed: the boy was a miracle. He sent the boy to Oxford at his own expense, to display his ability, and wherever he went he simply amazed great mathematicians. Rutherford said that a certain question that had been bothering him for years, the boy solved within seconds. And once he solved it, Rutherford saw that it was so simple — how had he missed it? Somehow he had gone round and round, just missing the point, and this boy simply jumped to that point. But he was not educated.

Intellect can be sharpened; there are ways to sharpen it. Modern psychology is trying to measure it. I say don't be foolish, don't waste time in measuring it — what is there to measure? The average person remains at the mental age of thirteen; he may be seventy but his mental age remains thirteen, and he uses five to seven percent of his intelligence. Now why waste time in finding more accurate methods to measure it? Why not use methods which can sharpen the intellect? That's what I have been teaching you.

If you doubt, your intellect will be sharpened.

If you believe, your intellect will go rusty; it will start gathering dust, because you are not using it. Doubt is bound to sharpen it, for a fundamental reason: you cannot remain at ease with doubt. You have to do something about it; you have to find the answer. Till you find the answer the doubt is going to harass you, nag you — and that's the way doubt sharpens your intellect.

But all the religions teach that to doubt is sin, to believe is to be religious. I say to you: to doubt is to be religious, and to believe is to be irreligious.

But those pseudo-religions were really cunning and clever. What psychologists have not found even now, they found five thousand years ago: that doubt is dangerous; it sharpens the intellect. Belief is comfortable, convenient; it dulls. It is a kind of drug; it makes you a zombie. A zombie can be a Christian, Hindu, Mohammedan — but all are zombies, with different labels. And sometimes they get fed up with one label, so they change the label: the Hindu becomes a Christian, the Christian becomes a Hindu — a new label, a fresh label, but behind the label the same belief system.

Destroy your beliefs. Certainly it will be uncomfortable, inconvenient, but nothing valuable is ever gained without inconvenience.

In three hundred years, science has used doubt as its method, and given the world so much in three hundred years. In ten thousand years religions have not been able to give even a thousandth part of what science has given. The religions have not given anything. On the contrary they have prevented everything in every possible way. They were trying to prevent science too, and they tried hard — they are still trying.

Now, the Catholic pope goes on teaching the Catholics that methods of birth control should not be used — they are against God. Strange, even the Holy Ghost must be using birth control methods, because Jesus says, "I am the only begotten son of God." What happened to God? Has he stopped creating sons, daughters? Either he has become a brahmacharya, a celibate, which is not very likely, or he is using birth control methods. But the pope goes on continually talking against birth control, because it is against God — but God is sending the people.

This earth is already overloaded; it is already such a situation that if we don't cut its population by half, humanity is going to die. There will be no need for a Third World War; just the population itself will be enough to kill everybody, to starve everybody.

And God is continually sending people. Either he has no idea: at least send a small piece of land with each child, or try some new way so nobody is hungry. Rather than real babies, make plastic babies which run on batteries; that would be easier. Once in a while you go and you can get your battery charged. And for God everything is possible. He has been doing all kinds of miracles, his son was doing all kinds of miracles. This will not be much of a miracle, creating a baby that runs on a battery.

But he goes on giving us stomachs and hunger, and no land — and the old land is losing its fertility every day. And the Catholic pope goes on saying no birth control, no abortion. Why no abortion? — because it is killing. But it is very strange coming from a pope's mind, because these popes have been conducting all kinds of crusades in the past and killing thousands of people. That has been their whole business: burning people, burning women just because of a fictitious idea... .

Anybody could write to the pope informing him: "In our village there is a woman who is a witch." That was enough to start an inquiry; and there was a special court to inquire into whether the woman was a witch or not. They would torture the woman so much that she would find it easier to accept that she was a witch rather than being continually tortured. They would torture her till she accepted that she was a witch; and once she accepted that she was a witch she had to be burned alive. They burned thousands of women alive.

Now suddenly, their interest is in non-violence since abortion is violence. And the same pope's predecessors blessed Benito Mussolini in the Second World War. Was that not violence? The archbishop of Canterbury in England blessed the British forces — and that was not violence? That was perfectly good? One wonders at what point abortion becomes violence.

At what point — a child is conceived this moment — is he alive or dead? He is alive, but from where has the life come? He was alive in the semen cells before he became conceived in the mother's womb; the semen cells are all alive. They have a small life span, just two hours, so if within two hours they can find a female egg, and can enter the egg, the child is conceived. The egg is alive. Half of your being, the feminine part, is in the egg, and half of your being is coming from your father's semen. And in a single intercourse millions of cells are rushing ... .

You will be surprised to know that it is there that politics starts. Everybody is running fast towards the egg, because whosoever reaches first becomes President Ronald Reagan. Those who are left behind, just a little behind — finished! Only one sperm is going to enter; then the woman's egg becomes hard and no more can enter. That is the natural process; it is available only to one. Only once in a while does it happen that two male cells reach exactly at the same time and enter. That's why sometimes you have twins, or three or four or five or six — even nine children have been known. But that is a very rare event.

Millions of sperm ... and they are really fast. It is almost like a car race. They are all racing, and they have to be quick. Within two hours if they don't reach, they are finished. In a single intercourse you are responsible for killing millions of beings. And what about an abortion? — just one. So whether it's one million or one million plus one, what difference does it make?

But the Catholic pope is ready, just as the Mohammedan chief imam is ready, and the Hindu shankaracharya is ready to let the population grow, because numbers have a political significance. It is the politics of numbers — how many Catholics are there? The pope is not interested in humanity, in the future, in a global suicide, no. His whole interest is in how many Catholics there are. The more Catholics there are, the more power he has. The shankaracharya is interested in more Hindus, so he has more power.

Everybody is interested in power. In the name of God they are simply trying to become more and more powerful. God is just a useful instrument in the hands of the priest. Whatsoever the priest wants, he makes God say. He writes the scriptures, he writes all kinds of nonsense in them. And it is a strange fact to be understood about human beings that people become very impressed with nonsense, because it seems mystical.

For example the Bible says: "In the beginning was the word." Now how can the word be in the beginning? Do you make any distinction between sound and word, or not? A word is a meaningful sound. Perhaps it can be said that in the beginning there was sound — but not word.

A word presupposes there was somebody who made the sound meaningful, who used a word. "In the beginning was the word." I am just saying hypothetically that sound would be better, more logical; in fact sound is also not possible. Scientifically sound is possible only if somebody is there to hear it, otherwise there is no sound.

I am speaking here. If nobody is here there will be no sound, because for sound two things are needed: me making a noise and your ears receiving it. Between these two the sound happens. When there is nobody near a waterfall, you may think there will be much sound still happening near the waterfall. You are wrong; there is no sound because there is no ear.

So even if sound is not possible, what to say about a word! But they say, "In the beginning was the word" — just see how nonsense becomes mystical. "In the beginning was the word. The word was with God." You have spoiled the first statement already. "In the beginning was the word. The word was with God," so already there were two — you have contradicted it immediately — and the third sentence, "And the word was God."

Now, such garbage impresses people: "Something very profound must be in it, that's why we cannot understand it." There is nothing profound in it — just some idiot writing. But Christian theologians have been commenting on it for centuries, different commentaries on what it means. What is "the word"? What does it mean that "The word was God," that "The word was with God"? — just three sentences, and all contradictory to each other.

If you analyze any scripture you will find these kinds of statements. And they say, "Don't doubt, believe, have faith and great will be your reward; doubt and you are misguided." But in this darkness, except for doubt, there is no light.

Doubt! And not half-heartedly: doubt with your total intensity so that doubt will become like a sword in your hand, and it will cut all the garbage that has gathered around you. Doubt is to cut the garbage, and meditation is to awaken yourself.

These are two sides of the same coin, because burdened with all the garbage you will not be able to wake up. That garbage will create sleep in you; that's its function. It is meant to keep you asleep. Have faith and go to sleep so that you don't bother the politicians, the priests; you don't bother the vested interests, you don't bother anybody. You yourself become a man without any soul, a mechanism, a slave.

So doubt, and meditate! And by meditation I mean a very simple thing: just be silent and start drowning in your silence.

In the beginning that too creates fear because silence is like an abyss — perhaps there is no bottom, and one wants to cling to anything available. Silence needs courage, just as doubt needs courage.

To doubt is to throw out everything that others have put in you. And meditation is, after everything has been thrown out, to enter into your self — which no God, nobody has put there. It has been your being for eternity and it is going to be your being for eternity.

Drown yourself in silence. Enjoy, drink it, taste it!

Just in the beginning there is fear. Once you have had a little taste, just a little taste on the tip of your tongue, then all fear disappears, because it is so sweet, so nourishing, so immensely centering and grounding. It gives you for the first time the feeling that alone you are enough, that no God is needed, no prayer is needed, that the temple is not outside but within. And as the feeling grows and you go on entering into it, you will be surprised:

In the beginning there was silence, not sound. In the middle there is silence. In the end there is silence.

It is perpetual, continuous, and it is your very being: so fulfilling, so tremendously fulfilling, giving you such contentment that for the first time you feel nothing is needed. All that is needed is provided already within you.

Existence is very generous. God is very miserly — of course, because misers have created the fiction in their own image. God is very miserly, very cruel, very jealous, very revengeful. Just for small things ... Somebody smokes cigarettes — now what kind of sin is he committing? I cannot conceive that he is committing any sin. Perhaps he is committing some mistake, but that is a medical thing, it has nothing to do with religion. Perhaps he is not taking proper care of his body, but that is his business. Perhaps he will die two or three years earlier, but if he thinks of what he is going to do for two or three years more, he will smoke more, so what is the point?

But there are religions like Buddhism and Jainism — smoke and you are in hell. Strange, here that man is smoking, and there you will throw him again into fire. Here he was throwing fire into himself; there you throw him into fire! What kind of revenge is going on? And he was not throwing anything on you; whatever he was doing, he was doing to himself. And he has suffered for it: he may have tuberculosis, he may have cancer, he may suffer for it. He has suffered, now what is the need of a hell? Small things, natural things, and the religions have made so much fuss about them because of the very tiny mind of God.

Existence is very generous, always forgiving, never punishing. But the only way to reach to existence is through your own innermost silence. That is the silence between the stars — the same silence; there is no difference.

There are no types of silence, remember that. There cannot be two kinds of silence. Silence is simply one: just the taste of it, and you have tasted the silence that is there millions of light years away, surrounding the whole universe.

By feeling your inner silence you have felt the pulse of the universe.

I say to you, with God there is no possibility of authentic religion. And I say to you also, that with the so-called religions that have existed up to now, there is no possibility of religion either. I teach you a Godless, religionless religion.

Of course, then my meaning of religion will be "religiousness." You are not a Christian, you are not a Hindu, you are not a Mohammedan. You are just a man of silence, a man of truth, a man of compassion, a man who is no longer searching — one who has arrived. And the feeling of arrival... Then there are no questions, no doubts, no beliefs, no answers either.

When Bodhidharma was dying his disciples asked him, "Master, your last message?"

He opened his eyes, and said, "I do not know anything at all — I have arrived. Knowledge is left far behind; who cares to know? There is nobody asking, there is nobody questioning, there is nobody answering; all has become silent. Hence," he says, "all that I can say is that I do not know."

That was the statement of Socrates also in the end. He said, "When I was young I thought: 'I know much and soon I will know all.' But as I went on searching, doubting, inquiring" — and he was a man not of belief, but of doubt ... He was far superior to any of your religious prophets, messiahs, avatars, tirthankaras — he was far superior. In the end he said, "The more I started to know, the more I started to feel that I don't know anything."

His statements are tremendously beautiful, because on the surface they look contradictory. He says, "The more I knew, the less I knew. The moment I came to know all, all was lost; only ignorance remained." So he said, "There is a knowledge which is ignorant, and there is an ignorance which knows."

With belief you will come to knowledge, which is ignorant. With doubt, inquiry, meditation, you will come to a state of ignorance, which knows.

There is no need for you to be labeled. There is no need for you to be part of a congregation. My commune is, in a way, strange, a contradiction. My function is to make you free of all congregations, to give you total freedom to be yourself

But perhaps alone you are not able to stand against the whole world. You need fellow travelers. You need people who are walking on the same path to give you courage, to keep you inspired, because the vast mass is out there. These people poisoned Socrates. These people killed Jesus. These people killed Al-Hillaj Mansoor and so many others. I would not like that to happen to any of you. Hence I had to commit a contradiction, and create a commune. But you have to remember that it is just out of playfulness; you have not to become serious about it.

It does not make you my followers. It simply means that you are available to me, receptive; that you can listen to me, putting all your prejudices aside. And I am not giving you any doctrine. I have none. I will take all doctrines away from you. I want you to become just emptiness. And that is the ultimate quality of a religious person, to know the inner emptiness. It is unbounded. It is as vast as the universe. It contains the whole universe in it.

When you are absolutely empty, stars start moving within you. The whole universe and you are no longer separate. You have found a subtle, secret door that goes from you to the whole.

God is not needed. It is an absolutely useless hypothesis. Nor are religions needed. But a religious consciousness is absolutely needed — more today than ever before.

If we cannot create a great movement for authentic religious consciousness there is no future for humanity — man is doomed. The priests, the politicians and other vested interests together have prepared your grave; any moment they will push you into it. Many of you, of your own accord, are sitting in that grave. The world has never before been at such a critical moment. If a great release of meditative consciousness is not made available, man is doomed.

But I hope that meditative consciousness is going to prevail, that man will pass through this dangerous moment and will come out of it far superior, far higher, far more humane.

Chapter 10
God — the nobody everybody knows

God did not create people like Adolf Hitler in his own image. He created people like Jesus Christ, Krishna and Buddha.

It is not a question. It is a statement, an answer, but I have not asked the question. The person seems even to know whom God created in his own image and whom God did not create in his own image. The person seems to be an eyewitness. What was he doing there? Did God create him in his own image? Then what is he doing here? But I can enjoy even answering an answer.

He says God did not create people like Adolf Hitler in his own image. What is wrong in Adolf Hitler? The followers of Adolf Hitler believe that he was the reincarnation of the great Jewish prophet, Elijah. It is as true as the Christian's belief that Jesus is the only begotten son of God, and the Mohammedan's belief that Mohammed is the only messenger of God. Nobody else believes it, but that is not the point. Christians believe it, the followers of Adolf Hitler also believe it.

And Adolf Hitler was a very religious man. Let me give you a little glimpse of Adolf Hitler's life. He lived like a monk, in an underground cell. He was not interested in so-called worldly things that everybody is interested in. He was a vegetarian; he never ate any nonvegetarian food in his whole life. He remained unmarried almost his whole life — except for three hours, the last three hours. That is almost his whole life — what do three hours count? And what is possible in three hours of marriage?

The marriage was arranged after he decided to commit suicide, because he had been continually harassed by this woman: "Why don't you get married to me?" And he always refused. He lived like a monk, absolutely alone in his cell, and he was worried that once he got married it would be difficult to live alone, this woman would force her way into his room. So he kept on postponing.

When he finally decided, Berlin was falling and the bombs were falling on the street outside the house; he could hear the bombs exploding from his cell. He immediately asked for a priest to be called so that the marriage could be arranged. Marriage for what? — to commit suicide together. Perhaps most people do the same, not knowingly. Perhaps their three hours are very long; and the longer they are, the more tedious.

A priest was somehow brought in. He quickly performed the marriage ceremony, and after the ceremony was over they drank poison and killed themselves. And his order was that petrol should be poured over them and they should be burned completely; not even a trace should be found — and that's how it was done.

This man used to wake up every morning before sunrise. Not all monks are so religious. I know monks are supposed to get up before sunrise — but human beings are human beings. Adolf Hitler was made of a different mettle. Even in winter he would get up before sunrise, and the whole year round he would take a cold shower after getting up — the first thing, a cold shower — a very disciplined monk. He would go to sleep exactly at nine at night. He was not interested in anything that you can call bad. He neither played cards nor smoked cigarettes. His food was very simple, very frugal and he never drank wine — no alcoholic beverages.

When Germany took over France, all his generals wanted him to come to the most beautiful city in the world, but he was not interested. Beauty was not a concern in his mind at all, but because everybody was asking him — and they had done a great job of conquering France — he went there, but he stayed for only twenty-four hours in his hotel room and did not go out to see Paris.

You say God did not create Adolf Hitler in his own image. Why not — because he killed so many people? But every day God is killing millions of people — who else is killing them? Adolf Hitler was simply sharing a little bit of God's job. People have to be killed, everybody has to die; so what is wrong in it if Adolf Hitler shares a little work, takes a little burden off God?

And he did perfectly well, far better than God himself. Sometimes it happens, the carbon copy comes out clearer than the original. He invented gas chambers, the most non-violent method of killing man, but you cannot call it killing; killing is too cruel. In a gas chamber the person never comes to know when he is and when he is not. It is so quick: just a switch flicked on and there is only smoke — you can call it holy smoke! He did his job perfectly.

In fact Hitler had this belief, this fanatic idea that he had been sent by God to destroy all that was not right, all that was hindering the growth of the superman on the earth. He was doing it in good faith.

You cannot suspect his faith, his intention, because if he had been a little bit doubtful it would have been impossible to do what he did: killing millions of people. It needs tremendous faith, fanatic blind faith that what you are doing is the right thing. There was no doubt in his mind, no doubt at all, that he was doing God's work: cleaning the world of all that was not in tune with the evolution of the superman.

You say God did not create Adolf Hitler in his own image. That raises a question: then who created Adolf Hitler? Are there a few other gods also? That means there is a choice; you can shop and choose in whose shape you want to be created. You can just go into the mall and choose your own god: "I want to be created in this god's image."

This is an old strategy of the so-called pseudo-religious people: that whatsoever is good belongs to God, and whatsoever is bad belongs to the Devil. Then who created the Devil?

God has to take responsibility at some point or other. I cannot leave him out of it. If he says that Adolf Hitler is being created by his enemy, the Devil, okay, but who created the Devil? God cannot shirk the responsibility; shrug it from his shoulders. He must have created the Devil, otherwise from where did the Devil come? And if the Devil can come from somewhere else, then anybody can come from somewhere else. So what is the need for God to create? Creation is being done somewhere else too.

God should be told, "You are not a monopolist, there are other potters — and perhaps there may be better potters, because the world that you have created does not seem to be a perfect world. And you seem to be absolutely impotent. If the Devil goes on smuggling his people into your world, what are you doing there? At least you can stop this smuggling business. And it is going on, on a tremendously vast scale. In fact your people seem to be very few, can be counted on one's fingers, and the Devil's people seem to be in millions."

It is strange that God goes on sitting on his throne, gossiping with the Holy Ghost, playing with his only begotten son, Jesus; and the Devil goes on running the whole world — goes on creating Adolf Hitler, Joseph Stalin, Benito Mussolini, Mao Zedong ... The whole of history seems to be ninety-nine point nine percent a creation of the Devil.

Then why go on giving credit to God as the creator? He may be an amateur potter — once in a while he makes a pot — but the Devil seems to be the professional. Genghis Khan, Tamerlane, Nadirshah, Alexander the Great, Napoleon Bonaparte and Ivan the Terrible — just go down through history — were all these people not created by God? They were, but you are afraid to accept the fact because then your God becomes almost a devil.

You say God created men like Jesus Christ, Hazrat Mohammed, Krishna and Gautam Buddha. Let us look at these people whom you think God created. Jesus was a Jew — born a Jew, lived a Jew, died a Jew. He had never heard the word Christian, and I don't think that he had any idea of creating a religion called Christianity. There is no indication anywhere to even create a suspicion that he had it in mind to create a new religion, no. For his whole life he was trying to do only one thing — to be accepted by the Jews as their messiah.

Now, the God of the Jews is a Jew, Jesus is a Jew, the high priest of the Jews is a Jew. The rabbis, who are in the highest posts in the great temple of the Jews, are all religious people, very scholarly and very knowledgeable. It is difficult to find more scholarly people than rabbis; their whole life is devoted to study, to scholarship. And the high priest must have been a great rabbi; that is why he had been chosen.

They decide to crucify Jesus. A Jewish God creates Jesus in his own image, but Jewish rabbis, their high priest, and the Jewish community, do not recognize that man at all, that he is an image of God. They look upon him as a mischief-monger, as a cheat, a deceiver.

Now, if God sends his own son, can't he send a small message to the high priest: "Please take care of my son, my only begotten son," and they are all Jews so they all understand the same language. There would not have been any difficulty — but he remains silent. Jesus is crucified and God is silent; his image is destroyed and he remains absolutely indifferent.

In fact, Jesus was not such a disciplined man as Adolf Hitler. Jesus drank wine and even turned water into wine, which should be a crime. You try turning anything into LSD!

Do that miracle and you will be in jail. Turn ordinary grass into "real grass" and you will find what it means to perform a miracle.

Now, this man was turning water into wine, and he was drinking wine without any feeling of guilt. No Hindu, no Mohammedan, no Jaina, no Buddhist will accept this man as an image of God. An image of God drinking alcoholic beverages! The image of God should be the pinnacle of consciousness, and drinking anything alcoholic is just the opposite of being conscious; it is drowning yourself in unconsciousness. It is one of the most anti-religious acts possible.

This man Jesus, although he taught about meekness and humbleness, was very arrogant himself. Buddha could not have accepted him as an image of God. His proclamation, "I am the only son of God," is the greatest egoistic proclamation ever made. Adolf Hitler's claim is not that great. Elijah... Who knows this Elijah? He must have looked into the Old Testament and found a name somehow appealing to him for some reason, because with Adolf Hitler you could never be sure what reason ... Perhaps he was counting the numbers which numerology gives to each letter of the alphabet, and found that Elijah was a good numerological name — because these were the things in which Adolf Hitler believed: numerology, astrology, palmistry.

You will be surprised that even his attacks on countries were not decided by generals but by astrologers. In fact, this was the reason for his continual victory in the first four years — it was not that astrology is right but that his enemies could not figure out where he was going to attack. If he had been listening to his generals, then of course every other country would have been able to figure out his plans, because all the generals think in a certain way. There is a military science based on simple arithmetic: you don't attack the enemy where he is strongest; obviously you attack him where he is weakest.

But Adolf Hitler would attack where the enemy was strongest. And the enemy would be thinking: "Here we are strongest; Adolf Hitler is not going to attack here," so they would move their armies to the weakest point. But he was not going to attack there, because he depended on astrology. The stars were in favor of another point, so at he would attack that point.

Now, if both sides were deciding through the generals, both sides would have been absolutely clear where the attack was going to happen, because both function according to the same logic, but here there was no question of logic. And Adolf Hitler's word was law. There was no "Why?" — that could not be asked of Adolf Hitler. You could not ask, "Why have you decided on this procedure?"

Nobody was allowed to ask — even the closest people were not close enough. Not a single man was close enough to put his hand on Adolf Hitler's shoulder. Nobody was a friend; Adolf Hitler never allowed any friendship. The reincarnation of the prophet Elijah was far above that with you ordinary human beings crawling on the earth — and you ask him why!

So he was continually winning for four years, until Winston Churchill himself had to come down to the same rules, against his will: "This is stupid, but what to do? If you are fighting with an idiot, you have to be an idiot, otherwise you are going to be a loser." He had to call astrologers from India, because that is where you can find the best astrologers. And the Indian astrologers felt tremendously proud, that finally even Winston Churchill had understood that: "Astrology is a science and we are far more advanced than you are."

And with astrology entering in, Winston Churchill certainly started winning, because now he was also going crazy. He was a great general but now he was doing things against himself, against his whole reason and experience — but what to do? "That other fellow will be listening to astrologers; you have to listen to astrologers. And it is a question of victory, so it is not the time to argue about astrology; the time for that argument we can find later on. First finish this man and this mad situation."

When Winston Churchill started listening to astrologers, he started winning because he also began attacking in a crazy way with no logic. And certainly he had stranger astrologers than Adolf Hitler, because Adolf Hitler's astrologers were western. You could find in London the same kind of astrologers who could tell you what those German astrologers would be suggesting to Adolf Hitler — but these Indian astrologers had a totally different astrology.

Adolf Hitler had no way to find out what these astrologers were suggesting, because both were different in their workings. Even in palmistry ... In western palmistry a line indicates something; in Indian palmistry the same line indicates something else — because there is nothing written on the line. It depends on you, what you want to make out of it.

Jesus died on the cross — that does not seem to be the right place for the son of God. And if you ask Jainas, Buddhists and Hindus, you will find meaning in what they say. You will be surprised by their answer, but their answer seems to be more rational. They say, "He must have committed some great sin in his past life and this is the outcome of that great sin — the simple law of karma. Otherwise, why should he be crucified?"

No Hindu avatar was crucified, no Jaina tirthankara was crucified, no buddha was crucified — that is impossible! In fact when Mahavira, the Jaina tirthankara, walked on the road — and in those days there were no tar roads or cement roads, just muddy tracks — if there was a thorn on the road it would immediately turn its pointed part downward so that Mahavira's feet remained unhurt and unharmed.

Because that man had finished with all his karmas, even a thorn could not hurt him — what to say of a cross! Even a thorn had to consider that: "A man is coming here who is finished with all his karmas. You cannot bother him; you had better put yourself in such a position that you don't hurt him." Now, these people — how could they accept Christ as the son of God, a messiah?

In Buddhist scriptures there are so many incidents described. A mad elephant was released towards Buddha to kill him. The mad elephant had killed many people; whoever came in his way, he finished them. He was kept in chains by the king, just for the simple purpose of killing criminals.

The whole royal family, their advisors and their ministers, would sit on the balconies of the palace and enjoy the game. Down on the ground the criminal would be standing; the elephant would be brought in and his chains taken off. He would rush immediately towards the man who would run and scream; and all those people would enjoy it, just as you enjoy a bullfight or Mohammed Ali's boxing. All these are of the same type, there is not much difference. What you are enjoying is violence, because the elephant was bound to kill him — where could the man escape to?

The elephant was sent to kill Buddha, but even this mad elephant, when he saw Buddha, recognized that this man had finished with all his karmas; you could not hurt him, rather this was an opportunity to touch his feet and to earn some good karma for your future life. So he touched Buddha's feet and sat down there. The king could not believe his eyes. They had all followed what had happened; they said to Buddha, "Only you can say what happened."

He said, "Nothing special. The elephant is wiser than you: seeing that all my karmas are finished and I have no more to suffer, my accounts are closed, the balance sheet is complete — whatever I have done, I have suffered for it, and I am completely clean. Seeing this, the elephant thought, 'Why miss this opportunity? Where will I find another such man?' So he touched my feet to be blessed. In fact he is already blessed; he has already gained enough virtue — he will be born in his future life as a great buddha. He will become enlightened himself, because if he can recognize a buddha even in madness, then he is not identified with his madness. He is still aware that he is different."

Now, do you think Buddhists will accept Jesus, the image of God, being crucified? Even an elephant can see when a buddha is there; yet those thousands of Jews were there and nobody could see, not a single person, that this man was the image of God and you should not destroy him. It is just your conditioning; otherwise no other religion is going in any way to accept Jesus.

He was mixing with people Mahavira would not allow his monks to mix with, what to say of Mahavira himself — Jesus was mixing with gamblers, prostitutes, thieves, the lowest strata of society. Mahavira would not allow it; Buddha would not allow it. And why was he mixing with those people? — because nobody else was ready to mix with him. The higher classes, the richer classes, the educated, cultured and sophisticated people were not ready to mix with this carpenter's son: uneducated, a village idiot who was declaring himself son of God.

Only one time had a professor come to him, and that too in the middle of the night. He was a rabbi and a known professor, Nicodemus. He came in the night when there was nobody around and all the apostles had fallen asleep. Jesus was saying his last prayer before he went to sleep. In the dark came this very respected, rich rabbi, a professor in the university, and he introduced himself. Jesus said, "Why don't you come in the day? It is the middle of the night; I was just going to sleep. I have just finished my last prayer."

Nicodemus said, "In the day I cannot come because people will see that I associate with a man like you. I have heard about you so much that curiosity has brought me here, but in the day I will not admit the fact that I came to see you." The higher class people were not mixing — what to say of mixing — they were not even ready to talk to this man.

This is the son of God, created in his own image — and nobody in the whole of Judea could recognize him except those few fools who had no religious education, no understanding. They were fishermen, woodcutters, farmers; they enjoyed the idea of being associated with the only son of God because that gave them the hope that: "When we reach the kingdom of God we will be with the son, close to God. Then all these rich people, these kings, these viceroys and these rabbis will see who we are. Right now we are only fishermen, woodcutters, farmers." So that was their hope. That's why it was so cheap to enter the kingdom of God with Jesus. This opportunity was not to be missed. But he could find only those twelve people in the whole of Judea.

No great religion in the East will accept him, because a man is known by his company — and his company was certainly not good. And that company became his apostles, that company created Christianity; so if Christianity is a third-rate religion there is no wonder about it — it has come from a very third-rate source. It hasn't the profundity of Jainism or Buddhism or Hinduism; there is no comparison.

You ask me about Krishna. You must have thought that I would at least accept Krishna and Buddha as the images of God — no. There is no God in the first place so how can there be any image? And whoever you bring before me as an image, I am going to hammer hard on. It is a fight with the fictitious God; it is not a fight with Jesus, Mohammed, Krishna or Buddha. If that fictitious God is finished with, much of the glory of these people will be demolished.

If there is no God, then "I am the only begotten son" cannot be said. Then, "I bring the message of God, and only my message is true because it comes from God" cannot be said. So I am trying to destroy the fiction of God. Of course I will have to beat the images too, because just by being God's image they go on giving life to a fiction.

Krishna was one of the most cunning politicians the world has ever known; and perhaps in the future it will not be possible to have such a cunning politician. He was not a man of his word at all; that's why I call him a politician. He would say one thing and would do exactly the opposite. He would make you a promise and he would break that promise any moment he found that it was in his favor to do so. You could not rely on him at all. His whole life was full of using people's trust, taking advantage, deceiving, but the Hindus go on saying, "This is God's play."

You can always find good words for anything. The young girls of the town were taking a bath in the river and he would collect all their clothes and sit in a tree. Now, they would be asking for their clothes, standing naked in the water. Anybody else doing such a thing would be immediately taken to the police station. But in many Hindu families you will find this picture hanging — of course not in those houses where I have stayed!

Once, I said, "You should be ashamed — keeping this picture here, just in your sitting room. You think you are displaying some great religiousness — this is religiousness? If I did the same with your wife and with your daughter, then... ?"

The man said, "What do you mean?"

I said, "Yes, if I actually do this, as Krishna was doing, that would be God's play. Why should he be an exception?" Sixteen thousand wives stolen by Krishna, forcibly taken away from people, from their husbands and from their children ... He must have created a great concentration camp for these wives. And I don't think that he would have recognized who was his wife and who wasn't. And I don't think that this is in any way an exaggeration.

It used to happen in India; kings used to have hundreds of wives. Even today, the Nizam of Hyderabad, who died just a few years ago, left five hundred wives behind him — five hundred widows ... one man. So sixteen thousand doesn't seem too big a number — only thirty-two times more than the Nizam of Hyderabad. The person's richness was counted by how many wives he had, and Krishna was certainly thirty-two times wealthier than the Nizam of Hyderabad.

A poor man could not afford even one wife; for a poor man to have one wife, only one wife, was difficult — he could not manage two meals a day for himself. So in ancient India the way to show how wealthy you were was to have many wives — and Krishna defeated everybody. Just to defeat everybody, sixteen thousand wives and sixteen thousand families were destroyed. The children may have become orphans or beggars — what happened nobody knows — and this man is thought to be the image of God! Can't you see his cruelty? And it was not for love's sake. He did not even know these women. How can you know sixteen thousand women? What love can you give to sixteen thousand women? What relatedness is possible with these women? They are just imprisoned to show your greatness.

With the same egoistic attitude, perhaps even stronger, Krishna said to his disciple, Arjuna, "Surrender at my feet, leaving aside everything — your doubts, your thinking — leave aside everything, just surrender at my feet. I am your salvation, I am your refuge."

Now, anybody saying that seems to be ugly. If it were true, then even Arjuna would recognize it himself. You need not declare it, you need not persistently say to him, "Surrender at my feet." Certainly he was not surrendering, hence the insistence. Arjuna was continually arguing, bringing doubts, questions; he was not convinced. I don't think he was ever convinced.

I have tried hard to look into the whole conversation between Arjuna and Krishna — that is the Shrimad Bhagavadgita, the whole conversation. The way Arjuna was arguing was perfectly right and the doubts he raised were perfectly valid, but what Krishna was saying, his answers, were not justified. They didn't dispel the doubts and they didn't dispel Arjuna's confusion; hence, tired of arguing with Arjuna, Krishna said, "Leave everything aside and simply surrender at my feet, because I am the perfect incarnation of God."

But if you have to say it, then I say, you are not! If the other recognizes it even though you deny it, then perhaps there is something to it. If you are denying it, but the other goes on seeing something which is more than can be understood by the mind, which is more than can be comprehended by intellect ... If the other goes on feeling it, the presence of it, the smell of it, and against your denial he says, "You can go on denying it, I don't care; I listen to my heart, and my heart is saying something to me," that is something totally different. But that does not happen in the whole conversation in the Gita.

Krishna simply forced him; and seeing the situation and the awkwardness of the situation — because they were standing on the battlefield, Krishna was functioning as his charioteer and both armies were facing each other, just about to begin the war for which they had been preparing for years and which was going to be decisive for the whole of India ... And it proved to be decisive; it destroyed the very backbone of the country.

I find three men responsible for India's downfall. The first was Krishna, because he destroyed India's zest, gusto for fighting. He drove India into a kind of Third World War, in which almost the whole country was devastated and destroyed. Everybody, whosoever was alive, became so shaken and afraid of war that they were ready to do anything rather than go to war.

And then came Buddha and Mahavira who started talking about nonviolence. That appealed very much to people who were so tired of war. And they had seen such a great war that they never wanted to have anything to do with it again. It would be better to be slaves rather than to have such a war and such destruction.

Mahabharata was the name of the war, the Great Indian War; since then there have been only battles, nothing like the Great Indian War. Its magnitude was almost universal: whatsoever was known of the world at that time, every part of that world joined in the war, either from this side or from that side. Both sides were cousin-brothers and the problem was: who should inherit the kingdom?

On one side were one hundred Kauravas, one hundred brothers. Now you can see ... The father was blind, yet he must have had thousands of wives — even a blind fellow managed to produce one hundred sons. His brother had five sons, the Pandavas. The conflict was: who is going to inherit the kingdom? They could not negotiate in any way, so that the only way to decide was go to war. And because it was one family, all the relatives were divided — somebody was fighting from that side, somebody was fighting from this side; a brother from that side, another brother from this side, and all their friends were there from all over the world.

You will be surprised to know that Arjuna had one wife from Mexico too — Mexican kings had come with their armies to fight on Arjuna's side. The Sanskrit name for Mexico is Makshika; Mexico is a distortion of Makshika. Now much historical evidence has been collected and it is certain that Makshika is Mexico. In Mexico, Hindu temples have been found, Hindu gods and goddesses and their statues have been found. And the latest discovery is that there was a time when the water between Asia and America, the ocean water, was so shallow that you could simply walk from America to Asia. You could simply walk over the ocean; it was one foot deep at the most.

So the whole known world of that time had gathered for this decisive battle and all were ready for the signal to be given. But they were waiting because Krishna was still persuading Arjuna. Arjuna wanted to leave; he said, "I want to renounce war because I don't see any point in it. All these people are my people: on this side are my people; on that side are my people. I see my friends on that side whom I will have to kill and I see my friends on this side. These people, these hundred Kauravas are my brothers, and I have to kill these people just for the kingdom? Millions of people will be killed in the war, and even if we win, who will be left to rejoice in the victory?"

And he was absolutely right: "Who will there be to rejoice in the victory over the corpses of millions of relatives and friends? These are the people for whom we would have fought, for whom we would have won the victory so that they could rejoice with us, celebrate with us — but all these people will be dead. There is no certainty we will win; there is no certainty that the other party will win, because both are equally balanced. But one thing is certain: whosoever wins, almost everybody will be dead." And that's what happened.

Finally Krishna argued: "You are a coward, you are an impotent man escaping from the warfield; you are a warrior, and the religion of the warrior is to fight. Are you afraid of killing, of murdering? These people are going to die anyway." Just see the argument, what he is saying: "These people are going to die anyway, any day." Nobody is immortal, so if you murder these people you are not doing anything that you have to be worried about. Perhaps you have taken a few years off this man's life, but in that too you are wrong to think that you are doing it. The doer is God, and whatsoever happens, happens through his will; we are only his instruments.

That's what I was telling you: that these religions have been reducing humanity to puppets. Krishna's whole Gita can be condensed into a single sentence: "Man is a puppet; the puppeteer is God." So whatever the puppeteer wants, you do. If he makes you dance, you dance; if he makes you jog, you jog — whatsoever he makes you do, leave everything to God. Simply act and don't think of the consequences or the results. That's the whole message of the Gita, on which the whole of Hinduism stands: go on surrendering everything to God, and don't bother about the result — the result is in his hands.

Now this is a very tricky argument. If I had been in Arjuna's place I would have slapped Krishna then and there, told him to get down from the chariot and said, "I am going — because this is the will of God. Who am I to think? Now my whole being is saying to renounce this war — I am going. This is God's voice. Who are you? And I am not going to think about the consequences: that people will think me a coward. Let them think it — that is their business."

In fact the argument that Krishna gave to Arjuna was so bogus that if Arjuna had a little insight into argumentation he could have turned the whole thing round. Krishna was saying, "Only do, and don't think of the result."

Arjuna should have said, "Great! So I will only do this, and I will not bother about the result" — and he should have turned his chariot towards the jungle. But he was befooled, perhaps by the situation or the pressure. He had collected all these people, he had invited all these people, and now at the last moment to escape ... "What will the world say? And Krishna is God's incarnation — that's what people say — and if he is saying, 'Fight and leave the consequences in God's hands,' then I should fight." So he fought and they won. But whatsoever he was afraid of did happen. The whole country has never been again alive in the same way as it was before. It lost its backbone; it lost its manliness.

I cannot say that Krishna is the image of God. He is far closer to Adolf Hitler, Joseph Stalin, or Mao Zedong than to God. This is what Adolf Hitler was doing, what poor Adolf Hitler was doing — why should he be condemned? He was doing God's will and not both- ering about the consequences. It was the same thing with Krishna: forcing Arjuna to do something that he wanted, argued for it — and destroyed the country for at least five thousand years. It is still not free of the shadow of the Mahabharata; that Great War still falls like a shadow on India.

And the last person the questioner asks about is Gautam Buddha. He must have thought that at least I will agree about Gautam Buddha — but he is wrong. In the first place Gautam Buddha does not believe in God, that God exists, so he will not agree that he is an image of God. He himself would disagree with this statement, that he is an image of God. He does not believe in God. He himself cannot say he is an image of God, and he has never said that.

The very idea of "the image of God" is inapplicable to Gautam Buddha — Krishna was born as an incarnation of God, Jesus was born as the only son of God, Mohammed was born as the only messenger of God, but this is not the case with Buddha. He was born a human being, and he went in search of truth. If he were made in the image of God he would have known the truth already, but he had to go in search, a long search.

Buddha took immense pains in every possible way to find out the truth. He did every- thing he was told. He went to all the teachers that were well known in the country until each teacher said, "Now I cannot teach you any more, because whatsoever I know I have taught you. Move on, go somewhere else; you know more than I know now." But this knowledge was not satisfying. He did everything, and that was his basic mistake: all the teachers got fed up with him.

Teachers never get fed up with a person who goes on committing mistakes. Then the teacher is always happy: "You committed this mistake, that's why you are missing; you committed that mistake, that's why you are missing." But this man was so particular that he was overdoing what the teacher was saying. No teacher — and he was with dozens of teachers — could say to him that he had failed because he had not done something, or he had missed something. No, every teacher understood that he had done everything — and nothing had happened.

He was standing there saying, "You said all these things were to be done; I think they have been done to completion. If not, tell me where the mistake is, and I am going to correct it. But nothing was happening. The teachers soon realized that they could not cheat and exploit this man; he was ready to go to any lengths.

But a point comes where the teacher becomes afraid because he himself does not know. He is just a scholar, a great scholar maybe; he can teach you all the methods but he himself has never done them. He knows no truth; he has not realized himself, so this man becomes a question mark to him, because he is doing exactly what is being told and yet nothing is happening.

Finally the last teacher he was with told him, "Don't waste your time with teachers. I am the greatest of all those teachers; many of them have been my students. Seeing in your eyes your sincerity, your authenticity, I would like to say to you that you have to go on your own. Nobody can take you there, nobody can lead you there; you have to go there on your own. So forget about teachers, forget about teachings and just move on your own. You have done enough of all these disciplines, Yogas, mantras, tantras, all that is available." And India is a great bazaar, buzzing with all kinds of things that you can do; it can drive you on for many lives. And those methods will not end; they are always there, and new ones too.

Buddha understood it because he had wasted twelve years and he was nowhere. But really, he had achieved something without being aware of it: he was finished with following. And that is a great achievement. To become religious; that is one of the greatest achievements: to be finished with following.

He went alone. He himself had gathered, in those years, five followers. He also told them, "Forgive me, all those teachers wasted my time and I don't want to waste your time — go on your own. Leave me alone and I will leave you alone. I am not your leader, and you are not my followers. From now onward I am alone. I will risk everything, and if there is any truth, I will find it; if there is none, I will find that."

This man had never claimed that he was a born God, deity, messenger, prophet or anybody's incarnation, no. And what he found was not God. He found absolute silence: no word, no idea, no image. He found tremendous contentment, but no God, nobody there even to thank. The whole universe was there, and he was grateful to the whole universe, but it was not separate so there was no question of saying thank you to it; he was part of it.

Buddha made no claim to be God or his image. That's why I have loved him the most, because he is the most human of all these people. Of course Buddhists corrupted all his teachings, made statues of him, started worshipping him and made a God out of him. But for that he cannot be held responsible.

You have not asked me a question you have made a statement. But I have still answered you, for the simple reason that anybody living close to me and carrying such statements in the mind will miss me, is bound to miss me.

You have to drop your answers. I am enough to wrestle with your questions; with your answers, you are the least able to wrestle.

Drop them and I will kill your questions.

The day there is no question and no answer within you, and you are just sitting here empty, you have come home — from ignorance to innocence

Chapter 11
Truth — not a dogma but a dance

? *Are you against all the religions? What is their most fundamental mistake?*

Yes, I am against all the so-called religions because they are not religious at all. I am for authentic religiousness but not for the religions.

The true religion can only be one, just like science. You don't have Mohammedan physics, Hindu physics, Christian physics; that would be nonsense. But that's what the religions have done — they have made the whole earth a madhouse.

If science is one, then why should the science of the inner not be one, too? Science explores the objective world and religion explores the subjective world. Their work is the same, just their direction and dimension is different.

In a more enlightened age there will be no such thing as religion, there will be only two sciences: objective science and subjective science. Objective science deals with things, subjective science deals with being.

That's why I say I am against the religions but not against religiousness. But that authentic religiousness is still in its birth pangs. All the old religions will do everything in their power to kill it, to destroy it — because the birth of a science of consciousness will be the death of all these so-called religions, which have been exploiting humanity for thousands of years.

What will happen to their churches, synagogues, temples? What will happen to their priesthood, their popes, their imams, their shankaracharyas, their rabbis? It is big business. And these people are not going to easily allow a true religiousness to be born.

But a time has come in human history when the grip of the old religions is loosening. Man is only formally paying respect to Christianity, Judaism, Hinduism, Mohammedanism, but basically anybody who has any intelligence is no longer interested in all that rubbish. He may go to the synagogue and to the church and to the mosque for other reasons, but those reasons are not religious; those reasons are social. It pays to be seen in the synagogue; it is respectable, and there is no harm. It is just like joining the Rotary Club or the Lions Club. These religions are old clubs, which have a religious jargon around them, but look a little deeper and you will find they are all hocus-pocus: no substance inside.

I am for religiousness, but that religiousness will not be a repetition of any religion that you are acquainted with. It will be a rebellion against all those religions. It will not carry their work further; it will stop their work completely and start a new work: of real transformation of mankind.

You ask me: "What is the most fundamental error of all these religions?" There are many errors and they are all fundamental, but first I would like to talk about the most fundamental. The most fundamental error of all the religions is that none of them was courageous enough to accept that there are things which we don't know. They all pretended to know everything, they all pretended to know all: they were all omniscient.

Why did this happen? It was because if you accept that you are ignorant about something then doubt arises in the minds of your followers. If you are ignorant about something, who knows? — you may be ignorant about other things also. What is the guarantee? To make it foolproof, they have all pretended, without exception, that they are omniscient.

The most beautiful thing about science is it does not pretend to be omniscient. Science does not pretend to be omniscient; it accepts its human limits. It knows how much it knows, and it knows that there is much more to know. And the greatest scientists know of something even deeper. The known they know, the boundaries of the knowable they will know sooner or later — they are on the way. And the unknowable: only the greatest scientists like Albert Einstein will be aware of the third category, the unknowable, which will never be known. Nothing can be done about it because the ultimate mystery cannot be reduced to knowledge.

We are part of existence — how can we know existence's ultimate mystery?

We have come very late; there was nobody present as an eyewitness. And there is no way for us to separate ourselves completely from existence and become just an observer. We live, we breathe, we exist with existence — we cannot separate ourselves from it. The moment we are separate, we are dead. And without being separate, just a watcher, with no involvement, with no attachment, you cannot know the ultimate mystery; hence it is impossible. There will remain something always unknowable. Yes, it can be felt, but it cannot be known. Perhaps it can be experienced in different ways, not like knowledge.

You fall in love — can you say you know love? It seems to be a totally different phenomenon. You feel it. If you try to know it, perhaps it will evaporate in your hands. You cannot reduce it to knowing. You cannot make it an object of knowledge because it is not a mind phenomenon. It is something to do with your heart. Yes, your heartbeats know it, but that is a totally different kind of knowledge; the intellect is incapable of approaching the heartbeats.

But there is something more than heart in you: your being, your life source. Just as you know through the mind, which is the most superficial part of your individuality, you know something from your heart, which is deeper than the mind. The mind cannot go into it; it is too deep for it. But behind the heart, still deeper, is your being, your very life source. That life source also has a way of knowing.

When mind knows, we call it knowledge. When heart knows, we call it love. And when being knows, we call it meditation.

But all three speak different languages, which are not translatable into each other. And the deeper you go, the more difficult it becomes to translate, because at the very center of your being there is nothing but silence. Now, how to translate silence into sound? The moment you translate silence into sound you have destroyed it. Even music cannot translate it. Perhaps music comes closest, but still it is sound.

Poetry does not come quite as close as music, because words, howsoever beautiful, are still words. They don't have life in them; they are dead. How can you translate life into something dead? Yes, perhaps between the words you may have a glimpse here and there — but it is between the words, between the lines, not in the words, not in the lines.

This is the most fundamental error of all religions: that they have deceived humanity by blatantly posing as if they know all. But every day they have been exposed and their "knowledge" has been exposed; hence, they have been fighting with any progress from knowledge.

If Galileo finds that the earth moves around the sun, the pope is angry. The pope is infallible; he is only a representative of Jesus, but he is infallible. What to say about Jesus — he is the only begotten son of God, and what to say about God ... But in the Bible, which is a book descended from heaven, written by God, the sun goes around the earth.

Now, Galileo creates a problem. If Galileo is right, then God is wrong; God's only begotten son is wrong, the only begotten son's representatives for these two thousand years — all the popes who are infallible — are wrong. Just a single man, Galileo, destroys the whole pretension. He exposes the whole hypocrisy; his mouth has to be shut. He was old, dying, on his deathbed, but he was forced, almost dragged, to the court of the pope to ask for an apology.

And the pope demanded, "Change it in your book, because the holy book cannot be wrong. You are a mere human being; you can be wrong but Jesus Christ cannot be wrong, God himself cannot be wrong, hundreds of infallible popes cannot be wrong. You are standing against God, his son, and his representatives. You simply have to change it!"

Galileo must have been a man with an immense sense of humor — which I count to be one of the great qualities of a religious man. Only idiots are serious, they are bound to be serious. To be able to laugh you need a little intelligence.

It is said that an Englishman laughs twice when he hears a joke: once, just to be nice to the fellow who is telling the joke, out of etiquette, mannerism; and secondly, in the middle of the night when he gets the meaning of the joke. The German laughs only once, just to show that he has understood it. The Jew never laughs; he simply says, "In the first place you are telling it all wrong... "

You need a little intelligence, and Galileo must have been intelligent. He was one of the greatest scientists of the world, but he must be counted as one of the most religious persons also. He said, "Of course God cannot be wrong, Jesus cannot be wrong, all the infallible popes cannot be wrong, but poor Galileo can always be wrong. There is no problem about it — I will change it in my book. But one thing you should remember: the earth will still go around the sun. About that I cannot do anything — it does not follow my orders. As far as my book is concerned I will change it, but in the note I will have to write this: 'The earth does not follow my orders, it still goes around the sun.'"

Religion was against each step of science. The earth is flat, according to the Bible, not round. When Columbus started thinking of going on a trip with the idea that the earth is round, his arithmetic was simple: "If I continue journeying directly, one day I am bound to come back to the same point from where I started — the whole circle." But everybody was against it.

The pope called Columbus and told him, "Don't be foolish! The Bible says it clearly: it is flat. Soon you will reach the edge of this flat earth and you will fall from there. And do you know where you will fall? Heaven is above, and you cannot fall upward — or can you? You will fall downward into hell. So don't go on this journey and don't persuade other people to go on this journey."

Columbus insisted that he was going; he went on the journey and opened the doors of the new world. We owe so much to Columbus that we are not aware of: the world that we know was brought to light by Columbus. If he had listened to the pope, the infallible pope who was talking just nonsense ... but his nonsense was very holy, religious.

All the religions of the world are bound to pretend that whatsoever there is, they know it. And they know it exactly as it is; it cannot be otherwise. Jainas say their tirthankara, their prophet, their messiah, is omniscient. He knows everything: past, present and future, so whatsoever he says is absolute truth. Buddha has joked about Mahavira, the Jaina messiah. They were contemporaries twenty-five centuries ago. Mahavira was getting old, but Buddha was young and was still capable of joking and laughing. He was still young and alive; he was not yet established.

Once you become an established religion, then you have your vested interests. Mahavira had an established religion thousands of years old, perhaps the oldest religion of the world — because Hindus say, and say rightly, that they have the oldest book in the world, the Rig Veda. Certainly it is now scientifically proven that the Rig Veda is the oldest scripture that has survived. And in the Rig Veda, the first Jaina messiah is mentioned; that is proof enough that the Jaina messiah has preceded the Rig Veda. And he is mentioned; his name is Rishabhdeva.

He is mentioned with a respect that it is impossible to have towards a contemporary. It is just human weakness, but it is very difficult to be respectful toward somebody who is contemporary and alive, just like you. It is easy to be respectful to somebody who has died long ago. The way the Rig Veda remembers Rishabhdeva is so respectful that it seems that he must have been dead for at least a thousand years, not less than that, so Jainism is a very long-established religion.

Buddhism was just starting with Buddha. He could afford to joke and laugh, so he jokes about Mahavira and his omnipotence, omniscience, and omnipresence. He said, "I have seen Mahavira standing before a house begging" — because Mahavira lived naked and used to beg just with his hands. Buddha said, "I have seen him standing before a house which was empty. There was nobody in the house — and yet this man, Jainas say, is a knower, not only of the present, but of the past and the future."

Buddha said, "I saw Mahavira walking just ahead of me, and he stepped on a dog's tail. It was early morning and it was not yet light. Only when the dog jumped, barking, did Mahavira come to know that he had stepped on his tail. This man is omniscient, and he does not know that a dog is sleeping right in his way and he is going to step on the dog's tail."

But the same happened with Buddha when he became established. After three hundred years, when his sayings and statements were collected for the first time, the disciples made it absolutely clear that "Everything written here is absolutely true, and it is going to remain true forever."

Now, in those statements there are so many idiotic things, which may have been meaningful twenty-five centuries ago, but today they are not meaningful because so much has happened in twenty-five centuries. Buddha had no idea of Karl Marx, he had no idea of Sigmund Freud, so what he had written or stated, is bound to be based on the knowledge that was available at that time.

"A man is poor, because in his past life he has committed bad actions." Now, after Marx, you cannot say that: "A man is rich because he has committed good actions in his past life." Now, after Marx, you cannot say that. And I don't think Buddha had any idea that there was going to be a Karl Marx, although his disciples said that whatsoever he said is going to remain true forever — another way of saying that he was omniscient.

This was good consolation for the poor, that if they did good works, in their future lives they would also be rich. It was a joy for the rich too: "We are rich because we have done good works in our past life." And they knew perfectly well what good works they were doing right then, with their riches increasing every day — the past life was finished with long ago and yet their riches went on increasing. The poor people go on becoming poorer and the rich go on becoming richer.

But in India no revolution has ever been thought about; there is no question of its happening — and India has lived in poverty such as no other country has lived. India has lived longer in slavery than any other country of the world. But slavery, poverty, suffering, everything has to be accepted because it is your doing. You cannot revolt against it. Against whom are you going to revolt? The only way is to do something to balance your bad actions with good actions. The very idea of revolution has never happened to the Indian mind. If slavery comes, you have to accept it.

The Hindus know all the answers. They say, "Without God's will nothing happens." So if you are a slave ... And for two thousand years India has been in slavery. It is a miracle that such a big country has remained in slavery for two thousand years. And the people who invaded India were small barbarian tribes; they were nothing compared to India. They could have been simply crushed by the crowd; there was no need even to take sword in hand.

But anybody — Hunas, Moguls, Turks, Mohammedans, Britishers — anybody who was ambitious and wanted to invade India was always welcome. It was ready — obliged that you came from so far away, and you took so much trouble! The simple reason was that the Hindus know the answer: it is God's will; nothing happens without God's will, so this slavery is God's will. And a man like Mahatma Gandhi — one would think that a man like Gandhi would show a little more intelligence, but no. If you are a Hindu you cannot show more intelligence than you are supposed to.

In Bihar, one of the provinces of India — the poorest province — there was a great earthquake. It was already poor; every year it suffers from floods. And then this earthquake ... thousands died. And what did Gandhi say? Gandhi said, "Bihar is suffering because of its bad actions." In the twentieth century, an earthquake and the whole population of Bihar... ?

It was understandable that you had been explaining to single individuals that they were suffering because of their bad karmas, but the whole state suffering because of its bad karmas ... ! — as if all these people in their past life were also in this same state, and they all committed such bad karmas that the earthquake happened. And the whole of the rest of India did not suffer from the earthquake because they had done good karmas in their past life. Strange!

It is even stranger because Bihar is the birthplace of Mahavira, of Gautam Buddha, of Makhkhali Gosal, of Ajit Keshkambal — great teachers and great prophets — and Bihar is suffering because it has committed bad karmas! In India no other state has given birth to so many prophets, philosophers, thinkers. And what wrong could Bihar have done? But Hinduism knows everything.

I want you to remember that the basic mistake that all the religions have committed is, they have not been courageous enough to accept that there are limits to their knowing. They have not been able to say on any point: "We don't know." They have been so arrogant that they go on saying they know, and they go on creating new fictions of knowledge.

That's where the true religion will be different, fundamentally different. Yes, once in a while there have been single individuals who had the quality of true religion ...

For example, Bodhidharma, one of the most lovable human beings; he went to China fourteen hundred years ago. He remained for nine years in China and a following gathered around him. But he was not a man belonging to the stupidity of the so-called religions.

Formally he was a Buddhist monk, and China was already converted to Buddhism. Thousands of Buddhist monks had already reached China before Bodhidharma, and when they heard Bodhidharma was coming, they rejoiced, because Bodhidharma was almost equal to Buddha. His name had reached them long before he came. Even the king of China, the great Emperor Wu, came to receive Bodhidharma on the boundary of China and India.

Wu was the medium to transform the whole of China into Buddhism, to convert it from Confucius to Gautam Buddha. He had put all his forces and all his treasures into the hands of Buddhist monks — and he was a great emperor. When he met Bodhidharma he asked, "I have been waiting to see you. I am old, and I am fortunate that you have come after all; all these years we have been waiting. I want to ask a few questions."

The first question he asked was: "I have devoted all my treasures, my armies, my bureaucracy — everything that I have — to convert this vast land to Buddhism, and I have made thousands of temples for Buddha." He had made one temple to Buddha in which there were ten thousand statues of Buddha; the whole mountain was carved. Because ten thousand Buddhas had to be carved, the whole mountain was finished — carved into Buddhist statues, so the whole mountain became a temple. He asked, "What will be my benefit in the other world?"

That's what the other monks were telling him: "You have done so much to serve Gautam Buddha that perhaps when you reach the other world, he himself will be standing there to welcome you. And you have earned so much virtue that an eternity of pleasures is yours."

Bodhidharma said, "All that you have done is absolutely meaningless. You have not even started on the journey; you have not even taken the first step. You will fall into the seventh hell — take my word for it."

The Emperor Wu could not believe it: "I have done so much, and this man says 'You will fall into the seventh hell'!"

Bodhidharma laughed and he said, "Whatsoever you have done is out of greed, and anything done out of greed cannot make you religious. You have renounced so many riches, but you have not renounced unconditionally. You are bargaining; it is a business. You are purchasing in the other world. You are moving your bank balance from this world into the other world, transferring it. You are cunning because this world is momentary — tomorrow you may die — and these other monks have been telling you the other world is eternal. So what are you doing? Giving momentary treasures to gain eternal treasures? Really a good deal! Whom are you trying to deceive?"

When Bodhidharma spoke to Wu in this way, before all the monks and the generals and the lesser kings who had come with Wu and his whole court, Wu was angry. Nobody had spoken this way to him before. He said to Bodhidharma, "Is this the way for a religious person to talk?"

Bodhidharma said, "Yes, this is the only way a religious person talks; all other ways are of people who want to cheat you. These monks here have been cheating you; they have been making promises to you. You don't know anything about what happens after death; nor do they, but they have been pretending that they know.

Wu asked, "Who are you to speak with such authority?"

And do you know what Bodhidharma said? He said, "I don't know. That is one point that I don't know. I have been into myself, I have gone to the very center of my being and come out as ignorant as before. I do not know."

Now this I call courage. No religion has been courageous enough to say, "We know this much, and that much we don't know; perhaps in the future we may know. And beyond that there is a space which is going to remain unknowable forever."

If these religions had been that humble, the world would have been totally different. Humanity would not have been in such a mess; there would not have been so much anguish. All around the world everybody is full of anguish. What to say about hell — we are already living in hell here. What more suffering can there be in hell?

And the people responsible for it are your so-called religious people. They still go on pretending, playing the same game. After three hundred years of science continually demolishing their territory, continually destroying their so-called knowledge, bringing forth new facts, new realities, still the pope is infallible, still the shankaracharya is infallible!

In Jaipur there was a Hindu conference and one of the shankaracharyas ... There are four shankaracharyas in India and they are equivalent to the pope: each one ruling one direction — for the four directions, four shankaracharyas. One of the shankaracharyas belonged to Jaipur; he was born in Jaipur. He was basically an astrologer, a great scholar, so when one shankaracharya died, he was chosen to be the shankaracharya of Jagannath Puri.

I had known him before he was a shankaracharya and this conference was the first time that I had met him since he had become a shankaracharya. I asked him, "Now you must have become infallible. And I know you perfectly well — you were not so before. Can you tell me on what date, at what time you became infallible?"

He said, "Don't ask inconvenient questions in front of others. Now I am a shankara-charya and I am supposed to be infallible."

I said, "Supposed to be!"

He said, "That is for your information. If you ask me in public, I am infallible."

A Polack has become pope. Have you ever heard of any Polack becoming infallible? But one pope, a Polack, has become infallible. How far has this world to fall? Now there is nowhere to fall. When the Polack dies — because popes die very quickly, for the simple reason that by the time they become pope they are almost dead. It takes such a long time to reach the Vatican, that if they survive a few years that is enough. Now after that pope whom are you going to choose? Can you find anybody else?.

A true religiousness will have this humbleness of accepting that only a few things are known, much more is unknown, and something will always remain unknowable. That something is the target of the whole religious search. You cannot make it an object of knowledge, but you can experience it, you can drink it, you can have the taste of it — it is existential.

The scientist remains separate from the object he is studying. He is always separate from the object; hence knowledge is possible, because the knower is different from the known. But the religious person is moving into his subjectivity, where the knower and the known are one.

When the knower and the known are one there is no possibility of knowledge. Yes, you can dance it, but you cannot say it.

It may be in the walk, the way you walk; it may be in your eyes, the way you see; it may be in your touch, the way you touch — but it cannot be put into words. Words are absolutely impotent as far as religion is concerned. And all these so-called religions are full of words. I call it all crap!

This is the fundamental mistake. But there are other mistakes too, worth remembering. For example: every religion is egoistic. Although every religion teaches its followers to drop the ego, to be egoless, to be humble, the religion itself is not humble; it is very arrogant.

Jesus says, "Be humble, be meek," but have you ever thought: Jesus himself is not humble, not meek, not at all. What more arrogance and what more egotism can there be? He declares himself to be the only begotten son of God! You cannot declare yourself to be another son of God — not even a cousin, because God has no brothers. You cannot have any relationship with God, that one relationship is closed; Jesus has closed the door.

He is the messiah and he has come to redeem the world — nobody seems to be redeemed, and two thousand years have passed. He himself died in suffering on the cross — whom is he going to redeem? But the idea that "I am going to redeem you, come follow me"... This has been one of the most important factors in destroying humanity — because all religions claim that they are the only right religion, and all other religions are wrong. They have been continually fighting, killing each other, destroying each other.

Just the other day I saw a panel on the TV. A rabbi, a Protestant priest and a Catholic monk were discussing me. And they came to the conclusion ... The rabbi suggested, "It is time now — we should make an effort to have a dialogue with this man." I could not believe it — a rabbi talking to the Catholic priest, suggesting that a dialogue is needed. Why? There were so many rabbis in Jesus' time, why wasn't a dialogue needed with Jesus? Was crucifixion the dialogue?

And this idiot Catholic agrees. He does not even say, "You, being a rabbi, do you believe in dialogue? Then what happened with Jesus? Was crucifixion a dialogue?" No, he does not ask that. Nor does the rabbi wonder what he himself is saying. Jesus was a Jew — it would have been perfectly right for rabbis to have a dialogue with a Jew. If he has gone astray, bring the Jew back on the right path; or perhaps he is right, then you come to his path. But was crucifixion the dialogue? It is not even a monologue!

But now they are all established. The Catholic, the Protestant and the rabbi have no trouble because they are now part of the vested business. And they all know that they are doing the same things, they are in the same business. Jesus was trouble; perhaps dialogue was not possible. It is not possible with me either, but the reasons are different.

With Jesus the dialogue was not possible because he was the messiah — who are you? A dialogue is possible only amongst equals. He is the son of God. Who are you — son-in-law? You have to be something; otherwise what dialogue? No, it was not possible because Jesus was so egoistic that the rabbis knew perfectly well a dialogue was not possible. Once or twice they had approached him.

Once a rabbi asked him, "On what authority are you speaking?"

He said, "On my own authority — and remember, before Abraham was, I am." Abraham was the forefather, the ancientmost; and Jesus says, "Before Abraham was, I am. What more authority do you want?" Now this man is saying, "Blessed are the meek," but he himself is not meek. "Blessed are the poor, blessed are the humble." But what is the reason? Why are they blessed? They are blest because they shall inherit the kingdom of heaven.

Strange argument! Here you lose; there you gain a thousandfold. But what do you gain? — the same things. Here you are poor, there you will be rich. Here you are a beggar; there you will be a king. But what is the qualitative difference? — just here and there: two different spaces. And these people are trying to be meek and humble and poor for a simple reason: to inherit the kingdom of God. Now this man is provoking and exploiting your greed. All the religions have been doing that.

A dialogue with me is also impossible, but for different reasons. First: I don't know myself — about that no discussion is possible — and that is the most fundamental thing to be discussed. What dialogue? Either you have been within or you haven't. If you have been within, then just looking into your eyes is enough — that's the dialogue. If you have not been within, then just looking in your eyes is also enough. The dialogue is finished before it begins.

With me a dialogue is impossible because I am not a scholar. I cannot quote scriptures; I always misquote. But who cares? I don't pay any respect to those scriptures. I don't believe them to be holy. They are just religious fictions, so misquoting from religious fictions is not a problem at all. In fact I have never read them carefully. I have gone through them, here and there, just looking, and even then I have found so much garbage.

So what dialogue is possible with me, on what points? There needs to be a certain agreement, and there is no agreement possible because I say there is no God. Now what dialogue is possible? You will have to prove God, then the dialogue can begin. Or bring God to the witness box; then we can discuss whether he is truly a God or just a phony American.

I don't believe that there is any heaven or hell. What dialogue is possible? Yes, in other religions you can have dialogues because these are the points of agreement. A Mohammedan, a Christian, a Hindu, a Jew — they can discuss God. One point is certain, that God is. Now, the question is only about his form, attributes, qualities — but the basic thing is agreed. They all agree on heaven and hell. Now, it may be that somebody believes in seven hells, somebody believes in five, somebody believes in three. This is only a question of numbers, not so important. With me what kind of dialogue is possible?

When I heard the panel, I started wondering, that if a dialogue has to happen, how is it going to start — from where? There is not a single point of agreement, because all those religions are pseudo, they are not true religions; otherwise there would have been...

With Bodhidharma I can have a dialogue. He says, "I do not know who I am." That's enough agreement. Now we can hold each other's hand and go for a morning walk. Now there is no need to say anything more, all is said.

After nine years, when Bodhidharma was returning to India, he gathered four of his chief disciples and he asked them, "Condense religion into a single statement so that I can know whether you have understood me or not."

The first one said, "Compassion is religion. That is Buddha's basic message: compassion."

Bodhidharma said, "You have my bones, but nothing else."

The second disciple said, "Meditation. To be silent, to be so utterly silent that not a single thought moves inside you: that is the essence of religion."

Bodhidharma said, "You have my flesh, but nothing more; because what you are saying, you are only repeating my words. In your eyes I don't see the silence; on your face I don't see the depth that silence brings."

The third one said, "It cannot be said. It is inexpressible."

Bodhidharma said, "You have my marrow. But if it cannot be said, why have you used even these words? You have already said it. Even saying, 'It cannot be said, it cannot be expressed,' you are saying something about it; hence I say you have only the marrow."

He turned towards the fourth. There were tears in the disciple's eyes and he fell at Bodhidharma's feet. Bodhidharma shook him and asked him again and again, "What is religion?" But only tears of joy, and his hands touching Bodhidharma's feet in gratitude... He never spoke a single word, not even, "It cannot be said, it is inexpressible."

Bodhidharma hugged him and said, "You have me. Now I can go in peace because I am leaving something of me behind."

Now with these rabbis, Catholic priests, Protestant priests, what dialogue! Two thousand years have passed and the rabbis have not apologized yet for crucifying Jesus. He may have been an egoist, he may have been wrong, he may have been teaching something faulty, but nobody had the right to crucify the man; he had not harmed anybody. All that was needed was a gentlemanly argument, but they were not competent enough to argue with him.

Crucifixion is not an argument. You can cut off my head — that is not an argument. That does not mean that I was wrong and you were right. In fact, cutting off my head simply proves that you were incapable of arguing your point. It is always the weak one who becomes angry. It is always the weak who want to convert you at the point of a sword. After two thousand years and still I wonder that not a single rabbi has apologized. Why should they? They think they were right then and that they are right now.

I wonder what kind of Catholic is this priest and what kind of Protestant is this priest who are sitting with the rabbi and discussing me. They should talk first about themselves, about why they are sitting together.

All these people have been egoists. Now, rabbis go on teaching people to be humble but they cannot give an apology. That is impossible. They have not even mentioned the name of Jesus in their scriptures, in their books. You will not find any mention of Jesus, his crucifixion or the birth of Christianity in Jewish sources, no. It is not even worth mentioning. But the same is the situation of other religions. Mohammed says, "I am the only messenger of God. One God, one messenger and one holy book, the Koran — if you believe in these three things, that's enough, you are saved."

That brings me to the second point that all these religions have been against doubt. They have been really afraid of doubt. Only an impotent intellect can be afraid of doubt; otherwise doubt is a challenge, an opportunity to inquire.

They have all killed doubt and they have all forced on everybody's mind the idea that if you doubt you will fall into hell and you will suffer for eternity. Never doubt. Belief is the "in thing." Faith, total faith — not even partial faith will do, but total faith. What are you asking from human beings — something absolutely inhuman? A man ... how can he believe totally? And even if he tries to believe totally, that means doubt is there; otherwise against what is he fighting? Against what is he trying to believe totally? There is doubt, and doubt is not destroyed by believing; doubt is destroyed by experiencing.

They say, "Believe!" I say, "Explore!"

They say, "Don't doubt!" I say, "Doubt to the very end, till you arrive, and know and feel and experience."

Then doubt evaporates by itself, there is no need to repress it; then there is no need for you to believe. You don't believe in the sun, you don't believe in the moon — why do you believe in God? You don't believe in ordinary facts because they are there, but they are not ultimate truth.

A roseflower is there in the morning; by the evening it is gone. Still you "believe" in it; there is no question of doubt. Your belief in a rose flower is a simple belief, not against doubt. Just so that you don't get confused between a simple belief and a complicated belief, I have a different word for it: it is trust.

You trust a roseflower. It blooms, it releases its fragrance, and it is gone. By the evening you will not find it; its petals have fallen and the wind has taken them away. But it was not an eternal truth; you know it as a fact. And you know again there will be roses, again there will be fragrance. You need not believe; you simply know from experience, because yesterday there were roses and they also disappeared. Today again they appeared — tomorrow nature is going to follow its course.

Why believe in God? Neither yesterday did you have any experience of God, nor today — and what certainty about tomorrow? From where can you get certainty for tomorrow? Yesterday was empty, today is empty, and tomorrow is only an empty hope, hoping against hope. But that's what all these religions have been teaching: destroy doubt.

The moment you destroy doubt you have destroyed something of immense value in mankind, because it is doubt which is going to help man to inquire and find. You have cut the very root of inquiry; now there will be no inquiry.

That's why there is rarely in the whole world, once in a while, a person who has the feel of the eternal, who has breathed the eternal, who has found the pulse of the eternal — but very rarely. And who is responsible? All your rabbis and all your popes and all your shankaracharyas and all your imams — they are responsible because they have cut the very root of inquiry.

In Japan they grow a strange tree. There are in existence, three-hundred or four-hundred-year-old trees, five inches tall. Four hundred years old! If you look at the tree, it is so ancient but such a pygmy of a tree — five inches tall. And they think it is an art! What they have been doing is to go on cutting the roots. The earthen pot in which the tree is has no bottom, so once in a while they take up the pot and cut the roots. When you cut the roots the tree cannot grow up. It grows old but it never grows up. It becomes older and older, but you have destroyed it. It might have become a big tree, because mostly those trees are bo trees.

Japan is a Buddhist country, and Gautam Buddha became enlightened under a bo tree. The bo tree is called a bo tree in English too, because under it Gautama Siddartha became a buddha, attained bodhi, enlightenment. The full name is bodhi tree, but in ordinary use it is enough to call it a bo tree. So all those trees are bo trees. Now no buddha can sit under these bo trees. You have stopped who knows how many buddhas from becoming buddhas by cutting these bo trees.

The tree under which Buddha became enlightened was so big that one thousand bullock carts could rest underneath it. It was so big. It is still alive — not the same tree of course, but a branch of the same tree. Mohammedans destroyed the tree. They could not tolerate that a tree exists underneath which somebody became far greater than their Mohammed. They burned the tree; they completely destroyed the tree.

But one of the emperors of India, Ashoka, had sent a branch of the tree as a present to Ceylon with his own daughter, Sanghamitra, who had become a sannyasin. Sanghamitra carried that branch of the bo tree to Ceylon where it grew into another tree, and from that bo tree a branch has been brought back again and put in the place where Buddha became enlightened. It is part of the same tree, but the third generation.

But what these people in Japan are doing shows something significant: it is what religions have done with man. They have been cutting your roots so you don't grow up — you only grow old.

And the first root they cut is doubt; then inquiry stops.

The second root they cut turns you against your own nature, condemns your nature. Obviously when your nature is condemned, how can you help your nature to flow, grow and take its own course like a river? No, they don't allow you to be like a river, moving zigzag.

All the religions have turned you into railway trains, running on rails, from one station to another — and mostly just shunting, not going anywhere but still on rails. Those rails they call discipline, control, self control.

Religions have done so much harm that it is almost incalculable — their pot of sins is full, overflowing. It just needs to be thrown into the Pacific, five miles deep, so deep that nobody can find it and start the same idiotic process again.

The small number of people in the world who are intelligent should get rid of all that their religions have done to them without their knowing. They should become completely purged of Jewishness, of Hinduism, of Christianity, of Jainism, of Buddhism. They should be completely clean. Just to be human is enough.

Accept yourself. Respect yourself. Allow your nature to take its own course. Don't force, don't repress.

Doubt! — because doubt is not a sin, it is the sign of your intelligence. Doubt and go on inquiring until you find. One thing I can say: whosoever inquires, finds. It is absolutely certain, it has never been otherwise. Nobody has come empty-handed from an authentic inquiry.

Chapter 12
Faith is the suicide of intelligence

? *What is the greatest harm that the so-called religions have done to humanity?*

The greatest harm that the so-called religions have done to humanity is to prevent humanity from finding the true religious consciousness. They pretended to be the true religion. All the religions of the world have conditioned the human mind from the very childhood to believe that theirs is the true religion, the religion in which the child has been born.

A Hindu believes his religion is the only true religion in the world; all other religions are false. The same is the case with the Jew, with the Christian, with the Buddhist, with the Mohammedan. They are in agreement on one point, and that is that there is no need to find the true religion; the true religion is already available to you — you are born into it.

I call this their greatest harm because without authentic religiousness, man can only vegetate, cannot really live. He remains a superficial being; he cannot attain to any profundity, authenticity. He knows nothing about his own depths. He knows about himself through others, what they say. Just the way you know your face through the mirror, so you are acquainted with yourself through other people's opinions; you don't know yourself directly. And the opinions that you depend on are of those people who are in a similar situation: they don't know themselves.

These religions have created a society of blind people, and they go on telling them "You don't need eyes." Jesus had eyes — what is the need for Christians to have eyes? All that you have to do is to believe in Jesus; he will lead the way to paradise, you simply have to follow. You are not allowed to think, because thinking may take you astray. It is bound to take you on different paths than they want you to go, because thinking means sharpening your doubt, your intellect. And that is very dangerous for the so-called religions. Those religions want you dull, dead, somehow dragging; they want you without intelligence. But they are clever in using good names: they call it faith. It is nothing but the suicide of your intelligence.

A true religion will not require faith from you. A true religion will require experience. It will not ask you to drop your doubt, it will help you to sharpen your doubt so that you can inquire to the very end.usness,

The true religion will help you to find your truth.

And remember, my truth can never be your truth because there is no way of transferring truth from one person to another. Mohammed's truth is Mohammed's truth; it cannot be yours just by becoming a Mohammedan. To you it will remain only a belief, and who knows whether Mohammed knows or not? Who knows, Jesus may simply be a fanatic, neurotic. That's what modern psychiatrists, psychologists and psychoanalysts agree upon: that Jesus was a mental case.

To declare oneself to be the only begotten son of God, to declare, "I am the messiah who has come to redeem the whole world from suffering and sin" — do you think it is normal? And how many people has he redeemed? I don't think that he was able to redeem even a single person from suffering and sin. He was certainly a megalomaniac.

How can you have faith? Even if a Gautam Buddha knows the truth, there is no way for you to know whether he knows it or not. Yes, you can recognize somebody knowing the truth, if you also know it; then you will have the capacity to smell it. Otherwise you simply believe in public opinion, you believe in mass psychology, which is the lowest.

Truth comes to the highest intelligence.

But if from the very beginning you are taught to believe, then you are crippled, you are destroyed. If from the very beginning you are conditioned to have faith, you have lost your soul. Then you will vegetate, you will not live. And that's what millions of people around the world are doing: vegetating.

What life can you have? You don't even know yourself. You don't know from where you are coming, to where you are going, what the purpose of all this is. Who has prevented you? Not the Devil but the popes, the priests, the rabbis, the shankaracharyas — these are the real devils.

As far as I can see, all these synagogues, temples, mosques, churches — they are all dedicated to the Devil, not to God, because what they have done is not divine, it is sheer murder: slaughter of the whole human mind.

But they have done many other things also. This fundamental harm cannot be done alone, it needs support from many other harms. For example: the religions have demystified the universe. I consider that to be one of the greatest crimes.

Let me repeat, they have demystified the universe, and I consider it to be one of the greatest crimes. They have done it so cunningly, so cleverly that you are not even aware what has been done.

What do I mean when I say demystifying the universe? I mean they have supplied ready-made answers for you. All the religions have a certain catechism. Christians have approached me: "Why don't you publish a small booklet which contains your catechism? Because you have so many books that it is difficult to read them all, to find out and figure out what your message is. It will be easy; just like the Christians have done, you can publish the catechism on a postcard."

I had to tell them, "It is impossible for me because I don't have a catechism at all. You will have to look into my books. You will have to enter into this jungle and you will have to find the message. And I don't know whether you will be able to find one, or whether you yourself will be lost; the second is the more probable possibility."

But all the religions have provided a catechism. What is a catechism? For questions which are unanswerable, they give you answers, even before you have asked. The child has not asked who has created the world; the child is not yet mature enough to ask such a question, but religions catch him before he becomes mature and the question arises. Once the question has arisen, their answer is not going to help.

Once the child asks who has created the world then the answer that God has created the world is not going to help, because the child is bound to ask, "Who has created God? The answer is not an answer because the question remains the same; it is just delayed a little bit — one step backwards. And finally religions say, "God has not been created by anybody." Very strange — because the logic behind their God is that everything that exists needs a creator.

I said to one of my religious teachers — I had to go every week to listen to his crap — "You gave me the logic: everything that exists needs a creator."

He said, "Of course."

I asked him, "Does God exist or not?"

He became alert: if he said that God exists, then he needs a creator — according to his own logic. And where this is going to land is a regress absurdum. You can go on: A created B, B created C, C created D — you can go on and the whole alphabet will be finished, and Z will be standing in front of you with the same question mark. Nothing has changed. The question was bogus; it was not answerable.

But no religion is courageous enough to say, "There are things about which you can ask a question, but don't expect the answer. Life is a mystery." And life can only be a mystery if there are questions which are unanswerable.

But then the religion loses all grip on your neck. If there are questions which are unanswerable, then what have your messiahs and messengers of God and incarnations of God … ? What have all these fools been doing? They have all answered questions which are basically unanswerable, and should be left unanswerable. An honest person, a sincere mind, will accept the fact that yes there is a question but there is no answer.

Hence I say poetry is far more religious than your so-called holy books. Music is more religious than your so-called sermons of great apostles. Painting is more religious because paintings are not answers, they are rather reflections of the mystery that is existence. Poetry does not answer anything for you, it simply reflects: the sunrise, the sunset, a cloud wandering in the sky, a bird on the wing, a rainbow. It does not give you any answers.

A Zen haiku says:

The wild geese fly over a lake.
The lake of course reflects them.

They neither ask, "Please reflect us," nor does the lake say, "Thank you for coming to be reflected in me." The lake is silent, the wild geese are silent; the reflection happens, but not a single word is uttered from either side. Not only that, the wild geese have no expectation that they should be reflected; if they are not reflected they won't feel offended. If the wild geese never come to the lake, the lake will not feel offended, rejected, humiliated. It has never asked, never invited them.

Things happen but there is no why to it. In poetry, painting, in music … Have you ever asked about great music: "What is the meaning of it?" Listening to Beethoven or Mozart have you ever asked, "What is the meaning of it?" Or looking at the paintings of Picasso …

It happened once: an American super-rich millionaire said to Picasso, "I want a few of your paintings."

Picasso said, "But my paintings are very costly."

The man said, "Money does not matter at all. Give me two paintings and whatsoever is the price — I will not ask the price — I will simply give it to you cash."

Picasso was in difficulty because he had only one painting ready right then. He went inside and cut the painting in two, brought out two paintings and sold them.

One of his friends who was sitting and watching the whole scene said, "In the first place the painting was absolutely meaningless; I have never been able to figure it out. In fact it is difficult to know how you manage to find which is the top and which is the bottom, and how you manage to hang it. I have tried it all ways, but it is still beautiful any way you hang it — and that means that it has no meaning. And now you have done a great miracle. You have cut the painting in two, and that man has left with two paintings which cannot be meaningful because each painting is only half — the other half is missing."

"But nobody will ever come to know," Picasso said, "that they are not two paintings. I could have even made it four. I don't know, myself, what it means, but it was such a joy to paint it." And tears were in his eyes that he had to sell it.

These painters, poets, musicians have given the human mind a richness because they do not demystify existence. In the beginning science was moving on the same lines as the so-called religions. In the eighteenth century science was doing the same stupid thing, perhaps because there was only one precedent: religions. It was trying to demystify existence, but soon it realized that the deeper you go into existence, the farther you are moving into mystery.

Soon science realized the great statement of Socrates: "The man who knows less, thinks he knows more; and the man who knows more, knows he knows less. The man who is just an idiot thinks that he knows all, and the man who is really wise knows only one thing, that he does not know anything at all."

As your intelligence becomes more and more mature and you enter into existence from different directions, and you start feeling and living and loving it; it becomes more like poetry, painting, music, dance, a love affair — but not theology. It becomes, slowly, slowly, so much more mysterious that you could never have imagined that you are sitting on immense treasures of mystery. But religions give you ready-made answers.

Existence is there and naturally the question arises, "Who created it?" Remain with the question. Don't accept anybody's answer — because there are peddlers all around: Christians, Mohammedans, Hindus, Buddhists, Jainas, Jews, all kinds of peddlers in search of customers, trying to sell you something which is simply poison and nothing else.

They will say, "God created it," or "Allah created it." Yes, they have given an answer, but do you know what harm they have done? If you accept their answer, your question dies. And with the death of the question, your inquiry dies; now you will never inquire. If you had inquired, I can say with my own authority … And my authority does not depend on the Vedas or the Bible or the Koran, it depends only on my experience, on my inquiry. I say with my own authority that if you go on questioning without accepting anybody's answer, including mine, by and by you will find that the answer is not found but the question disappears.

And that is the moment of feeling the mystery.

Do you see the difference? The so-called religions repress your question; they put an answer on top of it to cover it up, an answer which they give as if God himself has given it. Hindus say that the Vedas were written by God. Sheer nonsense — because in the Vedas there are so many things which have been proved absolutely absurd. If God wrote these absurdities then he should be dethroned.

They will all make their answer important, significant, infallible — as if coming from God himself or from God's son or from his messenger. All these strategies are used to make their answer penetrate your being and condition you so deeply that your question disappears into your unconscious.

The function of a true religion is to discard all these answers, to discard all these authorities and bring out your authentic questioning, your doubts, your inquiries, and help you to go in search of the unknown, of the uncharted. It is a dangerous journey.

Religions have given you comfortable lives, convenient ways of living. But there is no way to live unless you decide to live dangerously, unless you are ready to go into the dark, to seek and search for yourself. And I say to you, you will not find the answer. Nobody has ever found the answer. All answers are lies.

Yes, you will find reality, but reality is not the answer to your question. Reality will be the death of your question. And when your question disappears and there is no answer available, that space is mystery.

A true religion is mysticism.

In the beginning science tried to follow the well-trodden path of the old religions. But science could not go for long on those lines because science had to tackle reality, and religion, so-called religion, is fictitious. So religion could go on living in its fictitious world but science had to encounter reality sooner or later. Not even for one century could it continue with the idea: "Soon we will demystify the whole universe, soon we will come to know everything."

Now, ask Albert Einstein or Lord Rutherford … Ask these people who have penetrated into the deepest mystery of matter, and their statements look like the statements of mystics, and they are now very humble. The old egoism of the eighteenth century and nineteenth century scientist has disappeared from the world. Now the scientist is the most humble person in the world because he knows that it is impossible to know.

We can manage to live better, we can manage to live longer, we can manage to live more comfortably — but we cannot know what life is. That question will remain a question to the very end.

My whole effort here is to help you to become ignorant again.

The religions have been making you knowledgeable, and that is the harm they have done. They hand over to you the whole Christian catechism which you can learn by rote within an hour and can repeat like a parrot, so easily and so simply. But you will not come to know the truth, the real; the one that surrounds you within and without. The catechism is not going to give it to you.

But to drop knowledge is one of the greatest problems, because knowledge gives so much nourishment to the ego. The ego wants all knowledge within its power. And when I say you have to drop knowledgeability and you have to become again a child, I mean you have to start from that point where the rabbi or the priest distracted you. You have to come back to that point again.

You have to be innocent, ignorant, not knowing anything, so that the questions can start arising again. the inquiry becomes alive again, and with the inquiry becoming alive you cannot vegetate.

Then life becomes an exploration, an adventure. Everything starts having a mysterious aroma around it.

Then you cannot just pass by when a roseflower is calling you. What is his perfume if not a call? It is his language: "Please just for a moment be with me. It is too cold here, too alone." You cannot pass by; no child can pass by.

But the rabbi, the pundit, the maulvi, and the scholar are so burdened with books, their minds are so cluttered with junk — all these people are collecting antiques, dead skeletons — that the rose will not be heard. And anyway they know everything. They know even who created God, they know who created the world, they know who created the soul, so what about this poor roseflower?

But ask a poet and the poet can say, "A rose is a rose is a rose." Is that an answer? Is that a question? It is neither a question nor an answer. It is simply a description, a reflection; he is simply saying what he is seeing. He is not quoting scriptures. But there are people who go on ...

I was in Kolkatta some ten years ago, and a man came to me — a famous scholar, a professor of philosophy, Doctor Bhattacharya, a well-known name in the philosophical circles of the world. He asked me, "Can you say something — because this question has been bothering me a lot — is there such a thing as holy language, different from ordinary language?"

I answered, "A strange question — it has never occurred to me. Language is language; what has language to do with holy and unholy? But I can understand your question, because Hindus say Sanskrit is a holy language, a divine language." Hence brahmins, the priests, have kept a monopoly over it.

The large part of Indian society has been deprived of knowing Sanskrit. No woman is allowed to study Sanskrit. For women they have created different scriptures which are just stories, religious stories, just not of any significance. But something has to be given to the women so they don't start harassing them about the real scriptures.

They were not willing to publish, to print, those real scriptures because once they were printed then it would be very difficult to keep a monopoly on them. So for centuries the press was available but the Vedas were not published. It was with great difficulty that the Vedas were published. Then they started saying that they should not be translated into another language, because then all their holiness would be gone. So it took centuries of fighting to translate them, but the brahmins still believe that the translations have lost the quality of holiness. How can the Vedas be written in English or in German or in French? These languages, for the Hindus, are not divine.

But the same is the case with other fools; they are not different in their foolishness. For the Jews, Hebrew is the language of God. When he spoke to Moses he spoke in Hebrew. One of the sins of Jesus was that he was using Aramaic, not Hebrew. Aramaic was the language of the lowest class of people and he was a carpenter's son, not God's only begotten son; otherwise he would have known Hebrew. Even with God he was talking in Aramaic, and this was an unholy act — to use the language of ordinary people.

So I told Doctor Bhattacharya, "I understand your question although it is stupid, but it is scholarly."

He said, "Stupid and scholarly both!"

I said, "There is no contradiction. These people are the same people. Some people call them stupid, some people call them scholars, because who is going to become a scholar other than a stupid person, for what? When existence is available, when life is everywhere vibrant, you are pondering over a book!"

I am reminded ... but of that a little later on. First let me finish with Professor Bhattacharya. I told him, "Yes, you can make a distinction between holy language and unholy language."

You should not be deceived by the name of Professor Bhattacharya. Bhattacharya is the surname of high class brahmins in Bengal, but his father was a beggar, so he became converted to Christianity. And it was through Christianity that this man was brought up in convent schools, sent to the best colleges, sent to the West. He was a Christian, so I told him, "It is simply like this: ordinary people say, 'You son-of-a-bitch.'"

He said, "You are calling me that!"

I said, "No, I am not calling you that, I am simply giving you an example. People say, 'You son-of-a-bitch.' This can be translated into holy language: 'You son-of-the-Holy Ghost' — only this much difference. But I think the first is at least human, true, possible. The second is inhuman, untrue, impossible."

Now, let me tell you what I was reminded of. One of India's greatest poets was Rabindranath Tagore. He is the only Indian poet who got the Nobel Prize. The reason is not that there are not other poets, in fact there are many who are far greater than Rabindranath Tagore, but they write in their own languages.

India has thirty major languages of such tremendously beautiful qualities that they cannot manage to translate them into English. Rabindranath got the Nobel Prize for the simple reason that he could write in English — in the beginning he would write in Bengali, then he would translate it into English — just for that simple reason.

Otherwise in India right now you can find one hundred poets who deserve the Nobel Prize, but nobody will ever hear their names, for the simple reason that the Nobel Prize is not available to those languages in which they are writing.

But Rabindranath, being a very rich man's son, was brought up in England, educated in England, so it was easy for him. Although he himself never felt that what he has written in Bengali has really been expressed in English, he still got the Nobel Prize for one of his books, Gitanjali: an offering of songs. While he was writing Gitanjali it was his usual practice to go on a small houseboat and live on the river, moving alone, and he would stop the boat wherever he liked. Those were the days when he would compose his poetry.

A full-moon night and he was writing about the full moon, the beauty of the full moon, sitting inside the small room in the houseboat, not at all aware that outside the full moon was there. He was in one of the best beauty spots of the river, for miles there was nothing but silence. Once in a while a waterfowl would disturb the silence, but after this disturbance, the silence would become even deeper.

He was unaware — just by candlelight he was writing about the full moon, its beauty. In the middle of the night, feeling tired, he blew out the candle, and as he blew out the candle ... He writes in his diary, "A miracle happened. I was shocked, because as the candle was no longer there, from every nook and corner... " The hut that was on the houseboat was made of bamboos as they are in Bengal. So from every gap in the bamboos the moon started showering in.

For a moment he was struck dumb. He had never seen so much silence. He came out, he saw the moon and he wept. He went back and tore up the poetry he had written about the moon and the light of the moon and the beauty of it, and wrote in his diary: "I was very unfair to the moon, to the silence of the night. My poetry was just rubbish; it could not represent even a thousandth part. The moon was outside just knocking on my door, but I was so involved in writing my own book, I didn't hear the knock. I was talking about silence in my poetry and the silence was so profound outside — I have never before come across such silence, nor since. I would have missed it if I had gone to sleep without blowing out the candle. That small candlelight was enough to prevent the moon from shining in."

These people are full of books and words which are not their experiences. And unless something is your experience, don't go on deceiving yourself. Knowledgeability can be very deceptive; and these religions are responsible for making people knowledgeable.

They should help people to become innocent, they should help them to become ignorant; they should help them to inquire, search, seek. But rather than that, they have given you everything, presented to you on a plate all the answers that you have to find. And what you have lost in receiving their present, you are not even aware of.

You have lost everything. You live a borrowed life because they have told you how to live. They have told you how to discipline your life. They have told you how to control your behavior, your nature, and you have been blindly following them, not understanding a simple principle: Gautam Buddha is born only once. For twenty-five centuries millions of people have tried to become Gautam Buddha — not a single one has succeeded.

A simple fact, and I say it is fortunate that nobody has succeeded; it would have been unfortunate if somebody had succeeded. Nobody could succeed because every being has some uniqueness to him. Gautam Buddha has his uniqueness; you have your uniqueness. Neither has he to follow you, nor have you to follow him. Following creates imitators. The moment you become an imitator you lose contact with your life. That's what I mean when I say that you start vegetating. You are playing somebody else's role; you have completely forgotten your real life.

In my village, every year, the drama of Rama's life is played. Once it happened when I was present ... It was so hilarious, and so meaningful. In the story Rama's wife, Sita, was stolen by Ravana. Rama and his brother Lakshmana both gather armies and go to fight. After three years of Sita being imprisoned in Sri Lanka, they started fighting. Ravana was a great warrior; Rama and Lakshmana were also great warriors, but they were young. Ravana was very experienced; his first arrow hit Lakshmana, and it was known that whoever was hit by his arrow could not manage to survive.

The greatest physician was immediately called to do something. He said, "There is only one possibility. There is a mountain, Arunachal, in south India. On Arunachal there is found a small plant *sanjivani*, a life-giving plant. If within twenty-four hours that plant can be brought here, then there is a possibility; otherwise, after twenty-four hours nothing can be done, the poison will have spread all over" — he was already in a coma.

One of the disciples of Rama, Hanumana, who was a great warrior himself, said, "I will go immediately and I will find it, but just give me an indication — because by the time I reach there it will be night — how am I to find this *sanjivani*, this life-giving plant?"

The physician said, "It is very simple, particularly in the night. In the day it is very difficult to find, but that plant gives off light in the night, so you can find it easily wherever it is. You will find it surrounded by rays as if it is aflame."

In the story, Hanumana is the king of the monkeys and is himself a monkey. All the Hindus say that it is a fact. Hanumana flew — but monkeys can do that, perhaps with a little bit of jumping from tree to tree — I don't know how he managed but he flew. I know how it is done in the drama; a rope is tied to him; the rope moves and he is shown to the public, flying.

When he reached the mountain there was trouble. The trouble was that the mountain, the whole mountain, was aglow with light. Now, Hanumana was at a loss what to do. Which plant was the *sanjivani* — because so many plants were like flames, were they all *sanjivani*? He tried to look; those plants were different ... Now what to do? But he was a crazy devotee — he took the whole mountain!

And in religious stories everything is possible: Jesus walks on water, turns water into wine, turns stones into bread; everything is possible. So he came back with the mountain. But what happened in the drama?

He came in with the mountain — the mountain was made of cardboard — and he was carrying the mountain while suspended by the rope. Somehow the rope got stuck, and he was left hanging in mid-air! The people — at least fifty thousand people, because people would come from far and wide for the drama — were screaming and shouting. Rama was standing there, Lakshmana was lying down in a coma and the physician was sitting with him. The prompter went on telling Rama whatever his part was, so Rama went on saying, "Oh, Hanumana, where are you?" — and he was just above his head — "Where have you gone? Come back soon; otherwise if you are not back before sunrise, my brother will be dead!"

The manager of the drama was at a loss what to do. He ran onto the stage, tried to free the rope somehow, but nothing worked. He was in such a nervous state he cut the rope. Hanumana, with his mountain, fell on top of Lakshmana. Lakshmana stood up, but Rama was still saying what was being prompted: "Oh, Hanumana, you have come at the right time ... "

Hanumana said, "Shut up! You and your brother go to hell! First tell me who cut the rope. I will take care of him first, then the story can start again." And he was a wrestler in the town, so the manager simply escaped, afraid that Hanumana would give him a few fractures.

But I was watching and I saw one thing: although he was acting Hanumana, when he fell from the rope, just in that moment he forgot all about the drama. He said, "To hell with you" — he was saying "To hell" to his God! — "and to hell with your brother! First tell me where the manager is! Who cut the rope? First things first — this drama can wait a little." Of course he was heard by everyone, and the whole fifty thousand people were laughing at him.

The mountain was all in pieces and Lakshmana had already recovered, so there was no need... The physician simply slipped out by the back door. There was no need for *sanjivani* any more — Lakshmana was already standing up and looking at what had happened. They had to drop the curtains immediately and remove all those people from the stage. They changed Hanumana and when the curtain went up it was another person, because that Hanumana was so angry that he said, "Unless I see that manager I am not going to act. I am going to find him, wherever he is."

Just a single hit, and whatever you are — you may be acting a Buddha, a Christ, a Krishna — it will disappear, just by a simple hit on your head. Imitation cannot go to your being; it is going to remain just on the surface. You can practice it for thirty years, forty years ... There are monks who have been practicing for fifty years. There are monasteries,

Catholic monasteries, where once a monk enters, he never comes out; and thousands of people are living in such monasteries. What are they doing? Continually trying, making an effort somehow to become a little bit like Christ; if not the whole Christ, even a partial Christ will do. But that imitation is not going to help. It may give you a pseudo, phony mask, but scratch it just a little bit and you will find the real person is still there. You cannot deceive existence by imitation; you can only deceive yourself

These religions, by giving you ideals — what to do, what to think, what to be — have supplied everything. They have not left anything for you to do; you just have to follow blindly. And if the whole of humanity is functioning in a blind way, it is no wonder.

But who is responsible? All these religions are responsible for making you phony, plastic. They have told you in detail what to eat, what not to eat; when to go to sleep, when to get up — you are absolutely controlled. You are transformed into a robot, and the more you are a robot, the greater saint you are. Then you will be worshipped and will have the respect of your religion. The more you are unreal, the more respectable you are. And if any moment you show your reality, all respect for you will be withdrawn.

It happened when I was in Hyderabad that a Jaina monk, listening to me, became so interested that he dropped his monkhood. He came to the place where I was staying, and I told my host, "He has taken a great step, so be careful — the Jainas will now be murderous towards this man. This same man, they were touching his feet for years, but now they would like to kill him, so just be careful and be protective. I will be leaving after three days, then I will take him with me and send him somewhere where he can live for a few months without being troubled by the Jainas."

But that very day I was going to speak in the Corporation Hall of Hyderabad city, and the Jaina monk insisted, "I would like to come with you."

I didn't see that was any problem, so I said, "Okay, you can come."

But I became aware when I reached the town hall that the whole Jaina community was there. Hearing that I was going to give an address in the town hall, they figured it out, they guessed that the monk would also be coming — "and that will be our chance."

Seeing the situation, I told the monk, "Just come with me onto the stage, and sit behind me on the stage. Now we have to see what happens."

The mayor introduced me, but he was not even finished when hundreds of people stood up and said, "We want that Jaina monk to be removed from the platform."

The mayor was in difficulty. I was his guest and the monk had come with me; he was my guest. So I told the mayor, "Sit down and let me tackle the problem."

I asked those people, "Do you want to touch his feet again?"

They said, "Feet! We will cut off his head!"

I said, "Just see the point. How many years has he been a monk — twenty years? He became a monk when he was only twenty, now he is forty. For twenty years you have touched his feet, you have asked his advice — and just within a few hours you are ready to cut off his head. What has happened? The man is the same. You would have never allowed yourself to sit with him on the same floor, and now you are asking that he should be thrown off the stage and forced to sit on the floor where everybody else is sitting. What change do you see? Can you tell me what has changed?"

They said, "Everything has changed — he is no longer a Jaina monk."

I said, "That is true; he is not in the dress of a Jaina monk, but were you worshipping the dress? I have brought it with me."

I had carried his dress in a bag; he was not even aware of it. I brought the dress out, put it on the platform and said, "You can touch the feet of the dress — this is your monk. That man has nothing to do with you because you have never touched his feet. You need not be so angry that you want to cut off his head. You neither touched his feet, nor do you have to cut off his head. That man is absolutely a stranger to you, but this dress and his begging bowl, these are here. You can do whatsoever you want: if you want to touch the feet, you can. If you want to cut off the head, cut off the head."

I told them, "Can't you see a simple thing: that twenty years of following the discipline... "

And you cannot deceive Jainas because five monks have to live together. No monk is allowed to live singly because you can't trust just one monk; he may find some way to do something, which is not according to the rules. Four are spying on the fifth — in fact they are all spying on each other.

They are not supposed to stay in anybody's house, they can only stay in a temple, because in a house anything is possible. Women will be there, food will be there — and these people are hungry for food, for women, for everything. They are completely hungry.

They must eat only one time a day and they cannot touch a woman. What to say about touch, they are not allowed to see a woman. To avoid seeing them, the instruction is that they should walk looking at the ground four feet ahead, exactly four feet ahead, their eyes slowly becoming fixed to four feet ahead. That's the way they have to walk, so even if they happen to see a woman they will see only her feet, nothing else.

They are not allowed to stay in a house with a family, because, who knows, in the night they may open the fridge. Hungry people are hungry people. In the temple there is no fridge, no food and no water. They are not even allowed to drink water in the night.

I said, "This man was worshipped by you, like a god, for twenty years. Just because today he has thrown off his dress and changed his clothes, you are ready to murder him. You are non-violent people, but you are talking of cutting off his head."

And to the monk I said, "You see these people, all these people have been touching your feet. This was a mutual understanding, they gave you respect; you remained their slave. Become more and more their slave, and they will give you more and more respect. Lose your individuality completely, become phony and they will carry you on their shoulders. But a single moment of reality and they are your enemies."

No, nobody can give a discipline to you. You will have to find it through your own awareness. When people ask me how they should live, what they should do, what they should not do, I simply tell them, "You don't understand me. My single message is be more and more yourself.

The first thing is to be oneself.

And the second thing is to know who you are.

So remain yourself, remain natural. Try to become more and more aware of what this life current is that is running in you. Who is beating in your heart? Who is behind your breathing?

Just become more and more alert — about whatever you do, whatever you think, whatever you feel — just remain alert, a watcher on the hill. And that watching will help you to find the discipline that is your discipline.

The watching will help you to find what to eat and what not to eat, what to do and what not to do. Watching continuously will make you aware to drop many things you are unnecessarily carrying which have become burdens, and to choose only that which is in harmony with you — not a burden, but a relief.

If you live with alertness, you live rightly. If you live in imitation, you live wrongly.

To me there is only one sin, and that is not to be yourself. And to me there is only one virtue, and that is to know yourself.

All the religions have prevented this happening. It is time that we got rid of all this nonsense, which the past has left over our heads.

If you can become Adam and Eve again: no Moses, no Mahavira, no Mohammed, no Jesus, no Confucius, no Lao Tzu ... If you are Adam and Eve, just born, just getting out of the Garden of Eden — nobody to ask what to do, nobody to ask what discipline is right, no priest, no rabbi, no pope is available — what are you going to do?

Do that!

Chapter 13
Ecstasy is knowing that nobody is holding your hand

? *What is more important in your vision of religiousness — to be thyself or to know thyself?*

Do you think they are different? How can you know yourself if you are not yourself? And vice versa: how can you be yourself if you don't know who you are? To be thyself and to know thyself are not two separate things, hence the question of choice does not arise. They are two aspects of a single process.

You have to work on both together, simultaneously; neither can be neglected. But it is easier to start from being thyself, easier because you have been distracted from yourself by others. The masks that you are carrying are not your own imposition. Unwillingly, reluctantly, you have been forced to be someone other than you are; hence it is easier to throw it off.

Slavery of any kind is easier to get rid of, because intrinsically who wants to be a slave? That is not in the nature of any being, human or not human. Slavery is against existence, hence it is easier to throw it off. It always remains a burden, and deep down you continue to fight with it. Even though on the surface you follow it, deep down nobody can make you accept it. At the innermost core of your being it remains rejected forever, hence it is easier to throw off.

The process is simple. Whatever you are doing, whatever you are thinking, whatever you are deciding, remember one thing: is it coming from you or is somebody else speaking? And you will be surprised to find out the real voice; perhaps it is your mother — you will hear her speak again. Perhaps it is your father; it is not at all difficult to detect. It remains there, recorded in you exactly as it was given to you for the first time: the advice, the order, the discipline, the commandment.

You may find many people: the priest, the teachers, the friends, the neighbors, the relatives. There is no need to fight. Just knowing that it is not your voice but somebody else's — whosoever that somebody else is — you know that you are not going to follow it. Whatsoever the consequences, good or bad, now you are deciding to move on your own, you are deciding to be mature. You have remained a child long enough. You have remained dependent long enough. You have listened to all these voices and followed them enough. And where have they got you? — in a mess!

So once you figure out whose voice it is, say good-bye to it, because the person who had given that voice to you was not your enemy, his intention was not bad. But it is not a question of his intention; the question is that he imposed something on you, which is not coming from your own inner source — and anything that comes from outside makes you a psychological slave.

It is only your own voice, which will lead you into blossoming, into freedom.

Yes, the path in the beginning will look dangerous, because you were always holding the hand of your father, your priest, your rabbi, your mother; and when a child holds the hand of the father there is no fear, no danger. He can rely on his father. But now you are holding his hand only in imagination — there is no father; it is pure imagination. And it is better to know that you are alone and there is no hand supporting you, because then you will try to find your own way to protect yourself against dangers.

It is dangerous to go on believing that you are still protected when you are not really protected. That's what has happened to millions of people in the world. They feel they are protected, protected by God, protected by all kinds of things.

There is no God. There is nobody to protect you. You are alone, and you have to accept your aloneness joyously. In fact, it is a tremendous ecstasy that nobody is holding your hand.

My grandfather loved me very much, just because of my mischiefs. Even in his old age he was mischievous. He never liked my father or my uncles because they were all against this old man's mischievousness. They all said to him, "You are now seventy and you should behave. Now your sons are fifty, fifty-five, your daughters are fifty, their children are married, their children's children are there — and you go on doing such things that we feel ashamed."

I was the only one with whom he was intimate, because I loved the old man for the simple reason that he had not lost his childhood even at the age of seventy. He was as mischievous as any child. And he would play his mischief even on his own sons and daughters and sons-in-law, and they would be just shocked.

I was his only confidant because we conspired together. Of course he could not do many things; I had to do them. For example, his son-in-law was sleeping in the room and my grandfather could not go up onto the roof, but I could go. So we conspired together; he would help me, he would become a ladder for me to go onto the roof and remove a tile. And with just a bamboo and a brush attached to it, in the night, touching the face of the son-in-law... He would scream, and the whole house would run there: "What is the matter?" But by that time we had disappeared, and he would say, "There was some ghost or somebody just touching my face. I tried to catch him but I could not; it was dark."

My grandfather remained utterly innocent, and I saw the great freedom that he had. In my whole family he was the eldest. He should have been the most serious and most burdened with so many problems and so many anxieties, but nothing affected him. Everybody was serious and worried when there were problems; only he was not worried. But one thing I never liked — that's why I remembered him this moment — and that was sleeping with him. He had the habit of sleeping with his face covered and I would have to sleep with my face also covered, and that was suffocating.

I told him clearly, "I agree about everything else, but this I cannot tolerate. You cannot sleep with your face uncovered; I cannot sleep with my face covered — it suffocates me. You do it lovingly" — he would keep me close to his heart and cover me completely — "that's perfectly good, but in the morning my heart will not be beating. Your intention is good, but you will be alive in the morning and I will be gone. So our friendship is out of the bed."

He wanted me there because he loved me and he had said, "Why don't you come and sleep with me?"

I said, "You know perfectly well that I don't want to be suffocated by anybody, even if his intention is good. You love me and you would like to keep me close to your heart even in the night." Also, we used to go for a long walk in the mornings, and sometimes in the night when there was a moon. But I never allowed him to hold my hand. And he would say, "But why? You may fall, you may stumble upon a stone or anything."

I said, "That's better. Let me stumble, it is not going to kill me. It will teach me how not to stumble, how to be alert, how to remember where the rocks are. But you holding my hand — for how long can you hold my hand? How long are you going to be with me? If you can guarantee that you will always be with me, then of course I am willing."

He was a very sincere man, he said, "That I cannot guarantee; I cannot even say about tomorrow. And one thing is certain, you will live long and I will be dead, so I will not be here forever to hold your hand."

"Then," I said, "It is better for me to learn from now, because one day you will leave me in the middle, helpless. And if you have trained me to hold your hand, then there are only two ways: either I start living in a fiction: God the father... "

Why do you call God "the father"? Yes, there are two kinds of religions in the world. A few religions call God "the mother," and a few religions call God "the father." The majority of religions call God "the father" for the simple reason that the majority of societies are patriarchal, male chauvinist. But around the world, a very few, small tribes are still matriarchal, where the woman is higher than the man. Naturally God cannot be a man in those societies; in those societies God is the mother.

But no society calls God "uncle." It is strange, very strange, because uncle is an older word than father. Father is not very old; it is a very late addition to language. The further back you go, the more you will find there were societies all over the world — just as it is with other animals, birds — where the mother took care of everything. The father's function was finished once the woman was pregnant.

In fact, in olden days it was difficult to know who the father was. So all the males of the age of the probable father — somebody was the father — all the males of the probable age of the father were called uncle. So uncle is an older word, far more prestigious. Father only came later on when men became very possessive of women.

It came with private property. The word father is joined with private property. When people started having private property — their land, their house — then they wanted to be certain about their son, because he was going to inherit it. Then monogamy became the basic system: you had to marry one woman, and the woman had to remain absolutely surrendered and committed to you so that there was no possibility of her conceiving somebody else's son, and him possessing your property. This whole business of monogamy is a question of economics, not of psychology.

And man kept himself free. He created prostitutes and he created all kinds of ways to get out of monogamy without disturbing the woman. But the woman had to remain absolutely dedicated to the man — not only in life, even in death.

In India the woman had to die with the husband; she had to jump, alive, onto the funeral pyre where her husband was being burned, because the husband was so jealous: "What is the guarantee after I am dead that my wife may not start having some relationship with somebody else?" And the basic problem was that the property he had accumulated — he had earned it, exploited for it, robbed for it — should not go to somebody else; it should go to his own blood.

So if one day you find the father's hand is missing, you start creating a fiction: God the father — who is invisible of course — is holding your hand and he is leading you.

I told my grandfather, "I don't want to be left in the situation where I have to create a fiction to live in. I want to live a real life, not a fictitious life. I am not a character in a novel. So leave me alone, let me fall. I will try to get up. Wait, just watch, and that will be more compassionate towards me than holding my hand."

And he understood it, he said, "You are right — one day I will not be there."

It is good to fall a few times, get hurt, stand up again, to go astray a few times. There is no harm. The moment you find you have gone astray, come back. Life has to be learned through trial and error.

So the moment you start listening to the voices — and they are all recorded exactly as they were given to you — you will be surprised when you try to hear who is speaking to you. You will simply laugh: "Oh, this is my mother. I have not seen her for twenty years, and she is still trying to manipulate me." She may be dead, but from her grave she is still keeping her hand on your neck. Her intention is not bad, but she is crippling you.

I used to tell my father, "Don't give me any advice, even if I ask you. You have to be very straightforward about it. You simply have to say, 'Find out your own way.' Don't give me advice" — because when some cheap advice is available, who bothers to find one's own way?

I had been consistently telling my teachers, "Please remember one thing: I don't want your wisdom — simply teach your subject. You are a teacher of geography and you are trying to teach me morality? What relationship has morality with geography?"

I remember the poor man who was my geography teacher. He was in trouble because I had taken something from the pocket of the student who was sitting by my side. I had taken his money from his pocket and this teacher was telling me, "Don't do that."

I said, "That's not your business. You are a geography teacher and this is a question of morality. If you want, I am ready to go to the principal; you come with me. Nowhere in the geography syllabus ... I have read it and nowhere is it said that you cannot take somebody else's money. And money is simply money; whoever has it, it is his. Right now it is mine.

A few moments before it may have been his but he has lost it. He should be more alert. If you want to give advice, give advice to him.

"In the first place, what is the need to bring so much money to the geography class? There is nothing to buy, nothing to purchase, there is not going to be any shopping. Why did he bring his money here? Then if he has brought the money he should be alert. It is not my fault, it is his fault, and I have simply taken advantage of it, which is my right. To take advantage of situations is everybody's right."

I remember that poor man. He was always in difficulty, always in difficulty with me. He would see me out of class and he would say, "You can do whatsoever you want to do, just don't bring so much philosophy into poor geography. And I don't know anything about philosophy — I simply know about geography. And you turn the question in such a way that even in the night I go on thinking whether it was geographical or religious or philosophical."

Just in front of my school there were two beautiful Kadamb trees. The Kadamb is a very fragrant flower, and I used to sit in those trees whenever I could escape from the classes. That was the best place, because teachers would be passing underneath and the principal would be passing and nobody would be thinking that I might be hiding in the tree — and the trees were thick. But whenever this geography teacher would pass by there, I could not resist dropping at least one or two stones on his head. And he would look up, and say, "What are you doing there?"

One day I said, "This is not a geography class. You disturbed my meditation."

And he said, "What about those two stones that fell on my head?"

I said, "That is simply coincidence. I dropped the stones; it's strange how you appeared exactly at the right time. Now I will be wondering about it. You can also wonder about it, exactly how it happened."

He used to come to tell my father, "Things are going too far." He was a bald-headed man; and in Hindi the word for bald-headed is *munde*. His name was Chotelal, but he was known as Chotelal Munde. Chotelal was rarely used, just Munde was enough because he was the only completely bald-headed person. When just in front of his house, I would knock on the door and his wife or somebody else would open the door, and they would say, "Why do you torture him? You torture him in the school, you torture him in the market, you torture him in the river when he goes to take his bath."

One day his wife opened the door and she said, "Will you stop torturing Munde or not?" and he was just there, behind her.

He grabbed his wife and he said, "You also call me Munde! This boy has spread around the whole city the idea that my name is Chotelal Munde — and now my own wife has been converted by him. I will kill you if you call me Munde. I can forgive everybody else but my own wife, in my own house..."

But I was insistent with my teachers: "Please keep on your track and don't give me any advice that does not belong to your subject, so that I can explore my life in my own way.

Yes, I will commit many mistakes, many errors. I am willing to commit mistakes, errors, because that is the only way to learn."

There is no other way to learn. If you make learning completely foolproof, so that no mistake is possible no error is possible, then you will become a parrot. You may start repeating words, sentences, but you will not know exactly the meaning of what you are saying.

So, first find out the voices within you — and it is simple. Whenever you decide to do something, just sit silently and listen to the voice that is telling you to do this or not to do that. And try to find out whose voice it is. Once you have found it is your father, your mother, your uncle, your teacher, your aunt, your brother, it is very easy; then thank your brother and tell him, "It is so good of you; although you are dead you are still taking care of me. But please, now leave me alone."

Once you have told a certain voice clearly, "Leave me alone," your connection with it, your identity with it, is broken. It was capable of controlling you because you thought it was your voice. The whole strategy was the identity. You were thinking, "This is my voice, this is my thought," hence you were doing what it said. Now you know it is not your thought, not your voice; it is something foreign to your nature. Recognizing it is enough. Just be grateful to your father: "You are still taking care of me but I don't need any more care. You have made me mature enough that now I can start taking care of myself."

Get rid of the voices that are within you, and soon you will be surprised to hear a still, small voice, which you have never heard before; you cannot decide whose voice this is. No, it is not your mother's, it is not your father's; it is not your priest's, not your teacher's ... Then a sudden recognition comes that it is your voice. That's why you are not able to find its identity, to whom it belongs.

It has been there always, but it is a very still small voice, because it was suppressed when you were a very small child and the voice was very small — just a sprout, and it was covered with all kinds of crap. And now you go on carrying that crap and you have forgotten the plant that is your life, which is still alive, waiting for you to discover it.

Discover your voice! Then follow it with no fear.

Wherever it leads, there is the goal of your life; there is your destiny. It is only there that you will find fulfillment, contentment. It is only there that you will blossom — and in that blossoming, knowing happens.

How can you know yourself? — you have not even grown. Perhaps you are still in the seed, perhaps even the sprout was not allowed. Every religion takes care: take the child to baptism immediately, take the child to circumcision, take the child to some Hindu ceremony. And the child knows nothing of what you are doing to him.

Just wait — even for having the voting right he will have to wait twenty-one years; just for third-rate politics he will need twenty-one years of life. But, for religion no maturity is needed? Perhaps forty-two may be the right time for a person to decide about religion. But it is not when the child is born and others are deciding.

Yes, you can take him to the voting. You can give him the vote and you can hold his hand to drop the vote in the box, and you can make him choose the president, the prime minister — but the child is completely unaware of what is happening: what is this box about, and what is this card all about?

But you don't do that. You understand that for politics, at least twenty-one years — at least — are needed for a person to understand. But for religion you don't give any time at all. There is a reason why you don't give any time at all. You are afraid, because if you give him time and you don't mess his mind around before he starts thinking on his own, starts hearing his own voice, then there is no chance for you. You will never be able to make him a Jew or a Christian or a Hindu or a Mohammedan.

He may become someday religious, but that will be his own search. Someday he may find paths leading to silence, ways of moving to the innermost core of existence, but that will be his own exploration.

And remember one thing: whatsoever you find on your own gives ecstasy. Even if God is given to you ready-made, you will not find any ecstasy in it.

And just running on the seashore finding seashells of no value, you can see a child is ecstatic.

I used to come from the river when I was very small. All my pockets ... I used to have many pockets, I insisted on having many pockets. My father said, "It looks crazy. People ask me ... You are continually a trouble and for no reason at all. Why should you have four pockets in front and two pockets by the side?"

I said, "I need them. My needs and your needs are different. I never say to you that you should have so many pockets or that you should not have them; that is your business." I needed pockets because when I went to the river I found such treasures — so many beautiful stones, so colorful, that I was for hours walking on the sands to collect them. And I would come home full — almost double my weight.

My father would see me entering the house and he would say, "This is the use of the pockets? Are you mad or something? Why do you go on bringing all these stones? And we have to throw them out every day."

I said, "You don't understand. You can throw them out, but if you have any understanding of a simple thing ... I feel so ecstatic, so joyous when I see these stones. I am not interested in your money and I am not interested in anything else; I simply collect the stones." But the joy was in exploring for them, finding them far away by the side of the river — just to find one beautiful stone.

One day my father got so fed up that he brought four laborers and told them, "Go to the river and bring as many stones as possible, because he is wasting hours every day." So they brought buckets full of stones. They knew exactly from where to get them — I had no idea that there was a mine — and they poured them out in my small room where I had my own world, where nobody was allowed to enter. My father said, "You can keep all these. Now there is no need to go there because you cannot find anything more. All colors and all kinds of stones we have collected for you.... You waste so much time."

I said, "You have destroyed my joy. It was not the stones; it was my finding them. Now I see this: thousands of stones are here and I don't feel any joy. Take them away. You have destroyed something."

"But," he said, "I thought you loved stones."

I said, "No, there is no question of loving stones, it was the finding. Stones were just an excuse. Sometimes it is stones you are finding, sometimes it is butterflies you are finding, sometimes it is flowers you are finding, and sometimes it is truth you are finding — but remember, the beauty is always in the finding, not what you find. That is just an excuse."

He said, "Whatever is done, it seems difficult to make you happy."

I said, "That's true. Never try to make anybody happy. Nobody can do that. You can make me unhappy — that is possible — but happy? That is simply my absolute right, to be or not to be. You cannot force me to be happy — this is an enforcement. Pouring all these stones in front of me, are you trying to make me happy?"

But it was happening continually about everything. Slowly, slowly they started to understand that this boy seems to be eccentric, so leave him alone.

When I was very small I had long hair like a girl. In India boys don't have hair that long — at least at that time it was not allowed. I used to have very long hair, and whenever I used to enter — and the entrance was from the shop, the house was behind the shop, so to enter I had to pass through the shop — my father was there, his customers were there, and they would ask, "Whose girl is this?"

My father would look at me and say, "What to do? He does not listen." And he felt offended.

I said, "You need not feel offended. I don't see any problem. If somebody calls me a girl or a boy, that is his business; what difference does it make to me?"

But he was offended that his boy was being called a girl. Just the idea of a boy and girl ... In India when a boy is born, there are gongs and bands and songs, and sweets are distributed in the whole neighborhood. And when a girl is born, nothing happens, nothing! You know immediately that a girl has been born because there are no gongs, no bells, no band, no singing, nothing is happening, no distribution of sweets — that means a girl has been born. Nobody will come to ask because it will offend you: you will have to answer that a girl has been born. The father is sitting with his face down ... A girl is born.

So he said, "This is strange. I have a boy, and I am suffering from having a girl." So one day he really became angry because the man who had asked was a very important man; he was the collector of the district. He was sitting in the shop, and he asked, "Whose girl is this? It is strange, the clothes seem to be a boy's — and with so many pockets and all full of stones?"

My father said, "What to do? He is a boy; he is not a girl. But today I am going to cut his hair — it is enough!" So he came with his scissors and cut my hair. I didn't say anything to him. I went to the barber's shop, which was just in front of my house and I told him ... He was an opium addict, a very beautiful man, but sometimes he would cut half your mustache and would forget the other half. You would be sitting in his chair, with his cloth around your neck and he was gone, so you would search. Where had he gone? It was difficult; nobody knew where he had gone. And with a half mustache, where would you go to search for him? But he was the only one I liked, because it took hours.

He would tell you a thousand and one things, unrelated to anything in the world. I enjoyed it. It was from this man, Nathur — Nathur, that was his name — that I learned how the human mind is. My first acquaintance with the human mind came from him, because he was not a hypocrite. He would say anything that came into his mind; in fact, between his mind and his mouth there was no difference! He simply spoke whatsoever was in his mind. If he was fighting with somebody in his mind, he would start fighting loudly — and nobody was there. I was the only one who would not ask, "With whom are you fighting?" So he was very happy with me, so happy that he would never charge me for cutting my nails or anything.

That day I went there and I told him — we used to call him Kaka, Kaka means uncle — "Kaka, if you are in your senses, just shave my whole head."

He said, "Great." He was not in his senses. If he had been, he would have refused because in India you shave your head only when your father dies; otherwise it is not shaved. So he had taken a good dose of opium and he shaved my head completely.

I said, "That's good."

I went back. My father looked at me and said, "What happened?"

I said, "What is the point? You cut my hair with the scissors; it will grow again. I am finished with that. And Kaka was willing. I asked him; he said he was willing: 'Whenever there is no customer you can come and I will shave your head completely, and no question of money.' So you need not be worried. I am his free customer because nobody listens to him; I am the only person who listens."

My father said, "But you know perfectly well that now this will create more trouble."

And immediately a man came and asked, "What happened? Has this boy's father died?" Without that, nobody ...

Then my father said, "Look! It was better that you were a girl. Now I am dead! Grow your hair as fast as you can. Go to your Kaka, that opium addict, and ask him if he can help somehow; otherwise this is going to create more trouble for me. The whole town will keep coming. You will move around the whole city and everybody will think that your father is dead. They will start coming."

And they did start coming. That was the last time he did anything to me. After that he said, "I am not going to do anything because it leads into more trouble."

I said, "I had not asked — I simply go on doing my thing. You unnecessarily interfered."

But I never allowed him to give me advice. And soon everybody understood in my family that I was very averse to advice, because whatsoever they would say I would do just the opposite, to prevent them giving me any advice. I told them, "If you give me advice I will do just the reverse, so just don't give me any advice. I don't want to carry these voices all my life within myself — please leave my mind clean. I want to listen to my own voice, if there is any. If there is none, I am perfectly happy with that. I am happy with my authenticity."

Then slowly, slowly they understood that I should not be interfered with, and there was no point, it created more trouble because I would find a way which was more troublesome for them. Then a time came when I would be sitting in the room, and my mother would look around and say, "Nobody is here. I wanted somebody to go to the market to fetch some vegetables."

I said, "I don't see anybody either. There is nobody; only I am sitting here, there is nobody."

I was not counted as anybody at all — just nobody. She would see me in front of her and say, "I don't see anybody." And she would agree with me: "Neither do I see anybody, the room is empty" — and she would go back to find somebody else somewhere, to send to the market.

The moment they recognized me as nobody ... I can see in myself that since that moment I don't hear any voices. And it must have been at the age of nine or ten that they recognized it. They had to recognize me as nobody; not to count on me in any way, not to depend on me for any work, any small things.

My mother would say, "Go and bring a dozen bananas," so I would go. The market was not far away, just two furlongs; it was a small place. But in those two furlongs I would meet so many people and there would be so many discussions that by the time I reached the market, I would forget what I had come for. And moreover the time was also finished. I had to pick up something quickly because the sun was setting or had gone down long before.

I would come home to ask, "What was it that you wanted?"

And my mother would say, "You are good for nothing. I asked for a simple thing, one dozen bananas, and it took you five hours to come back empty-handed to inquire."

I said, "What to do? There were so many people on the way, so many problems, questions, arguments. By the time I reached the market I had forgotten, so I have come back to ask." They dropped the idea that I could be of any use; but it helped me tremendously. Slowly, slowly in my own house I became an absence. People would be passing but they would pass as if nobody was there. There was no need to say hello to me. There was no need to inquire anything of me.

I remember that since then I don't find any voices. But up to ten they had been trying their hardest, and when I started working on myself I had to pass through all those voices and consciously drop them. It is not a difficult process, you have simply to recognize that this is not your voice, this is your father's voice, your mother's voice, your rabbi's voice, and you have to give a grateful thankyou: "Great of you to follow me up to now, but no more, not any further. Here we part."

And once you are empty of all the voices, only then ... because in the crowd, in the marketplace that you have become inside it is almost impossible to hear your own voice. That is the beginning of being yourself, then much more happens, but that is very natural; you are not to do anything about it.

All you have to do is to negate the voices that have been covering your voice. Once that has happened you start growing your own insight. Slowly, slowly you start becoming aware of problems which you were never aware of before, because you were carrying answers. For the first time you start hearing questions of tremendous importance, which you were not even aware that you had.

And your question, just because it is yours, is significant, because in that very question is hidden the answer.

It has to be your question, only then it carries its own answer. But these so-called do-gooders go on giving you their questions, their answers. Nobody bothers whether it is your question or your answer. In fact, they are afraid that some day you may find your question. The day you find your question all their answers will become invalid, all their scriptures will be rubbish. And they are afraid that by finding your own being you will become an individual.

The society does not want you to be individuals. It wants you to be a Christian, a good Christian, a good Jew, a good Hindu, respectable. But they don't want you to be individuals, because individuals move, act, live in freedom. Individuals would be happy to die, but they cannot be forced to become psychological slaves.

And once you are an individual it is so simple to know thyself, because now you are thyself. Then it is only a question of closing your eyes and seeing who you are.

So don't divide the question into two. Don't ask me what is more important, being yourself or knowing yourself. I can see why the question has arisen, because the famous maxim of Socrates is "Know thyself," and one of the greatest findings of modern psychology is "Be thyself." Hence the question: which is more important?

Socrates is not somebody that you can put into the past. There have been a few people who will always remain contemporaries. Socrates is one of those people who will always remain contemporary. When he says, "Know thyself" he is implying that without being yourself, how can you know yourself? So if you want to know yourself you will have to be yourself; they are two aspects of the same coin.

But to start with, be yourself, because so much has been disturbed in you, so much has been diverted from you, so much has been taken away from you. Your being has been covered in so many layers of personality that you will have to do exactly what you do with an onion: you start peeling it. The moment you peel the onion and one layer is removed, a fresher layer is there. You remove it and there is another, even fresher and more alive. And that's how you are — covered with layers of personality.

The word *personality* is worth remembering. It comes from the root *persona*. In Greek drama the actors used to have masks, and they would speak through the mask.

Sona means sound. *Persona* means sound coming from a mask. You don't know who the person is, you only hear the sound and it is coming from a mask. From this word *persona* comes the English word, personality. It is literally true: your personality is nothing but many, many masks. And whatsoever you say and do is just coming through the mask; it is never truly your own, it has not your signature on it.

So, first drop all personalities.

And you don't have just one, remember. People ordinarily think they have one personality — absolutely wrong. You have many personalities. You have many stored personalities, so whenever you need a different personality you immediately change your mask. You become a different person immediately; not even a moment is lost. It has become almost automatic — the change from one personality to another. And there are so many, you will not even be able to count how many personalities you have.

The more personalities you have, the more sophisticated, respected a citizen you will be in society. Obviously your personalities give you more facilities. They make you capable of functioning in many ways in which others cannot function.

Gurdjieff used to play a game with his disciples. He would be sitting in the middle, one disciple on this side, another disciple on that side. And he had worked tremendously on personalities. He had worked so consciously that he had become capable, as many actors become capable, of showing... From this side of the mouth one disciple would see that he was in a very happy mood, and from that side, another disciple would see that he was very angry and it was not the time to say anything; he might hit you or do something. He was capable of smiling with half his mouth, and the other side would remain very somber and serious. It is difficult to learn, but one can be trained. It is not much of a problem — actors, great actors, are continually doing it.

You see the whole movie; you don't see that one moment the actor has to laugh, another moment he has to cry. While the movie is being filmed, he goes on changing personalities. You see only the story that is presented to you, but what happens to the actor? He falls in love with a woman whom he hates, and shows everything that even a lover may not be able to show: in his eyes, his face, his words, his hug, everything. For that moment he becomes the lover. He takes on the whole personality of the lover of the woman in front of him.

In the second scene maybe he has to cry — and actors become capable of crying, of bringing tears to their eyes. In the beginning they have to use chemicals to bring forth tears, but that is only for amateur actors. Once an actor really becomes capable then there is no need; he simply changes his personality. He brings the face of sadness, sorrow, and tears start flowing. He is not only deceiving you, he can deceive his own chemistry.

All these personalities are continuously moving with you. You are a crowd, many people together, all divergent — many enemies to each other in continuous conflict, fighting, wrestling. That's why you see people in such anguish. Otherwise, there is no reason to be in anguish if you do not have many voices inside you, conflicting, fighting, trying to control all the others — one voice trying to become the monopolist.

Gurdjieff calls them selves; it is the same. You can call personalities, selves or egos, and you can start looking for them — it is a tremendously charming game to look at them. In the evening, you decide that tomorrow morning you are going to get up at five. This you have been deciding for many years, and you know it: that every evening you decide. But this night is different — that too, you know. Every night you have been saying, "This night is different; tomorrow I am going to get up. There is a limit to everything!"

But you have been saying all these things every night. You are not saying a single new thing, but you are not aware of it. And at five o'clock when the alarm goes, you just press the button; and you are angry at the clock. You may throw the clock, turn over and say, "Such a cold morning, and this stupid alarm clock," and you go back to sleep. You are just going for a few minutes... And this has been happening for years.

Every morning, "just for a few minutes," you go back to sleep. When you wake up it is nine o'clock, and again you are repenting, sad, thinking, "How does it happen? I had decided to get up." And you will do it again but you will never see that the personality that decided in the evening must have been a certain personality, and the personality that threw the clock away is a different personality. These are not one personality; they cannot be one personality.

The personality that was saying, "Tomorrow I am going to get up," is no longer on top, is no longer on duty. Somebody else is on top and says, "Forget all about this nonsense," and throws the clock and says, "Go to sleep. It is so cold out — are you stupid or something?" And it feels so warm and good to turn over, and after the disturbance of the clock it feels an even better sleep. And at nine o'clock when you wake up again you are sad. This is a different personality. It has not thrown the clock; it was not the personality who said to you, "Just for a few minutes ... " And this personality decides, "Now, whatever happens, tomorrow morning I am going to get up."

You will do this your whole life, and you will never be able to see a simple fact: you have many personalities, and each time a different personality is speaking, speaks differently, has different ideas.

Just watch it; just watching it is such a great joy, such a great drama that one need not go to any movie. You can simply close your eyes and see the movie that continues there, with so many actors and so many actresses, everything is there that is needed: raw footage, unedited.

But before you can come to know yourself you have to be yourself. You have to drop all these personalities like clothes and you have to come to your utter nudity.

The beginning starts from there, and then the second thing is very simple. The whole problem is with the first thing; the second thing is very simple. When personalities have gone, the crowd has left you, you are alone, close your eyes; you will see who you are, because there is nobody else. There is only awareness of immense silence, of no object.

You will not meet any God there or any soul there or any angel there — all that is fiction. If you meet somebody, remember that you are again hallucinating. If you meet Jesus, throw him out! If you meet Krishna, tell him, "Get out. This is no place for you people, just leave me alone." Only Buddha had the courage to say, "If you meet me on the way, cut off my head immediately."

You have to cut off the head of the Buddha; otherwise you will not be alone — and without being alone how can you know yourself? In aloneness, suddenly out of nowhere, comes the fragrance called enlightenment. You become illuminated, for the first time full of light, all darkness dispersed.

The night is over, the sunrise has happened, and a sunrise that is never going to become a sunset.

Chapter 14
Society crowds you out; meditation outs your crowd

? *Why, in the first place, have people been distracted from their original self?*

Man is born with an unknown, an unknowable potentiality. His original face is not available when he comes into the world. He has to find it. It is going to be a discovery, and that's the beauty of it. And that's the difference between a being and a thing.

A thing has no potential; it is what it is. A table is a table; a chair is a chair. The chair is not going to become anything else, it has no potentiality; it has only actuality. It is not a seed of something. Man is not a thing. That brings all the trouble and all the joy, all the challenges, all the disturbances.

The child comes just empty, with no writing on him, no indications even of what he is going to be — all dimensions are open. This is the first basic thing to be understood: that a child is not a thing, a child is a being.

He is not yet; he is just going to become. He is a process, and there is no possibility to predict where he is going to end, what will be the ultimate outcome of his life's experiences, anguishes, anxieties, ecstasies, what is it going to finally amount to in the end? The final sum total of his whole life is not available in the beginning.

He does not bring a chart with him. All the astrologers have been befooling you, palmists have befooled you, and they could befool you because there was a chance to befool you. The parents are concerned what the child is going to be. And their concern is out of love; hence they can be exploited by all kinds of con men. Those con men can predict, "He is going to be this, or that," but they don't do much harm; they simply exploit a little bit. Their predictions never come true.

The greater problem arises from the priests, from the politicians, from the pedagogues. The politician is not interested in what the real potential of the child is. He is interested that the child becomes a part of his power trip. He has an investment in every child, because every child is a potential friend or enemy. It is good to start canvassing as early as possible. So before the child starts on his own, he is distracted onto a path which is going to fulfill the politician's desire, but which is going to kill the seed in the child himself.

The priest is interested; he has an investment. The pope is a bigger pope if he has more Catholics in the world. If Catholics disappear, what is the value of a pope, who cares about him? Each child that is born has some power, which can be exploited by politicians and priests.

Soon the child is going to become a fully-fledged citizen of the world — he should be grabbed. He should become a Catholic if he is born out of Catholic parents or if fortunately, he is an orphan, then Mother Teresa can look after him and convert him into a

Catholic. They are immensely happy. The more the world has orphans, the more Mother Teresas can get Nobel Prizes, and more orphans means more Catholics. The more poor people in the world... They can be easily converted to Christianity.

Jesus says man cannot live by bread alone. That is true of an authentic man but not true about the masses. As far as the masses are concerned, I say to you, man lives by bread and bread alone. And there are only masses. Where is the authentic man? These politicians, these priests, these pedagogues don't leave anybody to himself so that he can become authentic, so he can get his original face, so that he can find himself.

Everywhere there are people with vested interests in every child. And the child is simply a tabula rasa, nothing is written on him; it is a great temptation for everybody to write something on him. The parents, of course, would like to write their religion, their caste, their philosophy, their politics, because the child should represent them. The child should carry their inheritance.

If they have been Hindus for centuries, the child should be a Hindu, carrying the heritage of Hinduism to future generations. They are not interested in the child's own potential — nobody is interested in it — they are interested in their own investment, and of course everybody is investing.

Parents are investing too much in the child, giving birth to him, raising him, educating him; and everything is conditional — whether it is said or not, that is not the point. They will say one day, "We have done so much for you, now is the time that you should do something for us." They themselves may not be conscious of what they are doing, — because this is how they have been brought up by their parents, generation after generation, the same process.

The teacher is interested that the student should represent him. The religious teacher is interested that the disciple should be a model of his teachings. What I want you to remember is that everybody is interested in the child, for something which the child is not interested in at all.

And the child is very helpless, he cannot fight all these people. They are powerful. He's dependent on them; if they want to make something of him, he has to become that. This much is absolutely clear to the child: if he goes against the parents he is misbehaving, he is betraying them. These ideas are also given by the parents, the priests, the teachers, so he feels guilty.

Any assertion of his own self becomes guilt, and every pretense of the parents, of the religious priests, of the educationists, of the politicians — which is only a pretense — pays very well. The child starts learning politics from the very beginning, to be hypocritical, base — be authentic and you are punished. Now, the child has a simple arithmetic, and we cannot condemn the child.

In my childhood — because from there I can speak to you more authoritatively, I don't know your childhood, I know only my childhood — it was an everyday question. I was continually asked to be truthful. And I said to my father, "Whenever you say to me to be truthful, you have to remember one thing, that truth has to be rewarded; otherwise you are forcing me not to be truthful. I am willing."

Very easily I figured out that truth does not pay — you are punished. Lies pay — you are rewarded. Now it was a question of very decisive, very great importance. So I made it clear to my parents that it had to be understood clearly: "If you want me to be truthful then truth has to be rewarded, and not in a future life but here and now, because I am being truthful here and now. And if truth is not rewarded, if I am punished for it, then you are forcing me to lie. So let this be clearly understood; then there is no problem for me, I will always be truthful."

I don't think that every child tries to figure it out and makes a clear-cut contract with the parents. But this became a contract with my father. Howsoever the truth was against him, his morality, his family, his society, his respect, that did not matter, what mattered was that I was true. And for that I needed immediate reward, "Otherwise next time you know I will say what you want to hear — but remember, it will be a lie."

The day I said this to my father for the first time, he said, "Let me think it over, because you seem to be tricky. You are putting me into a subtle net. You do some mischief and are truthful, and I will have to reward you for your mischief."

I said, "It is your business to decide whether you want me to be truthful or not. Anyway, I am going to do what I want to do. The mischief would have happened anyway. It has happened, only afterwards the question arises to be true or to be untrue. So why bring mischief into it? It has already happened. Now nothing can be done about it. You cannot undo it.

"What can be done is: you can force me to lie, and I can lie. And I can lie with such a face that you will think I am absolutely truthful. I will learn. If that is the way, then let it be the way, but remember, you have been responsible for distracting me from truth because you were rewarding lies and punishing the truth. You can think it over. I am not in a hurry. You are asking me."

What had happened was that, living two or three blocks away from my family was a brahmin family, very orthodox brahmins. Brahmins cut all their hair and leave just a small part over the seventh chakra on the head uncut, so that part goes on growing. They go on tying it up and keeping it inside their cap or inside their turban. And what I had done was, I had cut the father's hair. In summertime in India, people sleep outside the house, on the street. They bring their beds, cots, on the streets. The whole town sleeps on the streets in the night; it is so hot inside.

He was sleeping, and it was not my fault ... He had such a long *choti* — that bunch of hair it is called a *choti*. I had never seen it because it was always hidden inside his turban. While he was sleeping, it was hanging down and touching the street. From his cot it was so long that I was tempted, I could not resist; I rushed home, brought the scissors, cut it off completely, and took it and kept it in my room.

In the morning he must have found that it was gone. He could not believe it because his whole purity was in it, his whole religion was in it — his whole spirituality was destroyed. But everybody in the neighborhood knew that if anything goes wrong, first they will rush to me. And he came immediately. I was sitting outside knowing well that he would come in the morning. He looked at me. I also looked at him. He asked me, "What are you looking at?"

I said, "What are you looking at? Same thing."

He said, "Same thing?"

I said, "Yes, the same thing. You name it."

He asked, "Where is your father? I don't want to talk to you at all."

He went in. He brought my father out and my father said, "Have you done anything to this man?"

I said, "I have not done anything to this man, but I have cut a *choti* which certainly cannot belong to this man, because when I was cutting it, what was he doing? He could have prevented it."

The man said, "I was asleep."

I said, "If I had cut off your finger while you were asleep, would you have remained asleep?"

He said, "How can I remain asleep if somebody is cutting off my finger?"

I said, "That certainly shows that hairs are dead. You can cut them but the person is not hurt, no blood comes out. So what is the fuss about? A dead thing was hanging there, and I thought that you are unnecessarily carrying this dead thing inside your turban for your whole life — why not relieve you of it? It is in my room. And with my father I have the contract to be true."

So I brought out his *choti* and said, "If you are so interested in it, you can take it back. If it is your spirituality, your brahminism, you can keep it tied and put it inside your turban. It is dead anyway, it was dead when it was attached to you; it was dead when I detached it. You can keep it inside your turban."

And I asked my father, "My reward?" — in front of that man.

That man said, "What reward is he asking for?"

My father said, "This is the trouble. Yesterday he proposed a contract that if he speaks the truth, and sincerely... He is not only speaking the truth, he is even giving the proof. He has told the whole story, and even has logic behind it that it was a dead thing so why be bothered with a dead thing? And he is not hiding anything."

He rewarded me with five rupees. In those days, in that small village, five rupees was a great reward. The man was mad at my father. He said, "You will spoil this child. You should beat him rather than giving him five rupees. Now he will cut off other people's *chotis*. If he gets five rupees per *choti*, all the brahmins of the town are finished, because they are all sleeping outside in the night; and when you are sleeping you cannot go on holding your *choti* in your hand. And what are you doing? This will become a precedent."

My father said, "But this is my contract. If you want to punish him, that is your business; I will not come into it. I am not rewarding him for his mischief, I am rewarding him for his truth — and for my whole life I will go on rewarding him for his truth. As far as mischief is concerned, you are free to do anything with him."

That man told my father, "You are putting me in more trouble. If I do something to this boy, do you think things will stop there? I am a family man, I have my wife, my children, my house — tomorrow my house will be burned down." He was very angry, and he said, "Especially now it's a problem, because tomorrow I am going to perform a ceremony in the next village, and people seeing me without my *choti* ... "

I said, "There is no need to worry — I am giving you back the *choti*. You can also reward me with something for giving your *choti* back. Just don't ever take off your turban in the other village, even in the night keep your turban on. That's all. It is not a big problem; it is only a question of one night. And in the night who is going to look for your *choti*? Everybody will be asleep.

He said, "Don't give me advice. I feel like beating you but I know better, because that will create a whole chain of events."

I said, "It has already been created. You have come to complain; you are not rewarding me for being so absolutely honest and sincere, and telling you that I could not resist the temptation. And I have not done any harm to anybody; no violence has happened — not a single drop of blood came from your *choti*. Just by complaining to my father you have already created a chain of reactions."

He said to my father, "Look!"

My father said, "That is not my business."

And I said to my father, "That's what the whole brahminism teaches: the chain of reactions."

My father said, "You keep your philosophy to yourself. And stop going to those lectures of the sadhus and the monks and mahatmas, because whatsoever you get from them, you then somehow manage to conclude such strange things."

I said, "But this is what I am saying, and it is not strange. That's exactly what the theory of karma is: you do one act, the reaction will follow. He has done an act of complaining against me, now the reaction will follow."

And the reaction followed, because he had told me that he was going to the other village. He was very angry with me, but when you are angry, you are angry — and he was really completely freaked out. So he was angry with his wife, with the children ... I watched everything, and he somehow managed to get his things together and went off in a horse buggy.

The moment he left, I told his wife, "Do you understand where he is going? He is going forever — and you don't know. He had come to say this to my father, that he is going forever and he is not coming back."

The wife suddenly started crying and screaming, "Stop him!" Other people ran and they stopped his buggy.

He said, "Why are you stopping me? I have to catch the train!"

They said, "Not today. Your wife is crying and beating her heart — she will die!"

He said, "But that is strange. Why should she beat herself, and why should she cry?" But the people would not allow him to go, and they were pulling at his bag and suitcase.

The man who was driving the buggy said, "I will not take you. If this is the situation, that you are leaving your wife and small children forever, I will not do such an act ... small children."

The brahmin said, "I am not leaving, I will come back, but right now I don't have time to convince you. The train will be missed, because the station is two miles away from my house."

But nobody was listening to him, and I was provoking people: "Stop him, otherwise his wife, his children ... you will have to look after them. Who is going to feed them?"

They brought him back with his bags, and of course he was angry and threw the bags at his wife. His wife asked, "What have we done? Why are you ... ?" And I was there outside in the crowd.

He said, "Nobody has done anything. That boy told me there would be a reaction. The reason is that three days before, in the temple, I was teaching the philosophy of action and reaction and this boy was present there. Now he is teaching me." He told me, "Forgive me and I will never say a single word about this action and reaction. And you can cut off anybody's *choti* if you want, I will not complain. You can cut off my head and I will not complain — because I want to stop this chain completely. My train has gone."

Then everybody asked, "What is the matter? We don't understand. Who has cut off your *choti*?

I said, "Look! The chain is impossible to stop. These people are asking, 'Whose *choti*? Who has cut it off? Where is the *choti*?'" I said, "Just look inside his turban." And a man who was considered to be a wrestler in the town came up and took off the turban and the *choti* fell out.

My father was also there, and saw it. When we were returning home he said to me, "I will reward you but don't take advantage of our contract."

I said, "I am not. It is not a contract between me and you. My contract is that I will always speak the truth to you, and you will reward me for it." And he remained consistent. Whatsoever I had done, howsoever wrong in his eyes, he continually rewarded me. But it is difficult to find a father like that — the father has to forcibly impose his ideals on you.

My father was condemned by the whole city: "You are spoiling the child."

He said, "If that is his destiny, to be spoiled, let him be spoiled. I will not be responsible for interfering in his destiny; he will never be able to say, 'My father spoiled me.' And if he is happy with being spoiled, then what is wrong in being spoiled? Wherever, and whatsoever happens in his life, I don't want to interfere. My father interfered with my life, and I know that I would have been a different person if he hadn't.

"And I know that he is right, that every father turns the child into a hypocrite, because I have been turned into a hypocrite. When I want to laugh, I am serious. When I want to be serious I have to laugh. At least let one person laugh at the time when he wants to laugh. And let him be serious when he wants to be serious." He said, "I have eleven children but I think of myself as having only ten." And he always thought that he had only ten. He never counted me among his children because, he said, "I have given him total freedom to be himself. Why should he carry any image of me?"

In a better society ... and when I say in a better society, I mean a society which understands each person's integrity, respects even a small child's being, and does not impose on it. But that society seems to be far, far away, because all people have got their vested interests, and they cannot stop their trips; they have to use and exploit people.

Somebody becomes a president; you never think that he has become president at your cost, that something in you has been killed so that this man can become the president of the country. If everybody was left unique, original, it would be impossible for the people who are presidents and prime ministers, who are ruling the whole world and who have been destroying the world for thousands of years and go on destroying it, to continue doing this.

With individuals there will be totally different kinds of societies: there will be communes, not societies. There will be no nations, because there is no need.

What is the need of nations? The whole earth is one. Only on maps do you go on drawing the lines, and over those lines you go on fighting and killing and murdering. It is such a stupid game: that unless the whole of humanity is mad, it is impossible to think how it goes on continuing. What is the need of nations? What is the need of passports and visas and boundaries? This whole earth belongs to us and wherever one wants to be, one has the right to be there.

The sun is nobody's property, the earth is nobody's property, the moon is nobody's property; the wind, the clouds, the rain — nothing is anybody's property. Why do you draw these lines?

You can understand it easily; soon you will see lines on the moon. Right now there are none, but soon you will see a Russian zone, an American zone, a Chinese zone. Nobody lives there; nobody will ever live there. There seems to be no possibility of life growing on the moon. The moon is a dead planet — not a single drop of water. Yes, you can be there for a few hours with all your gas masks and oxygen cylinders and everything, but this is not the way that people can live there. But already they have put their flags ...

There is nobody to see the flag, there is nobody to salute the flag — not even a bird sometimes, to shit on the flag! The first thing the Americans did was to place a pole, and put up the flag. How idiotic, and for whom? But soon other fools will follow. They will go to Mars, they will go to other planets, and they will do the same thing everywhere.

There is no need for nations, except that politicians need nations because without nations there will be no politics; except that generals need nations because without nations there will be no wars; except that the factories that produce weapons will go out of production. What will happen to your nuclear weapons plants and all the energy involved in them? If there are no nations there is no need to create nuclear weapons, for whom?

The simplest solution to save humanity is to remove all the lines from the map, and just from the map — on the earth there are no lines. Just simply remove all the lines from the maps and you won't have a Third World War, and you will not need so many armies all around the world.

Millions of people are doing nothing except turning left, turning right ... If somebody is watching from above, he will be surprised. Why do people go on turning right, then left, then about turn, then march, then come back, disperse? Every day millions of people all around the earth ... He will certainly think something is wrong — some nut, some bolt, needs to be put right.

These nations can exist only if your personality is false. These churches and religions can exist only if you don't have your original face — because a man who has his original face, what business has he to do, that he needs to go to the pope? For what? There is no reason he should go to any religious teacher or to any temple or to any synagogue. And why should he become a Mohammedan, a Christian, a Hindu? Why?

With your original face you will feel so contented, so immensely fulfilled and at home, that there is no search left; you have found it. But these people will not allow you to find it. They will distract you, for the simple reason that they have some trips, they have some ideas of their own, and you have to be sacrificed for their ideas. Politicians will sacrifice you for their politics. Religions will sacrifice you for their kind of politics. Nobody is interested in the child, and the reason is clear: the child has to be molded into a certain pattern, which fits into a society, into a nation, into a particular ideology.

In Russia the child had to be taught communism from the very beginning. He had to know the names of Karl Marx, Friedrich Engels, Lenin — they are the communist gods. In non-communist countries it is the same thing only the names differ. Everybody is sacrificed to some stupid ideology, theology, politics, religion. That's why people get distracted.

But the child allows it for the simple reason that he does not know who he is going to become. Naturally he depends on his parents, elders: those who know better. And he is not aware that they don't know better; they are in the same boat, as ignorant as the child. The only difference is the child is innocent also. They are cunning but ignorant, and just because of their cunningness they go on hiding their ignorance in borrowed knowledge.

My grandfather used to take me to any mahatma, any saint, and he used to say to me, "If you don't come then I am not going, because then it is so dull. You make it alive." And I was simply raising very simple questions. What can a child do?

One Hindu monk, Swami Vidyananda used to come to the town every rainy season. For four months he lectured there — he was a well-known teacher. The first day I went with my grandfather, I simply stood up, and because of my grandfather nobody could throw me out or tell me to sit down.

Everybody knew about him, that he was a dangerous man in that matter. If anybody said, "Boy, sit down, you don't understand such great things," my grandfather would say "But I don't understand either, and I am seventy years old. So you keep quiet, understand! And he would tell me, "Ask."

It was clear that they could not throw me out, they could not stop me, so I simply asked Vidyananda, "One thing I want to know about what you are saying: is it borrowed or experienced? Now, remember that you are sitting in the temple of God." It was a Rama Mandir, the best place in the town, the most precious temple of the town with a very beautiful marble hall — so all the best discourses were arranged there.

I told him, "Look at the statue of Rama; and remember that you are in a sacred place and remember your robe, that you are a monk. Don't disgrace your robes and don't disgrace your God; just say the truth — whatever you are saying, has it been experienced? Do you know God? Have you seen God just the way you are seeing me? Have you talked with God the way you are talking with me? Or have you just learned from the books?" There was a great silence. The man hesitated.

I said, "Your hesitation says everything. You better tell the truth because if you have seen God, why should you hesitate? You feel a little afraid — I can see perspiration on your forehead, and it is cool inside."

The man said, "I have never thought about it. But being a sannyasin and being in the temple of God, I cannot speak untruthfully. I have no experience. I am saying whatsoever I have heard and read and studied."

Then I said to him, "Get out! Get out from this place immediately. Then find a person who himself has known, and bring him here. You are throwing borrowed rubbish on these poor people's heads, and giving them the idea that they also know — because I know these fools, they are all from my own town, and they talk as if they know."

And I told the people, "Listen to your guru!" He was the guru of almost the whole city, because for years — he must have been sixty at that time — for years he had been visiting the town for four months every year. But that was the last time. Since then I have not heard about him.

When I was traveling in India I went on inquiring about what happened to Vidyananda, whether he died or he was still alive — what happened? Finally I met him in a place I had never expected, near Madras, in Adyar. Adyar is the headquarters of the Theosophical Movement. I had gone to deliver a few talks in Chennai, and my host wanted to go and see Adyar. Adyar is beautiful: the theosophists had done a really good job. They had made a beautiful place, but it is now lying deserted, nobody goes there. They had made beautiful houses, cottages, a great garden — a whole colony.

Adyar has perhaps the biggest bo tree. When the Theosophical Movement was alive, they used to have their conventions underneath that bo tree; thousands of people can sit under its shade. And Adyar has perhaps one of the most precious libraries in the world. Theosophists had collected manuscripts from China, Tibet, Ladakh, Mongolia,

Korea — strange places, strange languages — and they have a very great underground library of ancient scripts. I found this man there in the library; he was working as a librarian, but he was no longer a monk.

I asked him, "What happened?"

He said, "That day you changed my whole life. After that I could not speak with the same authority as I had before. I lost my courage. I tried, but every time the question arose in me that I don't know, so why am I telling these people? Perhaps it is not right, perhaps it is right — who knows? I am committing a sin, because these people will start thinking that they know. That day in your city... "

He had not been able to recognize me. I had to remind him because he had last seen me as a child. I could recognize him, although by then he was near-about ninety — but from sixty to ninety years nothing much... Yes, you become older, but no basic change happens. He was older, fragile, but in a way younger, more alive.

I said to him, "You are thirty years older now, but I can see your eyes are younger, more alive."

He said, "Yes, because I have dropped that life of phoniness. Now I am simply what I am. I don't know — I am searching but I don't know that it will be possible to know in this life, because so much is lost.

I said, "Don't ever be pessimistic. It can happen any day — it can happen today. If it is not happening that means that somewhere you are still carrying the borrowed. Can I ask you another question again, after thirty years?"

He said, "I will be obliged because that first question has done me a great service. It has taken away my monkhood, my mahatma-hood, my followers — everything."

I said, "Why did you start working in the library as a librarian? — because again this is the same kind of business. Now you are searching in ancient scripts found in Tibet, found in Ladakh, found in Nepal. You are still not looking into yourself. First you were searching for truth in printed books, now you are searching for it in hand-written ancient scripts, thinking that these people must have known. But again you are doing the same foolishness. Neither the printing press knows... It goes on printing Bible after Bible — millions of Bibles — and the printing press remains just a printing press; it does not even become a Christian.

"And do you think you will be able to find the truth, in handwritten scripts? These people were just working as writers. They were simply copying, and they were being paid for it. It is not that they were knowers, they were copiers, and they were doing a primitive method of printing. In those days printing was not possible so people used to write, copying from one manuscript to another manuscript, and from that to another manuscript, and they would sell them. Do you think these people knew?"

He said, "Again you are right. I have been here for twenty years in this underground library, looking into all kinds of strange methods, ideologies — very impressive, very logical — but certainly I am doing the same thing; I am not looking in. So from now on you will not find me anywhere."

He dropped his job that very day. While I was still in Adyar he left. When I came back after walking around ... It is a big place and once it was a very throbbing commune; when Annie Besant was alive thousands of people lived there. When I came back to the main office and inquired about Vidyananda they said, "He has left. What have you told him? — because after you met him in the library he came into the office and he said, 'I am leaving, and leaving forever. I am finished with books. Although I am much too old ... But perhaps a few days may be enough, or at least before I die I should begin rightly. Perhaps in the next life I can complete my search, but at least I should begin.'"

Nobody is asking, "What do you know, is it your knowledge?" If it is not your knowledge, put it aside, it has no value. "What you are doing, is it your aspiration? Do you really feel a bell ringing in your heart?" If it is not so then don't waste a single moment more.

People go on doing things which other people have forced them to do — and people are going to continue to force them. It is most improbable that parents will stop forcing their children to be just images of their own ideas, that teachers will stop forcing on them whatsoever they know — as if they really know, but they will go on pretending they know.

My principal in high school was a mathematician. I was not a student of mathematics but I used to go to his office whenever I saw that he was alone and talk about higher mathematics — because now the older mathematics is not applicable any longer to physics, biology, chemistry, biochemistry. They are going beyond it. So he told me, "Why don't you start attending my classes?"

I said, "I have no problem, I am not a student of mathematics, but whenever I am free and you have a class I would love to come if you allow me. But then don't get disturbed by me because I will not just be dead there, I will be alive."

He said "What do you mean by being alive?"

I said, "Exactly what it means: being alive. Just give me a chance and see."

I was always interested in many things, trying to find out whether they were really based on knowing or were only hypothetical — because if they were hypothetical then they were not really true; they were just pragmatic, helpful, convenient. For example, Euclidian geometry — that's the class he was teaching when he allowed me for the first day... Now Euclid's definitions — even a child can see that they are wrong. Euclid says: "A line has length but no breadth." Now, without breadth, how can a line be? It is so simple, one does not need to be a mathematician.

I am not a mathematician, and I was not at all at that time. And I said to him, "This is stupid what you are saying, that it has length but no breadth — it does have breadth. Draw a line on the board without breadth, just with length, then I will accept your hypothesis."

He said, "Now I know what you mean by being alive. I have done post-graduation mathematics and this question never came to my mind. Euclid says so; every school, every college, every university teaches it, so I never thought... But perhaps you are right. I can see, there is... "

And I said, "It is measurable. With the chalk you draw a line on the blackboard, and still you're saying that it has no breadth. 'And the point' Euclid says, 'has neither length nor breadth.' Then how can it be? It may have a very, very small length, a very, very small breadth, but that does not mean that it has none. You just need a magnifying glass. Just wait and I will run to the chemistry lab and bring the magnifying glass and show you.

He said, "There is no need to go; I can understand. But then what am I to teach? Euclid is finished, because these are basic definitions."

I said, "These are hypotheses. You have to accept just one thing: that these hypotheses are practical, but not truth."

So you have to find out about whatsoever you know: whether it is just hypothetical, useful in life, or really a truth that you know, that you have felt, that you have experienced. If it is only a hypothesis, put it aside and you will feel such an unburdening. All hypotheses, all borrowed knowledge that has gathered there and which you are carrying — you are dragging a mountainous load, you are being crushed under it — just put it aside.

Be ignorant; accept that "I am ignorant." And from that point you can start the search.

Every child is going to be burdened. I hope that someday it will not be so. In fact there is no need, because when you are teaching Euclid, you can teach very simply that this is not truth, it is only a hypothesis. With this hypothesis it becomes easier to understand the triangle, the circle and everything. But remember that at the base there is a hypothesis, and the whole palace is hypothetical.

Similarly, your God is a hypothesis and the whole pyramid of theology is based on nothing but that hypothesis. If you start looking into things it does not need great intelligence, it needs only simple innocence to see.

That principal called me into his office and he said, "You are not to come again to my classes because now it will be difficult for me to deal with the children. They have seen me as ignorant and up to now I was an authority. You destroyed that." But he was a sincere man in a way. He said, "I can understand you, but don't do it to any other teacher, because they may not understand it. And now I know why so many complaints go on coming against you: that you are a disturbance. But this was not a disturbance. You have opened my eyes; I will never again be able to be the same. But what puzzles me is that I never thought about it, I simply accepted it."

And that's the point I want you to notice. You have accepted everything up to now; what they have said, you have accepted. You have to start questioning, doubting. Don't be afraid of authorities; there is no authority. Krishna or Christ, Mohammed or Mahavira: nobody is an authority. And if they are an authority, then they are an authority to themselves, not to you.

You will be an authority only to yourself if someday you come to know the truth of your own original face. Then too, you will not be an authority to somebody else. Nobody can be an authority to anybody else. This whole idea of authority has to disappear from the world. Yes, people can share their experience, but that is not authority.

I don't want to force anything on you — not a single word, not a single concept. My whole effort is to somehow make you alert and to beware of all authorities. And the moment you see there is some authority hanging around your being throw it out.

Be finished with all that has been given to you, forced upon you, and the original face will start showing up. You never know, you cannot even imagine what your original face will be, what your true being will be. You will know only when you know, when you are face to face with yourself, when there is no hindrance of any kind and you are left totally alone.

In that aloneness have flowered all the beings that have flowered.

Not many have flowered. Only once in a while... It is a strange tragedy that millions of people are born and only once in a while a person blossoms. That's why I say there is no gardener, no God looking around, watching, caring — otherwise millions of trees and only one tree comes to flower ... ? Spring comes and goes and only one tree blossoms; millions of trees simply remain barren, unproductive. What kind of gardener is looking after the garden?

This is enough proof that there is no gardener, no God, but that does not mean that you have to become pessimistic. In fact that gives you a new dimension: that you have to be your own gardener. It is good that there is no God, because you can be your own gardener. But then the whole responsibility is yours; you cannot blame anybody.

I am taking God away, so that you cannot blame the poor old man. He has been blamed enough for everything: he created the world, he created this, he created that. I take all that blame away from him — he does not exist.

You have created him just to throw your responsibility on him. Take your responsibility back.

Accept your aloneness. Accept your ignorance.

Accept your responsibility, and then see the miracle happening.

One day, suddenly you see yourself in a totally new light, as you have never seen yourself before. That day you are really born. Before that it was only a pre-birth process.

There are reasons why people have been distracted from their originality. First, you don't know what your originality is. Second, there are people who are in a hurry to impose some idea of their own on you, because once that idea is imposed, you are psychologically enslaved.

A Christian cannot find truth, a Hindu cannot find truth, because Christianity is a prison, Hinduism is a prison; somebody is burdened by the Koran and somebody else is burdened by the Torah.

So it is not a question of what has to be thrown out, whatever it is. That's why with me, a Jew, a Christian, a Hindu, a Mohammedan, a Jaina, a Buddhist, a Parsi, a Sikh ... Anybody can find something transpiring in him, because what I am saying is applicable to all.

Whether you are burdened with the Bible or the Koran makes no difference. I am not interested in you throwing away the Bible; I am interested in you throwing away any kind of garbage that you are carrying. And I call it garbage because it has been given to you by others; it is not yours.

Remember it: only what you experience is yours.

What you know, only that you know. Let it be very small, don't be worried; seeds are very small, but a seed has potentiality. It is not a thing, it is a being who is ready to burst forth — it just needs the opportunity.

And that's what to me the function of the master is: to create the opportunity. Not to give you knowledge, not to give you discipline, not to give you a doctrine or a dogma, but to create an opportunity where all these things slowly, slowly disappear. They are not clinging to you, you are holding onto them hard.

So when I say they disappear, I mean slowly, slowly you open your fist. Of course you take time because for so long you have thought that you are holding something precious, but even if you understand me, again and again the idea comes that perhaps if you drop it you may lose something precious. But there is nothing precious there.

Remember one criterion: anything precious is only that which you know, and there is no way to lose that which you know. Anything that can be lost, and which you have to cling to, cannot be precious because it can be lost. That shows that it is not your experience.

So we have to accept that the society is going to continue the way it has continued, but we can find intelligent people and take them out of the society. That's what I mean by sannyas.

People cannot understand it because they think that I am trying to create a certain religion by giving you a certain atmosphere to meditate, a certain identity. No, I am not creating any religion. It is absolutely religionless religion.

This atmosphere I am giving you is simply so that you start having a distance from the crowd, so that the crowd pushes you out and does not allow you in. Otherwise you would like to be inside. Who wants to be outside the crowd? It is so cozy there, so warm.

I give you this simply as a strategy, a device so that people will avoid you; wherever you go, people will turn away. That's the only way to save you; you cannot mix with the crowd. Otherwise it would have been easier for me and easier for my sannyasins if I had not made you seem so different from other people. Many more people would have come around me more easily. But I am not interested in many more people. I am not a politician, I am not a pope; what do I have to do with many people?

I am interested only in those chosen few who are intelligent, courageous, capable of coming out in the cold and dropping the coziness of the crowd and the mob. Only in the beginning it feels cold; soon your body has its own system of creating warmth. Your being soon starts creating its own aroma.

So we have to go on pulling people from the crowd, and continue to destroy whatsoever the crowd has given to them, because when you pull a person out of the crowd that person brings the crowd in his mind. You can pull the person out of the crowd very easily — it is not so difficult — but the person brings the crowd in his mind. Then the second part of the work is more difficult: to push the crowd out of his mind.

Both things have to be done: pull the person out of the crowd, and then push the crowd out of the person, so he is simply left alone.

And to me there is nothing greater than to be left utterly alone, in your pure, essential being-hood.

Chapter 15
They say believe; I say explore

? *Is it possible for a politician to be an authentically religious man,
or for an authentically religious man to be a politician?*

I t is absolutely impossible for a political man to be authentically religious, because the ways of politics and authentic religiousness are diametrically opposite. You have to understand that it is not a question of adding something to your personality — authentic religion is not an addition. If you are political, you can be a painter, you can be a poet, you can be a musician — those are additions.

Politics and music are not diametrically opposite; on the contrary, music may help you to be a better politician. It will be relaxing, it will help you to get unburdened of the whole day and the anxieties that a politician has to go through. But religiousness is not an addition; it is a diametrically opposite dimension. So first you have to understand the political man, exactly what it means.

The political man is a sick man, psychologically sick, spiritually sick. Physically he may be perfectly okay. Usually politicians are physically okay; their whole burden falls on their psyche. You can see that. Once a politician loses his power he starts losing his physical health. Strange, when he was in power, he was so burdened with many anxieties and tensions, but he was physically perfect.

The moment power has gone, all the anxieties have also gone; now, they will be somebody else's business. His psyche is unburdened, and in that unburdening all his sickness falls on his body. The politician suffers, as far as his physiology is concerned, only when he loses power; otherwise politicians tend to live long, and are physically well. Strange, but the reason is that their whole sickness is taken by their psyche, and when the psyche takes on the whole sickness, then the body can live unburdened. But if the psyche releases all its sickness, where is it going to go? Lower than the psychic is your physical existence — all sickness falls onto the body. Politicians out of power die very soon. Politicians in power live very long. It is a known fact, but the cause is not well known.

So the first thing to be understood is that the political man is psychologically sick, and psychological sickness tends to become spiritual sickness when it becomes too much, when the psyche cannot hold it any more. Now, be careful: if the politician is in power, then his psychic sickness is bound to spread to his spiritual being, because he is holding his psychic sickness so it does not fall downward. It is his power, he thinks it is his treasure; he won't allow it to fall down.

I am calling it sickness. To him it is his whole ego trip. He is living for it; there is no other purpose for him. So, when he is in power he holds his sickness tightly, but he does not know anything about the spiritual realm, so those doors are open. He cannot close those doors; he has no idea that there is something more than his mind. When he is in power, if his psychological sickness is too much, after a certain point it overflows his psyche and reaches to his spirituality.

If he is out of power then he tends not to hold all that stupidity. Now he knows what it was, now he is aware that it was nothing worth holding. And anyway there is nothing to hold; the power has gone, he is a nobody.

Out of desperation, he relaxes — perhaps I should say, relaxation comes to him automatically. Now he can sleep, he can go for a morning walk. He can gossip, he can play chess; he can do anything. Psychically he finds himself loosening. The doors that he had kept closed between his psyche and the body start opening, and his body is bound to suffer now: he may have a heart attack, he may get any kind of sickness; everything is possible. His psychic sickness will flow to the weakest part of his body. But in power it flows upward, toward his being, of which he is unaware.

And what is the sickness? The sickness is the inferiority complex. Anybody who is interested in power is suffering from an inferiority complex; deep down he feels himself worthless, inferior to others.

And certainly in many ways everybody is inferior. You are not a Yehudi Menuhin, but there is no need to feel inferior because you never tried to be, and that is not your business. Yehudi Menuhin is not you either; so what is the problem, where is the conflict?

But the political mind suffers from a wound of inferiority, and the politician goes on scratching the wound. Intellectually he is not an Albert Einstein — he compares himself with giants — psychologically he is not a Sigmund Freud. If you compare yourself with the giants of humanity you are bound to feel completely shrunk, worthless.

This worthlessness can be removed in two ways: one is religiousness, meditation; the other is politics. Politics does not really remove it, it only covers it. It is the same sick man, the same man who was feeling inferior, who sits as a president. But just sitting on a chair as the president, what difference can it make to your inner situation?

My first conflict with Morarji Desai happened exactly in such a situation. One of the great Jaina monks — great to the Jainas, not to me, to me he is the phoniest person you can find, in fact it is very difficult for me to compare him with any other phony person, he will defeat all — had called a religious conference. That was their annual celebration, the birthday of their founder. Morarji Desai was invited. I was also invited. There were at least twenty guests from all over India, from every religion, from every direction of thought and ideology, and at least fifty thousand of Acharya Tulsi's followers.

Before the meeting, Acharya Tulsi greeted the guests, those twenty special guests. It must have been 1960, in a small, beautiful place in Rajasthan, Rajsamund. It has such a beautiful lake, so big and vast, hence the name, Rajsamund. Samund in Rajasthani means the ocean, and raj means royal. It is so beautiful that the name suits it exactly. It is a royal ocean, very emperor-like. The waves on it are almost as big as in the ocean. It is only a lake but you cannot see the other shore.

He called us to meet — before we all went and talked to the fifty thousand people who had gathered there — just to be introduced, and because he was the host who had invited us there. But from the very beginning, trouble started.

The trouble was that he was sitting on a high pedestal and all the guests were sitting on the ground. It was not a problem to anybody except to Morarji Desai, the politician. He was the only politician among those twenty people — somebody was a scientist, D.S. Kothari who was chairman of the atomic energy commission in India, somebody was a vice chancellor... Those people had come from different directions, but it was not a problem for any of them.

Morarji said, "I would like to start the conversation." He was just sitting by my side. Neither he nor I knew that now a lifelong friendship was starting. He said, "My first question is that you are the host, and we are the guests. Guests are sitting on the floor and the host is seated on a high pedestal. What kind of courtesy is this? If you were addressing a meeting it is understandable that you should sit higher so the people can see and hear you. But here there are only twenty persons, and you are not addressing a meeting, just chit-chatting, just introducing people to each other before the conference, the real conference starts."

Acharya Tulsi was at a loss. It would have been so easy for a real religious person to come down, and apologize: "This is really a most idiotic error on my part." But he did not budge from his place. Instead he told one of his chief disciples, who has now become his successor, Muni Nathmal, "You answer the question."

Muni Nathmal was even more nervous — what to say? Morarji Desai at that time was finance minister of India and that's why they had invited him. They were making efforts to create a university for Jainism, and he was the man ... If he was willing, then finance would not be a problem. Muni Nathmal said, "It is not any discourtesy to the guests, it is just our tradition that the head of the sect sits higher. And just a convention is being followed, nothing else is meant by it. Nobody is insulted by it."

Morarji is not an easy person to be silenced by such answers. He said, "We are not your disciples, you are not our head. None of these twenty people here recognize you as their master or head. You may sit on any pedestal you want amongst your disciples, your sect, your people — but we are guests. Secondly, you proclaim yourself a revolutionary saint, so why cling to a convention, tradition, which is so uncivilized, uncultured?" That was one of the claims of Acharya Tulsi, that he was a revolutionary saint.

Now Nathmal was silent, Acharya Tulsi was silent, and all the other guests started feeling a little uneasy; this was not a good beginning. I asked Morarji Desai, "Although this is not my business, I am not concerned at all, but seeing the situation, would you like me to answer you? It is just to start the conversation so this group does not end in an awkward situation."

He said, "I am concerned about the answer. Yes, you can answer."

I said to him, "A few things: first, there are nineteen other persons, you are not alone here. Nobody else asked the question — why did only you ask it? It didn't occur to me."

And I asked the people, "Had the question occurred to you? If it has not occurred, please raise your hands." All the eighteen hands were raised — that it didn't occur to them.

Then I said to Morarji, "You are the only person who felt hurt. You must be carrying a wound, you must be suffering from some inferiority — you are a psychological case. You can see — you know Doctor D.S. Kothari perfectly well, because he is chairman of the atomic commission of India; you know these other prominent people — nobody is bothered by it. And what does it matter?

"Do you see the spider walking on the ceiling? He is higher than Acharya Tulsi. Just being higher, do you become greater? But somehow it hurts you. There is a wound in you which has not been filled even by being the finance minister of India. You would like one day to be the prime minister of India."

He was very angry. He said, "You call me psychologically sick?"

I said, "Certainly. These eighteen hands were raised for what? They are supporting me, they are saying, 'This man seems to be very vulnerable as far as his ego is concerned, shaky' — just a monk sitting a little higher, and it disturbs you."

I said, "Let us assume, for example, if Acharya Tulsi invites you also to sit with him on the high pedestal ... " And let me remind you, even then Acharya Tulsi did not invite him. I said, "For example, if he invites you and you are on the pedestal, will you ask the same question again for these eighteen poor souls who are sitting on the floor? Will the question ever arise?"

He said, "That I have never thought of. Perhaps the question will not arise, because in hundreds of meetings and conferences, I have been sitting on the high pedestal, but the question has never arisen."

I said, "That makes it clear that it is not a question of why Acharya Tulsi is sitting higher than you. The question is why you are sitting lower than Acharya Tulsi. Change the question to, 'Why am I sitting lower than Acharya Tulsi' — this is what you should have asked. It would have been more authentic. You are projecting your sickness on somebody else.

"But perhaps that somebody else is also as sick as you, because if I was in his place, in the first place, I would not have sat there, if I was the host and you were my guests. Secondly, if by chance, by some coincidence I had been sitting there, the moment you asked the question I would have come down. That would have been enough of an answer: 'There is no problem; it is just our convention and I forgot that you are my guests, because only once a year do I meet guests, but every day I meet my disciples. So just forgive me and let us start our conversation for which we have gathered.'

"But he did not come down. He has no guts. He is sitting there almost dead, he cannot even breathe he is so afraid. And he has no answer — he asked his secretary to answer you. And the question that you have raised, about which he is also silent, is that he has been proclaiming himself a revolutionary saint. He is neither a revolutionary nor a saint, so what answer can he give to you? But my basic concern is not with him, my basic concern is you. This is the political mind which is always thinking in terms of lower and higher, in terms of power."

Of course he was angry, and is still angry, and has remained angry for all these twenty-four, twenty-five years. And he has been in positions from where he could have harmed me, but he has no guts either. He was deputy prime minister and then became prime minister. Before he became prime minister, he had even asked for my help. He had called me, unaware ... Later on he came to know that to call me was absolutely absurd. He was Indira Gandhi's deputy prime minister — the post is not in the constitution itself.

The first prime minister of India, Jawaharlal Nehru, had a clash with another disciple of Gandhi's, Sardar Vallabhbhai Patel. The clash was such that if voting had been allowed then Vallabhbhai Patel would have won. He was a real politician. He was just like Joseph Stalin.

Joseph Stalin was the secretary of the communist party when the revolution happened. He was not a great leader or anything. His function was in the office; he was the head clerk of the Communist Party to put it exactly. But because he was the secretary he knew everything, everything passed through his hands. Every person had to be acquainted with him, and he had a tremendous grip on people.

The same was the situation with Sardar Vallabhbhai Patel. He was a very strong man, I told you, just like Joseph Stalin. Stalin is not his real name, it was just given to him because it means in Russian, "man of steel." Strangely, Sardar Vallabhbhai Patel was called in India, lauha purush, that also means "man of steel." It is exactly the translation of Stalin.

Sardar Vallabhbhai Patel had a grip on the organization, an inside grip. He was not an impressive person like Jawaharlal in public. If the whole of India was going to vote, Jawaharlal would have won, nobody was going to win against him. But if the voting was going to be inside the congress party, the ruling party, then Vallabhbhai could have defeated anybody.

To avoid this voting, because this was going to be a party decision, Gandhi said, "It will be good to create a post of deputy prime minister, so Sardar Vallabhbhai Patel will be happy that he is, if not the first, at least the second man." And there is every chance, anytime, for the second man to be the first man, once you throw the first man out or he dies or something happens.

And Sardar Vallabhbhai Patel was clever enough to throw out the man who was in front of him. Jawaharlal was innocent in that way. He was not a politician at all. So without any constitutional basis for it, immediately an amendment was made that there would be a post of deputy prime minister. It was created for Sardar Vallabhbhai Patel.

Once Nehru and Patel both died the post was dissolved, because it was unconstitutional, but it was again revived with Indira and Morarji Desai. The same conflict: Indira was Jawaharlal's daughter, and Morarji Desai was almost a politically adopted son of Sardar Vallabhbhai Patel. He was his disciple in politics, the chief disciple.

Morarji became aware later on, that it was my suggestion to Indira to throw him out. And I had suggested it just by the way. I was talking for almost an hour to her. She listened, and in the end said only, "Whatever you are saying is right and should be done, but you don't know my situation: my cabinet is not mine, my deputy prime minister is not mine. There is so much conflict and continual fighting in the cabinet; he is trying to throw me out by hook or by crook any way, and to become the prime minister.

"If I say the things that you are saying, everybody will be with him; nobody is going to be with me, because the things that you are suggesting are so much against the Indian mind, the Indian tradition, the Indian way of thinking, that nobody is going to support me. If you want, I can propose it before the cabinet, but the next day you will hear that Indira is no longer prime minister."

Then just by the way, I said, "Then why don't you throw out Morarji Desai first, because he is the man who will manipulate all others. All those others are pygmies. They don't have any national character; they are all provincial people. In certain states, in Bengal or in Andhra or in Maharashtra they are important, but a provincial person cannot fight with you, he has no grounds.

"Only one man can manipulate all those pygmies, and that is Morarji Desai, so first finish him. And they will all be with you if you finish him — because of him none of them can become the second man. So create the situation that this man is blocking everybody's way; throw him out, and nobody is going to support him."

And exactly that happened: within eight days Morarji Desai was thrown out, and nobody supported him. They were all happy because now they were all equal; nobody was of national importance except Indira. So once Indira had gone, died, or something happened, then those pygmies were bound to have the power; otherwise they could not have it. So Morarji's removal was almost half the journey finished; now Indira was the only problem.

Morarji was not aware of it, but later on he became aware. Indira's secretary, who was listening from the other room, told him. But before the secretary told him, Morarji Desai had asked me to help him. He said that he had been thrown out and it was unfair, unjust; without being given any reason, any cause, he had just been told to resign.

And he said, "The strangest thing is that just eight days before there was no question of any change, there was no conflict between me and her. And another strange thing is: I had always thought that the other people would support me against Indira. When I was thrown out, not a single cabinet minister was against it. They rejoiced! They had a party, a celebration." He said to me, "I need help."

I said, "You have asked the wrong person. I would be the last person in the world to help you. If you were drowning in a river, and I was going along the side, and you shouted, 'Help! Help! I am drowning.' I would say, 'Do it quietly. Don't disturb my morning walk.'"

He said, "What! Are you joking?"

I said, "I am not. With politicians I never joke; I am very serious."

Later on he found out that it was basically my suggestion that got stuck in Indira's mind; it was clear mathematics that if she threw this man out, then there was nothing to be worried about. All the others were provincial people, then she could do whatever she wanted to do and nobody could oppose her, because nobody represented India as such. And India is such a big country — thirty states — that if you represent one state, what does it matter? So it stuck in her mind. And Morarji became even more inimical.

Just as he had asked for my help, he was asking everybody's help, whomsoever he thought had some kind of power over people, he was asking everybody. He was a beggar. And he found one man who was a national character, Jaiprakash Narayan, but he was never in politics. He had renounced politics, and he was a sincere man, but as I go on explaining to you, even the sincerest man...

He was a great public servant, he did much service for India in many ways, but he proves my point. He devoted his whole life to the freedom struggle, and after freedom Jawaharlal wanted him to be his successor — he refused. Naturally, anybody would think that he was a humble man — what more humility, what more meekness? He accepted to remain nobody when Jawaharlal was offering him: "Just be in my cabinet and I will make you my successor. I am ready to declare it." And he was capable of being the right successor to Jawaharlal.

Morarji went to him too, and Jaiprakash Narayan agreed to help him for a strange reason — that's why I am telling the story so that you understand that even such a man, who could renounce the premiership of India, was still a deep egoist. That renunciation was not out of humbleness, the renunciation was out of ego: that "I don't care." Perhaps the very idea that Jawaharlal was offering him the successorship was not acceptable to his ego. He can become the prime minister on his own. Who are you to announce, proclaim, declare that he is your successor?

He had his own authority, and he was very influential — perhaps next to Jawaharlal in India, he was the most loved by the people. And the love became more and more as Jawaharlal became more and more engulfed in politics, and became farther and farther away from people. Jaiprakash became more and more close to the people, and the people started loving him because: "Here is a man who can renounce." And in India, renunciation is the last word; you cannot go beyond that. That is the highest point. But a small thing triggered him and all the humanity, all the meekness, everything, disappeared.

I have told you that the richest man in India, Jugal Kisore Birla, had offered to give me a blank checkbook if I was ready to spread Hinduism to the world at large, and create a movement in India to force the government to ban cow slaughter. When I refused him he said, "Young man, think twice because Jawaharlal gets money from me, Jaiprakash Narayan gets money from me, Ram Manohar Lohia gets money from me, Ashok Mehta gets money from me." All these were the topmost leaders.

He said, "And every month I am giving them money, as much as they need. Even to Ashok Mehta who is the president of the Socialist Party of India, which is against the rich people — even he is my man." He said, "I give to all party presidents, important people;

whoever comes to power will be my man. Let them say what they say; talking does not matter — I have purchased them."

I told Indira about Jaiprakash, just in that conversation in which I talked about Morarji: to throw him out. She was shocked! She could not believe it because she called him uncle; he was almost like a brother to Jawaharlal. He had been Jawaharlal's secretary for many years and their relationship was very close. And Indira was brought up in front of his eyes; when just a small child she used to call him "Kaka" — uncle.

And when I said, "Jugal Kisore himself has told me, and I don't think that old man was telling a lie. In fact, how does Jaiprakash maintain himself? — because he does not belong to any party. He does not have any group of supporters; he has renounced politics. He does not earn a single pai. How does he manage to have two secretaries, a typist? How does he manage to continually travel in airplanes? Money must be coming from somewhere, and he has no visible source. My feeling is that Jugal Kisore was not lying."

Indira mentioned this to Jaiprakash: "Do you get a salary every month from the Birla house?" And that was the thing that hit him hard; that was when he decided that Indira could no longer be tolerated. He willingly became a partner of Morarji Desai and all the people — it always happens whenever you are in power that you manage to create enemies — all the enemies together. But Jaiprakash was the key. Morarji was not capable of gathering anybody — he is simply retarded — but Jaiprakash was an intelligent man.

He managed to overturn the government and to show his last renunciation: that although he had overturned the government, he was not going to be the prime minister. He wanted to prove that he was higher than Jawaharlal. That was his only, his deepest longing: to be higher than Jawaharlal. So he placed Morarji Desai in the prime ministership just to show to history: "Somebody was trying to place me as premier, but I don't care about these premierships, I can create my own premiers." But it was all egoism.

I used to speak in Patna, and because Jaiprakash also belonged to Patna, his wife used to come to attend my meetings. I was puzzled. I inquired of my host, "The wife comes, but I never see Jaiprakash."

He laughed, he said, "I asked the same question of Prakashwati, Jaiprakash's wife. She said, 'He comes but he sits in the car outside and listens from there. He cannot gather courage to come in and let it be seen by people that he has come to listen to somebody.'"

The ego is so subtle and so slippery. And the politician is sick because of his ego. Now there are two ways: either he can cover the wound by becoming a president, a prime minister. He can cover the wound, but the wound is there. You can deceive the whole world but how can you deceive yourself? You know it. It is there; you have covered it.

I am reminded of a strange story. It happened in Prayag, the very holy place for Hindus, where three rivers meet. You know in India the whole country is treated as a toilet; there is no demarcation where the toilet is and where it is not. Wherever you can find a place, that is the toilet.

One brahmin, early in the morning, must have gone to take his bath, and before his bath he went to defecate. Perhaps he was in a hurry, perhaps he had some stomach trouble or something, but he just went on the ghat. Ghat means the paved place where people put their clothes and go to take their bath. It is not allowed; nobody prevents you, but it is not conventionally allowed that you defecate, on that paved place where people are going to put their clothes.

But the man must have been in trouble. I can understand, I don't doubt his intention — I never doubt anybody's intention. He defecated there, and as he was finishing he saw people coming. So he simply covered his shit with the flowers that he had brought to worship with. What else to do?

The people arrived and they asked, "What is this?"

And he said, "A shivalinga, I am worshipping." And he started worshipping, and because a brahmin was worshipping, others started pouring their flowers on it — a shivalinga had appeared! It is thought to be a great miracle in India — whenever any statue just appears or whenever you want to create a miracle, this is the simplest way. Other people started chanting mantras, and what to say of that man ... He was feeling so bad. Not only had he dirtied the place, he had lied. One lie begets another lie, and then ... Now what was he doing? He was worshipping it, and others were worshipping it!

But how can you forget it? Is there any way for this man to forget what is under the flowers? The same is the situation of the politician: just pus, wounds, inferiority, feeling worthless.

Yes, he had reached higher and higher, and on each step of the ladder, the hope was that on the next step the wound would be healed. Inferiority creates ambition, because ambition simply means an effort to prove yourself superior.

There is no other meaning to ambition but an effort to prove yourself superior. But why make an effort to prove yourself superior unless you are suffering from inferiority?

I have never voted in my life. My uncles, my two uncles — I have two uncles who both were in the freedom struggle — both have been to jail. Neither of them could complete his education because they were caught and imprisoned. One uncle was just here for the festival. He was only in his matriculation class when he was caught, because he was part of a conspiracy to destroy a train, to bomb a bridge. They were making a bomb — and he was a student of chemistry, so he used to bring from the chemistry lab things needed to make the bomb. He was caught when he was just going to take the examination, just ten days before. And his education was finished, because after three years when he came back it was too late to start again and be ...

So he went into business. My elder uncle was in his BA final when he got caught, because he was also part of a conspiracy group against the government. My whole family was political, except my father. So they were all asking me, "Why don't you register, why don't you vote, and why are you wasting your energies? If you move in the direction of politics you can become the president of the country, you can become the premier of the country."

I said, "You have completely forgotten with whom you are talking. I don't suffer from any inferiority, so why should I be interested in becoming the president of the country? Why should I waste my life in becoming the president of the country? It is almost as if I have no cancer and you want me to be operated on for cancer — it is strange. Why should I be operated on unnecessarily?

You suffer from some inferiority complex, and you are projecting your inferiority complex on me. I am perfectly okay as I am. I am absolutely grateful to existence wherever I am. Today whatsoever happens is good. More than that I have never asked, so there is no way to disappoint me."

They said, "You talk of strange things. What is this inferiority complex and what has this inferiority complex to do with politics?"

I said, "You don't understand simple psychology and neither do your great politicians understand simple psychology."

All these politicians on top in the world are sick people, so one way is to go on covering their wound. Yes, they can deceive others. When Jimmy Carter smiles you are deceived, but how can Jimmy Carter deceive himself? He knows it is just an exercise of the lips. There is nothing else inside, no smile.

People reach to the highest rung of the ladder; then they become aware that their whole life has been a wastage. They have arrived, but where? They have arrived at the place for which they had been fighting — and it was not a small fight; it was tooth and nail — and destroying so many people, using so many people as means, and stepping on their heads.

You have arrived at the last rung of the ladder but what have you gained? You have simply wasted your whole life. Now to even accept it needs tremendous courage. It is better to go on smiling and go on keeping the illusion: at least others believe that you are great. You know who you are. You are exactly the same as you were — perhaps worse, because all this struggle, all this violence has made you worse. You have lost all your humanity. You are no longer a being.

It is so far away from you, that Gurdjieff used to say that not every person has a soul, for the simple reason — not that it is literally true, but he used to say — "Not everybody has got a soul, only a very few people who discover their being have." They have it; others are simply living in the illusion, because scriptures say, and all the religions preach, that you are born with a soul.

Gurdjieff was very drastic. He said, "It is all nonsense. You are not born with a soul. You have to earn it; you have to deserve it." And I can understand what he means, although I will not say that you are not born with a soul.

You are born with a soul but that soul is only a potential, and whatsoever Gurdjieff is saying is exactly the same. You have to bring that potential to actuality. You have to earn it. You have to deserve it.

The politician recognizes it when his whole life has gone down the drain. Now, either he has to confess — which seems very stupid because he is confessing that his whole life has been the life of an idiot ...

Wounds are not healed by covering them. The authentic religion is a cure. The word meditation and the word medicine come from the same root. Medicine is for the body; what medicine is for the body, meditation is for the soul. It is medicinal, it is a cure.

You ask me, can a politician be authentically religious? Remaining a politician, it is impossible. Yes, if he drops politics, then he is no longer a politician; he can become an authentically religious man. So I am not dividing, not preventing the politician from becoming religious, meditative. What I am saying is: as a politician he cannot be authentically religious because those are two different dimensions.

Either you cover your wound or you cure it. You can't do both together. And to cure it you have to uncover it, not cover it. Uncover it, know it, go deep into it, suffer it.

To me that is the meaning of austerity — not standing in the sun, that is an idiotic act. And particularly in Oregon you should not do that. Stand in the sun, the Oregonian sun and the Oregonian atmosphere, and immediately you will become the Idiot General of Oregon. Avoid it! Or starving yourself or standing in the cold, in the river, for days together, this is not the way to cure yourself; you are just being befooled. Anybody who knows nothing is going to give you advice: "Do this and you will be cured," but it is not a question of doing something for the cure.

What is needed is an exploration of your whole being, unprejudiced, without condemnation, because you will find many things which you have been told are bad, evil. So don't shrink back, let them be. You simply need not condemn them.

You have started on an exploration. Just note that something is there, note it and go on. Don't condemn it; don't name it. Don't bring any prejudice against or for, because that's what prevents you from exploring. Your inner world closes immediately, you become tense — something evil. You go inside and you see something, and you become afraid that it is evil: greed, lust, anger, jealousy. "My God! All these things, in me — it is better not to go in."

That's why millions of people don't go in. They simply sit on the staircase outside their house. They live on the porch their whole life. It is a porch life! They never open the door of their house. And the house has many chambers; it is a palace. If you go in you will come across many things which others have told you are wrong. You don't know, you simply say, "I am an ignorant man. I don't know who you are. I have just come to explore, to do a survey." And a surveyor need not be bothered about what is good and what is bad, he simply goes on looking, watching, observing.

And you will be surprised by the strangest experience: that what you have called love up to now, hidden just behind it is hate; just take note. What you have been saying up to now is humbleness, just behind it is hidden your ego; just take note.

If somebody asks me, "Are you a humble man?" I cannot say, "I am," because I know humbleness is only the ego standing on its head. I am not an egoist, how can I be humble? Do you understand me? It is impossible to be humble without having an ego. And once you have seen that both are together, the strangest thing happens, as I was telling you.

The moment you see that your love and your hate, your humbleness and ego are one; they evaporate.

You have not to do anything at all. You have seen their secret. That secret was helping them to remain in you. You have seen the secret, now there is no place for them to hide. Go in again and again, and you will find less and less things there. Gatherings inside you are withering; crowds are going away. And the day is not far off when you will be left alone, and there is nobody, emptiness is in your hands. And suddenly you are cured.

Don't compare at all, because you are you, and somebody else is somebody else. Why should I compare myself with Yehudi Menuhin or with Pablo Picasso? I don't see the point at all. They are doing their thing; I am doing my thing. They are enjoying doing their thing, perhaps — because about them I cannot be certain. But I am certain about myself that I am enjoying whatsoever I am doing or not doing.

I said I cannot be certain about them because Pablo Picasso was not a happy man, in fact very unhappy. His paintings show his inner misery in many ways and he has spread that misery on the canvas.

And why did Picasso become the greatest painter of this age? The reason is because this age knows inner suffering the most.

Nobody would have thought him a painter five hundred years ago. They would have laughed, and they would have put him into a mental institution. And five hundred years ago, mental institutions were not easy places to be in. They did all kinds of things, particularly beating, because they thought it was possible to beat the madness out, because madness was thought of as something like an evil spirit possessing you. A good beating every day, and they thought the madness would go.

They used — just three hundred years ago — to take blood out of the madman, so he became weakened. They thought that his energies were being possessed by an evil spirit; if you took his energies out, the evil spirit would leave the place because there was nothing to feed on: it was feeding on his blood. Good logic — and they were doing just that.

Nobody would have thought that these were paintings. Only this century could believe that Picasso is a great painter, because this century suffers, is a little alert of suffering, of inner misery — and this man has put it in color. What you cannot put even in words, Picasso has been able to put in color. You don't understand what it is, but somehow you feel a deep at-one-ment. It has an appeal; something clicks in you. It is not intellectual because you cannot figure out what it is, but you remain stuck watching, looking, as if it were a mirror and something of your inside, of your intestines, is there. Picasso's paintings became the greatest in this age because they served almost like an X-ray. They brought your misery out. That's why I said perhaps. And about anybody else I can only say perhaps.

Only about myself can I be certain. I know that if you go on exploring your inner world without condemnation, without appreciation, without thinking at all, just watching the facts, they start disappearing. A day comes, you are left alone, the whole crowd has gone away; and in that moment, for the first time you feel what psychic healing is.

And from psychic healing the door opens to spiritual healing.

You need not open it, it opens on its own. You just reach to the psychic center and the door opens. It has been waiting for you, perhaps for many lives. When you come, the door immediately opens, and from that door, you not only see yourself, you see the whole existence, all the stars, the whole cosmos.

Hence I can say absolutely: no politician can become authentically religious unless he drops politics. Then he is not a politician, and what I am saying does not refer to him.

You have also asked: can an authentically religious man become a politician? That is even more impossible than the first because there is no reason at all for him to become one. If inferiority is the cause that drives you into ambition, then how can a meditator become a politician? There is no driving force. But once in a while it has happened in the past, and it may happen in the future, so let me say this to you.

In the past it was possible because the world was dominated by the monarchy. Once in a while, the king's son might turn out to be a poet. It is very difficult for a poet to become the president of America; who is going to listen to him? People think he is crazy, and he will look like a hippie. He cannot shape up himself, and he is trying to shape up the whole world?

But in the past it was possible because of the monarchy. The last emperor of India, from whom the Britishers took over, was a poet — that is why Britishers could take over India — Bahadurshah Zafar, one of the greatest Urdu poets. Now, it is not possible for a poet to become an emperor; it was just accidental that he was born a son of an emperor.

The enemy forces were entering the capital and he was writing poetry. When his prime minister knocked on the door and said, "It is absolutely urgent, because the enemies have entered the capital," Bahadurshah said, "Don't disturb me. I am writing just the last four lines. I think I will be able to finish these four lines before they come here. Don't disturb." And he started writing. He finished his poem; that was more important for him.

And he was such a simple and good man; he came out and he said, "What is this nonsense of killing people? If you want the country you take it, what is the fuss about? I was burdened with all the anxieties, now you can be burdened with all the anxieties. Leave me alone."

But they would not leave him alone because they were politicians and generals. To leave this man in New Delhi was dangerous: he may collect his forces, he may have resources — nobody knows. They took him from India into Burma; he died in Rangoon. In his last poem that he wrote from his deathbed, he said, "How poor I am. I cannot get even six feet in my beloved's street." He is talking about New Delhi, which he loved, which he had created; and he was a poet so he made the city as beautiful as possible. He said, "I cannot get even six feet to be buried in my own beloved's street. How unfortunate Zafar" — Zafar was his poetic name — "How unfortunate, Zafar, you are."

He was buried in Rangoon; they did not even bring his dead body to New Delhi. He insisted, "At least when I am dead take my body to my city, to my country. A dead body cannot be dangerous." But politicians and generals think in different ways. Bahadurshah was the emperor loved by the people. Seeing him dead, "There may be a revolt, there may be some trouble, why get into trouble? Bury him there in Rangoon. Nobody will even hear for years that he has died."

So in the old monarchical days it was possible that in the western hemisphere a man like Marcus Aurelius could happen. He was a religious man, but this was just accidental. Marcus Aurelius could not become a president or a prime minister today because he would not go asking for votes; he would not beg — for what?

In India it happened a few times. Ashoka, one of the great emperors of India, was an authentically religious man, so much so that when his son asked — the only son, who was going to be the successor — to become a monk, he danced. He said, "This is what I have been waiting for, that one day you would understand." Then his daughter, his only daughter, he had only two children, one son and one daughter, when the daughter, Sanghamitra, asked him — she also wanted to go into the world of meditation — he said, "Go. This is my only happiness." But today it is impossible.

In India there was one great king, Poras; he fought against Alexander the Great. And you will be surprised at how western books have been unfair to this man Poras. Alexander the Great becomes a pygmy before Poras. When they reached India, Alexander played a trick — he was a politician. ...

Alexander sent his wife to meet Poras, on a particular day. There is a day in India, the day of the sisters, when the sister just binds a thread on your wrist. You may be her real brother, you may not be her real brother, but the moment she binds the thread on your wrist you become a brother to her. And it is a double oath: the brother says, "I will protect you," and the sister says, "I will pray for your protection."

On that particular day, Alexander sent his wife to Poras. He was staying outside Poras' kingdom. There is a river that was the boundary of Poras' kingdom; he was staying outside, and he sent his wife. And when it was declared in Poras' court, "The wife of Alexander the Great wants to meet you," he came out to greet her, because in India that was a tradition. Even if the enemy comes to your home, he is a guest, and the guest is a god.

He took her into his court, gave her a throne to sit on, and said, "You could have called me. There was no need for you to come such a long way."

She said, "I have come to make you my brother. I have no brother, and today, I heard, is the sisters' day; I could not resist."

This was a political game. And Poras could understand what Alexander and his wife understood about sisters' day, and why Alexander waited up to this day to send his wife, but he said, "This is perfectly right. If you don't have any brother, I am your brother." She had brought the thread; she tied it and Poras touched her feet. The brother has to touch the feet of the sister; whether she is younger or older does not matter.

A tremendous respect for womanhood has been there, side by side with a tremendous bitterness against women. Perhaps the bitterness was created by the monks and the priests, and the respect was created by the religious people. Immediately Alexander's wife said, "Now you are my brother, and I hope you will save me, but the only way to save me is not to kill Alexander. Would you like your sister to remain a widow all her life?"

Poras said, "There is no question about it. You need not speak about it — it is settled. Alexander will not be touched at all. Now we are related."

And this happened: the next day Alexander attacked, and a moment came in the fight when Poras killed Alexander's horse. Alexander fell from the horse and Poras was on his elephant — because in India, the elephant was the real fighter's animal, not the horse — the elephant was just going to put his feet on Alexander, and Alexander would have been finished. Just by habit Poras pulled out his spear and was going to kill Alexander, when he saw the thread on his wrist. He put his spear back, told the mahout, the man who guides the elephant, "Move away, and inform Alexander that I will not kill him."

That was the moment when Alexander would have been killed, and all his desire for conquering the world would have been finished; the whole of history would have been different. But Poras was a religious man, made of a different mettle: ready to be defeated but not ready to be demoralized. And he was defeated — he missed his chance.

Poras was brought before Alexander in his court, a temporary court, with chains on his hands and his legs. But the way he walked ... Even Alexander said to him, "You are still walking like an emperor, even with chains on your feet and chains on your hands."

Poras said, "This is my way of walking. It has nothing to do with my being an emperor or a prisoner; this is my way of walking. This is how I am."

Alexander asked him, "How would you like to be treated?"

Poras said, "What a question! An emperor should be treated like an emperor. What a stupid question."

Alexander says in his notes, "I have never come across a man like Poras. He was in chains, imprisoned — I could have killed him immediately, then and there — but the way he walked, the way he talked ... " Alexander was really impressed. He said, "Take away his chains; he will remain an emperor anywhere. Give his kingdom back to him. But," he said, "before we leave I would like to ask you one question. When the chance was there when you could have killed me, why did you pull your spear back? Just one more second and I'd have been finished, or your elephant could have crushed me, but you prevented it. Why?"

Poras said, "Don't ask that. You know it; you are a politician, I am not. This thread — do you recognize it? You had sent this thread with your wife; now she is my sister, and I cannot kill my own brother-in-law. It is not possible for me to make her a widow. I chose to be defeated rather than to kill you. But there is no need for you to feel obliged towards me; this is just how a really centered man should behave."

So in the past it was possible because of the monarchy. But within the monarchy idiots also became kings, madmen also became kings, everything is possible. So I am not supporting monarchy, I am simply saying that it was possible within the monarchy for am authentically religious man, by accident, to become an emperor.

In the future, democracy is not going to last long, because the politician is already ignorant before the scientist; he is already in the hands of the scientist. The future belongs to the scientist, not to the politician.

That means we will have to change the word *democracy*. I have a word for it: meritocracy.

Merit will be the decisive factor. Not whether you can gather votes by canvassing all kinds of promises and hopes, but your merit, your real power in the scientific world will decide. And once government comes into the hands of the scientist, then everything is possible because I have called science, objective religion; and religion, subjective science.

Once it comes into the hands of science, the world map will be different, because what is the fight between the Russian scientist and the American scientist? They are both working on the same projects; it will be far quicker if they work together. This is sheer stupidity, that all over the world the same experiments are being repeated in every nation; it is unbelievable. All these people together can do miracles. Divided, it becomes more expensive.

For example, if Albert Einstein had not escaped from Germany then who would have won the Second World War? Do you think America and Britain and Russia would have won the Second World War? No. A single man's escape from Germany, Albert Einstein escaping from Germany, has shaped history. All these bogus names: Roosevelt, Churchill, Stalin, Hitler, they don't mean anything. That man did the whole thing because he created the atom bomb. He wrote a letter to Roosevelt: "The atom bomb is ready with me, and unless you use it there is no way to stop the war."

He regretted it his whole life, but that's another story. The atom bomb was used, and the moment it was used there was no question of Japan going on fighting. The war was won: Hiroshima and Nagasaki burning ended the Second World War. Albert Einstein was working on the same project in Germany. He could have written to just a different address — instead of to Roosevelt, to Adolf Hitler — and the whole history would have been different, totally different.

The future is going to be in the hands of the scientist. It is not far away. Now there are nuclear weapons, politicians cannot manage to be on top. They know nothing about it, not even the ABC.

It was said while Einstein was alive that only twelve persons in the whole world understood his theory of relativity. One of those twelve people was Bertrand Russell who wrote a small book for those who could not understand it: *The ABC of Relativity*. He thought that at least they could understand the ABC — but even that is not possible, because if you can understand the ABC then the whole alphabet becomes simple. It is not a question of only understanding ABC; then XYZ is not far away. The real problem is to understand the ABC.

Now all these politicians don't understand anything at all. Sooner or later the world is going to be in the hands of the people who have merit. First it will move into the hands of the scientists.

This you can take almost as a prediction that the world is going to move into the hands of the scientists. And then a new dimension opens up.

Sooner or later the scientist is going to invite the sage, the saint, because he cannot manage it alone.

The scientist cannot manage himself. He can manage everything but he cannot manage himself. Albert Einstein may know all about the stars of the universe but he knows nothing about his own center.

This is going to be the future: from politicians to scientists, from scientists to religious man — but that will be a totally different kind of world. Religious people cannot go asking for votes. You will have to ask them. You will have to request them. And if they feel that your request is sincere and the need is there, they may act in the world. But remember it will not be politics at all.

So let me repeat, the politician can become religious if he drops politics; otherwise it is impossible. The religious man can become part of politics if politics changes its whole character; otherwise it is impossible for a religious man to be in politics. He cannot be a politician.

But the way things are moving, it is absolutely certain that first the world will go into the hands of the scientist, and then, from the scientist it will go to the mystics. And only in the hands of the mystics can you yourself be safe.

The world can be really a paradise. In fact, there is no other paradise unless we make one here.

For more information
www.OSHO.com

A comprehensive multi-language website including a magazine, OSHO Books, OSHO TALKS in audio and video formats, the OSHO Library text archive in English and Hindi, and extensive information about OSHO Meditations. You will also find the program schedule of the OSHO Multiversity and information about the OSHO International Meditation Resort.

To contact OSHO International Foundation visit: www.osho.com/oshointernational

About the Author

Osho's teachings defy categorization, covering everything from the individual quest for meaning to the most urgent social and political issues facing society today. His books are not written but are transcribed from audio and video recordings of extemporaneous talks given to international audiences over a period of 35 years. Osho has been described by the *Sunday Times* in London as one of the "1000 Makers of the 20th Century" and by American author Tom Robbins as "the most dangerous man since Jesus Christ."

About his own work Osho has said that he is helping to create the conditions for the birth of a new kind of human being. He has often characterized this new human being as "Zorba the Buddha" – capable both of enjoying the earthy pleasures of a Zorba the Greek and the silent serenity of a Gautam Buddha. Running like a thread through all aspects of Osho's work is a vision that encompasses both the timeless wisdom of the East and the highest potential of Western science and technology.

Osho is also known for his revolutionary contribution to the science of inner transformation, with an approach to meditation that acknowledges the accelerated pace of contemporary life. His unique "Active Meditations" are designed to first release the accumulated stresses of body and mind, so that it is easier to experience the thought-free and relaxed state of meditation.

Two autobiographical works by the author are available: *Autobiography of a Spiritually Incorrect Mystic*, by Osho, St. Martin's Griffin (2001) ISBN: 978-0312280710, and *Glimpses of a Golden Childhood*, by Osho, The Rebel Publishing House ISBN: 8172610726

About OSHO International Meditation Resort

The OSHO International Meditation Resort is a great place for holidays and a place where people can have a direct personal experience of a new way of living with more alertness, relaxation, and fun. Located about 100 miles southeast of Mumbai in Pune, India, the resort offers a variety of programs to thousands of people who visit each year from more than 100 countries around the world. Originally developed as a summer retreat for Maharajas and wealthy British colonialists, Pune is now a thriving modern city that is home to a number of universities and high-tech industries. The Meditation Resort spreads over 40 acres in a tree-lined suburb known as Koregaon Park. The resort campus provides accommodation for a limited number of guests, in a new 'Guesthouse' and there is a plentiful variety of nearby hotels and private apartments available for stays of a few days up to several months.

Meditation Resort programs are all based in the Osho vision of a qualitatively new kind of human being who is able both to participate creatively in everyday life and to relax into silence and meditation. Most programs take place in modern, air-conditioned facilities and include a variety of individual sessions, courses and workshops covering everything from creative arts to holistic health treatments, personal transformation and therapy, esoteric sciences, the "Zen" approach to sports and recreation, relationship issues, and significant life transitions for men and women. Individual sessions and group workshops are offered throughout the year, alongside a full daily schedule of meditations. Outdoor cafes and restaurants within the resort grounds serve both traditional Indian fare and a choice of international dishes, all made with organically grown vegetables from the resort's own farm. The campus has its own private supply of safe, filtered water.

www.osho.com/resort.